To Barbara and Bill
Always cherish your time together. Love and Light

MOMENTS
AND
WINDSTORMS

Take Back Your Power

Albert Clayton Gaulden

ISBN: 978-1-54390-835-0 (print)

ISBN: 978-1-54390-836-7 (ebook)

DEDICATION

To each person I have ever had the privilege to work, fight, cry, laugh or struggle with to get free from the bondage of your backstory, this book belongs to you. Each of you taught me more than I can ever express.

And to my Gorgeous Geniuses, Livia and Augusta Carney who teach me a lot every time we speak.

CONTENTS

INTRODUCTION xiii

PART ONE 1

PRELUDE 3

CHAPTER ONE
Asleep but Not Dead 5

CHAPTER TWO
The Haze 12

CHAPTER THREE
Acting Out 21

CHAPTER FOUR
The Teacher Learns a Lesson 26

CHAPTER FIVE
Pretending 35

CHAPTER SIX
Flying High 43

CHAPTER SEVEN
Fantasy 48

CHAPTER EIGHT
Conjuring 53

CHAPTER NINE

John Travolta and Me 64

CHAPTER TEN

Hitting Bottom 77

CHAPTER ELEVEN

Tough Love 82

CHAPTER TWELVE

Starting Over 91

CHAPTER THIRTEEN

Creating 101

PART TWO 107

CHAPTER FOURTEEN

Correcting 109

CHAPTER FIFTEEN

God is Everywhere and in All Things 119

CHAPTER SIXTEEN

Men and Women are the Same 127

CHAPTER SEVENTEEN

Sober and Straighter 135

CHAPTER EIGHTEEN

You're Not Who You Think You Are 142

CHAPTER NINETEEN

You Have Been Here Before 146

PART THREE... 149

CHAPTER TWENTY

The Protocol of the Sedona Intensive – Take Back Your Power 151

CHAPTER TWENTY-ONE

Day One – The Backstory 155

CHAPTER TWENTY-TWO

Day Two – The Harm Game..163

CHAPTER TWENTY-THREE

Day Three – Hidden Deal Breakers 167

CHAPTER TWENTY-FOUR

Day Four – Anger and Rage Letters 171

CHAPTER TWENTY-FIVE

Day Five – Forgiveness Letters..176

PART FOUR 181

CHAPTER TWENTY-SIX

Switching Over..183

CHAPTER TWENTY-SEVEN

E-Enemy.Com..203

CHAPTER TWENTY-EIGHT

Charlotte's Web...209

CHAPTER TWENTY-NINE

The Story of Jared...213

CHAPTER THIRTY

The Lies That TJ Told...216

CHAPTER THIRTY-ONE

Her Royal Highness Called Me Boss 221

CHAPTER THIRTY-TWO

The Obsessions of Laura..226

CHAPTER THIRTY-THREE

The Life and Death of Anthony 231

CHAPTER THIRTY-FOUR

The Actor Caught Between Acts...234

CHAPTER THIRTY-FIVE

Medicine Woman Surrenders to Win...240

CHAPTER THIRTY-SIX

What Money Couldn't Buy..247

CHAPTER THIRTY-SEVEN

When the Roll is Called Up-Yonder 252

PART FIVE 257

CHAPTER THIRTY-EIGHT

The Late and Great Mrs. Arthur Hornblow, Jr.............................259

CHAPTER THIRTY-NINE

The Comeback Kid 266

CHAPTER FORTY

Rex Reed and the Welles at the Dakota.....................................271

CHAPTER FORTY-ONE

Her Name is Bishop Reverend Doctor Barbara King 279

CHAPTER FORTY-TWO

The Strange Gift of Mr. Darby...283

DENOUEMENT

The Doomsday Clock – Two Minutes to Midnight 287

ACKNOWLEDGEMENTS 290

BIBLIOGRAPHY 293

Ozymandias

I met a traveller from an antique land,
Who said—"Two vast and trunkless legs of stone
Stand in the desert. . . . Near them, on the sand,
Half sunk a shattered visage lies, whose frown,
And wrinkled lip, and sneer of cold command,
Tell that its sculptor well those passions read
Which yet survive, stamped on these lifeless things,
The hand that mocked them, and the heart that fed;
And on the pedestal, these words appear:
My name is Ozymandias, King of Kings;
Look on my works, ye Mighty, and despair!
Nothing beside remains. Round the decay
Of that colossal Wreck, boundless and bare
The lone and level sands stretch far away.

INTRODUCTION

The Oracle of Ozymandias

I am a part of all that I have met; yet all experience is an arch where through gleams that untraveled world whose margin fades forever and forever when I move.

— Alfred Lord Tennyson

The Oracle of Ozymandias was inspired by Percy Bysshe Shelley's poem *Ozymandias*. Ozymandias was a Greek name for the Egyptian pharaoh Ramesses II. The poem explores the fate of history and the ravages of time: that all prominent figures and the empires they build are impermanent and their legacies fated to decay into oblivion. The premise I expound on in this book offers a correction of the inevitability of Man's demise with how each of us has a path to his own redemption.

I have chosen to write about my own life journey and comment on the life and times of the Worldview as it bears the outcome that Shelley presented. Renowned English historian Lord John Acton's said, "Power tends to corrupt and absolute power corrupts absolutely." It's as timely today as it was when he said it.

I am a flawed man. One day I heard a still, small voice. He identified himself as Paul, my High Self. Paul explained who I was born to be. In time the awareness from that Presence healed me. With the help of ordinary people I was reborn to live an extraordinary life.

Whatever compulsions and obsessions girdled me, with the help of divine intervention I became who I am today. Doing what I do. My mission is to uncover truth as well as balance and harmony for clients who seek my service. I grow exponentially. It is my privilege to work with others. Each who comes to me leaves me a better person.

The book's title, *Moments and Windstorms,* was inspired by an Elizabeth Kubler-Ross lecture. Through the recommendation of a client, Kubler-Ross requested that I pay her a visit in May of 1996.

The subtitle *Take Back Your Power* insinuates that each of us has lost our sovereignty and control through addictions, compulsions and glittering persuasions that overlay us from childhood forward.

When I walked into Kubler-Ross' house that morning, she was in a wheel chair but otherwise in fine fettle. That soon morphed into a very trying four hours.

"I understand that you are a wise man who works with birth charts. I gave your assistant my birth information. I have one question. When can I die?"

I paused and took both of her hands in mine.

"I will say to you what you would say to me if I had asked that question. Draw me a picture," I said.

She did. And we talked for hours about everything on her mind. Much of the conversation was dark. Kubler-Ross was desperately unhappy because of her strokes and confinement to a wheelchair.

Elizabeth wrote in one of her books, "I always say that death can be one of the greatest experiences ever. If you live each day of your life right, then you have nothing to fear."

In May 1997 she was interviewed by Don Lattin, a Chronicle religion writer. He published some of their conversation: "My only regret is that for forty years I spoke of a good God who helps people, who knows what you need and how all you have to do is ask for it. Well, that's baloney. I want to tell the world that it's a bunch of bull. Don't believe a word of it."

Elizabeth Kubler-Ross died in August 2004 in Scottsdale, Arizona. Despite her agony in her latter days, she was a great woman who did so much to make the world aware of death and dying. She was one of the first advocates for hospice.

Not even the best of us escapes those moments of despair and negative overlays. The problem I experience with my own work is that too many people expect perfection and an irrefutable acolyte of highest consciousness.

Saint Francis of Assisi was a rabble-rousing drunk as a young man. He became a great healer known throughout the world for being able to communicate with animals. The controversy surrounding Mother Teresa, who died in 1997 and was canonized in 2016, is far from new. Her saintly reputation was gained for aiding Calcutta's poorest of the poor, yet it was undercut by persistent allegations of religious evangelism in the institutions she founded.

All of us are imperfect but seldom do many of us have the service record to mankind as do Elizabeth Kubler-Ross, Saint Francis or Mother Teresa. And none of us is above reproach. Beware of any tendency to put anyone on a pedestal.

I had always been a misfit. I was a child of make believe. Visions of how the world was meant to be danced through my head. But I was in a place I did not understand. Sometimes I wanted to be anyone but who I was, to be anywhere but on my street. Coping was a no-brainer. I did what I was told. I was a perfect student who went to Sunday School and church.

I had three best friends as a young boy, and I was always trying to be No. 1 with each of them. Soon they were onto me and my shenanigans. Being tiny Albert tortured me. Wearing braces to strengthen my legs brought attention I did not want.

The first forty years of my life I lived in fear. A woman in the Spiritualist Church once told me that fear is a result of actions taken in contradiction to the perfect soul I was meant to be.

In these pages you will find out how God is a Light Source. Each of us without conscious awareness is pulled along a golden railroad track. God is guiding us even when we don't believe in him. God allows free choice: right or wrong or light or dark. Wherever we go, it depends on the choices we make. And when we are done with one life, we go back to the Upper World and, in incomprehensible time, are reborn.

Fear seems to be a common thread among all the people I have worked with. You will soon find out from my point of view that so many organizations and institutions have formed a hierarchy to control us because they feel that they know better. In my parlance, I call it entitlement. The construct of what we call "growing up" has a lot of pitfalls represented by those who think they know what's best for us, whose message is, "Here's how it's gonna be, so get in line and follow the rules."

But things are changing in the world today. Masses are mad at those authorities who promise only what each of us can give ourselves. With the stories I hear, so many feel that they have been in a trance state to a religion or politics and now are lost with no road map.

Acceptance of my plight was a coward's way of embracing what I was too weak to change. Years later I would understand that being manipulated and controlled were strategies of my own Ego.

To use a Winston Churchill quote: "I am a riddle wrapped in a mystery, inside an enigma." I don't know anything. I don't believe anything. I know what I know by experience. Don't get me wrong. One of my sobriety steps states, "We came to believe that a power greater than ourselves could restore us to sanity." But I always tell other recoverers that I came to *know*. That's where the notion of belief ends for me. Beliefs are based on dogma and dicta that someone or something tries to get us to accept because "they" or "it" say so.

How did I ultimately discover what I know? I asked a lot of questions. Some of the answers kept me moving forward. The toughest question I ever asked was, "Mama, why was I born with clubfeet?" She said that God made me that way. Nonsense, I made me that way. It was because of my actions in other places in different times. I found that out through conversations with connected people. I decoded revelations. To wit, I never figured anything out.

Years later I wrote a fan letter to Dr. Gina Cerminara, whose best-selling book *Many Mansions,* published in 1953, was considered by observers to have launched the Spiritual revolution. *Many Mansions* is based on the life of Edgar Casey, who many of us consider the Father of Reincarnation. To my surprise, she answered with a telephone call.

"Dr. Cerminara, why would you ever call a total stranger?" I asked.

"Did you ever get one of your letters?" she asked.

We both had a good chuckle. She insisted I call her Gina.

She had just moved to Ojai, California. I was in Long Beach. Gina invited me to visit her that next weekend. The two of us spent many hours together.

The most compelling thing we discussed was my having been born with clubfeet.

"Gina, why did my granny take me to Duke Hospital for help with my deformed tootsies? How did the surgeon know to perform an experimental procedure on me? Why do I have two perfect feet today? I had a professor who was born with clubfeet. On one foot he wore a very high heel and he hobbled when he walked," I said.

Gina was quiet for a few moments and then said, "You lived at the time criminals were crucified. Your job was to nail their feet while they hung on the cross. One day you stopped nailing and started healing. For more than thirty years you helped rehabilitate criminals. This is also the karmic suggestion that you must stand on your own two feet."

We talked about my work as an intuitive Jungian therapist. She reminded me of the linchpin of Dr. Jung's work: "You can be neither healthy nor happy until you individuate."

What I learned from Gina Cerminara was to take the obvious and backtrack to where a situation or an illness started. Listen for past life clues. Get quiet. Ask a question. You will get an answer dependent on how open you are to the guidance you receive.

Other questions followed.

Me: "Why was I born to the family I was?"

Gina: "They provided the best opportunity for you to face the mistakes of past lives."

Me: "Why did I become an alcoholic? None of my brothers and sisters is."

Gina: "The defects of character were passed down from father to son in the bloodline until the disease reached you. And more to the point, you had condemned alcoholics in former lives. You reap what you've sown."

It went on and on until I cleared a lot of the cobwebs from my mind. Acceptance did become the path to confessing. Cracking the code of all my bad-boy behavior was freedom.

Reincarnation is a concept you might want to explore. Lord knows for me, it answered some age-old questions I only silently asked:

"Why are some people born beautiful and rich and smart and the majority of us are hatched ordinary-looking, with average intelligence and limited financial means?"

"Why is there so much angst according to the religion we were born to believe?"

"Why is there so much hatred toward one another when our religion purportedly teaches love?"

"Where do we come from and is there really a heaven?"

There were a zillion more whys, whens and how-comes that I asked in puberty and beyond. It was a lot of pain and trial and error that brought me to those answers in a clear space with my mind and heart.

It became obvious to me that if I am a part of all that I've met, it's my job to introduce you to a lot of those people I encountered on my journey. Someone told me along the way that your enemy teaches you more than your friend. He also said that pain is the touchstone of growth.

My mother raised her six children without my father. She divorced him because he was an abusive alcoholic. Rich people join country clubs. Poor people go to church.

My father was a failed baseball player whom my mother married when she was 16 and he was 25. Daddy was Irish from Durham, North Carolina and Momma was of German heritage from Live Oak, Florida. Old sepia pictures of my mother showed her to have had a mean streak with ready-to-fight clinched fists. She evidently was a tomboy from the cradle.

In recovery circles we talk about being in a blackout, usually to mean we were so drunk we remembered nothing. Without the hooch for most of my early life, I erased everything from my mind as quickly as things happened. My recall button functioned like someone awakening from a coma that has flashes of his past.

I remember bits and pieces of being in and out of the hospital to have my clubfeet corrected. When I was two, I recall moments of my second birthday in my grandfather's backyard with four or five little kids. I retrieve a memory of a car wreck my family had when we moved from Florida to Alabama.

In Birmingham, we lived in a big white house in Ensley Highlands, a middle-class neighborhood. The screened-in back porch had a long flight of stairs with residue of cinder chunks on the ground below.

When my parents divorced, my father moved us to the tiny kingdom of Childersburg, Alabama, where there was a cemetery behind our house. One day a few of us were playing and came across a tombstone that said, "Asleep but not dead."

It would be my first cartouche to awaken me to past lives.

PART ONE

Prelude

The French doors were open to the chill blowing in from the Pacific Ocean. I was sitting in my 12-step sponsor's house in Sunset Beach, California. One of his requirements for sponsees was that we had to do our fourth step – coming clean about the hurtful things we did to ourselves and others – by the time we were sober 365 days. The next day, Feb. 18, was my first anniversary.

Fil was not the kind of sponsor I would have picked if I were a pledge in a fraternity. He was uncouth, tall with a beer belly and he acted so much like a Texan that he wore pointed-toe Tony Lima boots. As long as he was my sponsor, he was who God chose to squeeze the truth out of me and spot Ego stuff across the room at 12-step meetings.

His wife's name was Val. She was a former two-fisted drinker who could knock the big boys under the table when they gave her trouble. The night I met her she was the speaker at the Sunset Beach meeting at the Women's Club.

In her pitch, she said that she used to drink at the Crystal Pistol Bar in Phoenix. One night she shot out the lights in the crystal and shouted, "Now that I have your attention, who wants to buy a lady a double?"

Val brought Coca-Colas and a pile of fatty pastries into the den where Fil and I were going over my fourth step. We sobering-up alcoholics gobbled up sugar like it was our new high.

Fil had stepped into his office for a phone call with an oil man from Mexico.

"Val, I don't think Fil likes me. He is always calling me a 'sick sorry son of a bitch,'" I meowed.

"Albert, he only talks like that to the ones he loves and cares about. He thinks you're going to be a big winner. Whatever you do, tell the whole truth about any lies you've been hiding," she advised and left the room.

Here is the long and painfully honest backstory I told him. You are about to be privy to what I said to start the real feet-on-the-ground recovery with an amazing sponsor.

Chapter One
Asleep but Not Dead

———

I was born sometime between creation and now. I am always trying to get a firmer footing for whenever and wherever I return to Earth.

The 50s was the most uneventful decade this country had seen in a long time. I remember those years as dull and boring. No credit cards and no social media. The general mien was the quiet after the storm of combat. General Dwight Eisenhower was president.

The Bop was all the rage. Best-selling books were *Advise and Consent*, *Compulsion*, *Atlas Shrugged* and *Auntie Mame*. Sack dresses were en vogue. This was also the era when Elvis Presley shook up the world. Chubby Checker, Perry Como and Patti Page sang a lot of hit records.

Today many of us read *Fifty Shades of Grey*, *The Girl on the Train* or vampire books. The music is written and sung by the likes of rappers, zappers and self-involvers like Jay-Z and Kanye West. Thank God for Adele.

Today's world is much more complicated. Social media is an addictive outlet. And it is dangerous. The national debt is heavier than ten tall buildings. Why don't we live on what we make? What a concept.

Difficulties are paths to triumph if we forebear setbacks. Being born is but a new beginning. We get to start over. Listening for the still, small voice of intuition helps us machete through the bramble bushes we have to get through.

Mama and Daddy and the street we grow up on, the church and mixed messages we swallowed whole, are harbingers of what lies ahead.

It was when we got to Ensley Highlands that the eerie, netherworld people and things began to crop up. Miss Morrison was our spooky neighbor across the street that walked back and forth in front of her shaded window. She was either preaching or sinning with her words. When she came out at first light to get her mail we off-to-school kids crouched behind a tree until she went back inside.

"Little boy, are you all alone in that big house?" Miss Morrison asked me one afternoon, catching me off guard.

"No, ma'am, there are lots of people at my house and they are waiting for me right now," I said as I skedaddled home.

After we moved a few years later, a friend of ours called Mama to tell her that Miss Morrison had died. She was dead for three weeks before anyone found her. When Mama told us kids the news, one of us said, "Maybe she was roaming the streets looking for a lost kid."

From an early age I lived in two worlds. There was the awakened world and the dream state. I took a dream workshop in Sedona in 1984. In that class, I came to understand that the sleep state/dreams had a life of its own. My teacher was a firm believer that dreams offered insights for solutions to problems that we woke up to on a daily basis. When awakening from sleep, there is often a pall over our state of mind. Perhaps the difference between awake and asleep is contradictory awareness. One teacher opined that the pang of fear upon awakening has a lot to do with not wanting to come back to the world we all created.

When I was five years old, I picked up my older sister's textbooks and said, as I stepped into the outdoors, "I'm going to school."

I stumbled and fell face-first onto a bed of cinder. In healing, my face was left with layers of burned but healed flesh. When the doctor picked the scabs from my face, he said he had never had a young boy not cry from such a painful process. As I unraveled the mysteries of life in later years, I knew I had left my body to avoid the pain.

I'll never forget my first grade teacher Miss Cooper. She was so nice and kind. That was my first experience at being teacher's pet. It would happen so often I wondered throughout my school days if being the pet got me all As.

The first week I started grammar school, each student had to stand before the class and tell, among other silly facts, what our ancestry was.

"I am Scotch-Irish on my Dad's side of the family and my mother is all German," I admitted.

"Nazi," a boy peeped up under his breath.

The next day, my mother went to school and asked to speak to the boy who chirped in with that racist comment.

"Charles, my family and I migrated to this country before any of my parents' children were born. We are proud to be Germans. What is your ancestry?" Mother asked the child.

"We're Italians, ma'am," Charles answered.

"Albert goes to the Catholic Church more than he does to the church where we are members. He was even in their nativity pageant last Christmas," Mother added.

"I'm sorry I said that word, Mrs. Gaulden. Albert and I are friends," he said.

"No harm done. As a matter of fact I must have really come to class today to meet one of Albert's favorite pals," Mother said.

She hugged him before thanking him for speaking with her.

Charles and I were best friends all the way through grammar school and high school.

What really imprinted me most when we moved to the west side of Birmingham were the financial struggles. We made the move in 1948 when I was in fourth grade. I have two brothers and three sisters. We got new school clothes in September, and if we were lucky, something new to wear to church on Easter Sunday.

We lived in a federal housing project, euphemistically called the Village. Medical students and divorced mothers were the general makeup of families who lived there.

There were embarrassments to us youngsters around the lack of money. Our church saw to it that we went to the Fresh Air Farm several summers for free because we could not afford the tuition. To make matters worse, I refused to drink milk. I hated the taste and still do.

The camp nurse called me in to discuss why I would not drink milk.

"My mother never nursed me when I was a baby because I lived in the hospital from infancy for correction for my clubfeet. I have always refused to drink milk," I explained.

"Well, Albert, that makes perfect sense. Thanks for telling me your reason," the nurse explained.

My father's mother, Granny, came to visit us kids when we were at the Fresh Air Farm. She was the one who told me, "Take notes." Another admonition of hers was, "Never let anything get you down. You were born to win."

She died shortly after that visit. At the height of my drinking, when I thought all was lost, she appeared as an apparition at the foot of my bed and said, "Don't despair. It's going to be alright."

I got sober a few years later.

There were two events in my youth that affected me greatly. When I was in eighth grade, I was in the finals of the city spelling bee and I misspelled "blossom." I spelled it "blossum."

My aunt and mother were in the audience. Mother consoled me, but my aunt chastised me: "I drove all the way out here from Fairfield and dummy misspells a word that first graders could get right!"

When she was dying of cancer years later, I went to her daughter's house with balloons and a huge coconut cake with mounds of icing. She and I laughed like we were in a funhouse.

As I was leaving she told me she loved me and to forgive her for all the mean things she had ever said to me and my brothers and sisters.

"Gee, Aunt Mary, I only remember that you made the best desserts in the world. Looking back, you were good to us. You always invited us to Sunday lunch after church," I said.

Aunt Mary died a few weeks later.

The next year I was awarded second place in the Birmingham City Poetry Reading Contest for reciting *Abou Ben Adhem* by Leigh Hunt:

> Abou Ben Adhem (may his tribe increase!)
> Awoke one night from a deep dream of peace,
> And saw, within the moonlight in his room,
> Making it rich, and like a lily in bloom,
> An angel writing in a book of gold:–
> Exceeding peace had made Ben Adhem bold,
> And to the presence in the room he said,

"What writest thou?"—The vision raised its head,
And with a look made of all sweet accord,
.Answered, "The names of those who love the Lord."
"And is mine one?" said Abou. "Nay, not so,"
Replied the angel. Abou spoke more low,
But cheerly still; and said, "I pray thee, then,
Write me as one that loves his fellow men."

The angel wrote, and vanished. The next night
It came again with a great wakening light,
And showed the names whom love of God had blest,
And lo! Ben Adhem's name led all the rest.

In the eleventh grade I ran for vice president of the Ensley High School student body against a boy named Jerry Philips. His sister, who was the prettiest and smartest kid in school, was his campaign manager.

Losing was bad enough, but going into classes to see how badly was unbearable. Names and votes were on every classroom blackboard that day. Jerry was so nice to me in my loss. He consoled me by saying things like, "You're too nice to be in politics," and, "You're so smart you'll end up in Harvard or Yale."

That year I was tapped into the National Honor Society and I received a partial scholarship to Yale, but I could not go because the family could not afford the rest of the tuition.

At the high school graduation day picnic, everyone else in the class brought ice tubs full of beer. Except me. I brought Coca-Colas – more from being self-righteous than from not wanting to join in with the beer guzzlers.

It is hard for those who have known me over the last forty years to ever believe I was shy and retiring. The early years were when my minister and others in the church built a timeline of obedience to their tenets that I would one day disavow.

Going to church and being a good little boy makes sense to a lot of churchgoers. But to me, in hindsight, being an alcoholic and tearing my world apart with bad-boy behavior and too much hooch eventually saved my life and gave me a life worth living.

In retrospect, my first 18 years were a blueprint for everything I would one day disavow. What served me was to challenge my free-range Ego. Quiet but brilliant and insightful teachers and books would help me undo my past and replace the rutted dogma with what I discovered within me that would allow me to become authentic.

Getting sober would be the answer to all my prayers. But it would take a long time after tumbling into too many deep dark abysses.

Chapter Two
The Haze

When I graduated from high school, my self-righteousness stood tall as I took soda pop to the class picnic while all the other teens drank beer for the first time. Not me. I was a teetotaler. My minister told me I was going to be a pastor. So off I went to Howard College in Birmingham, Alabama. We newbies pastored small churches in South Alabama that could not afford to pay a full-time minister.

I was quickly into hero worship. Today they're called bromances. Mine was Joe Lawley, captain of the football team. Joe was a senior and I was a freshman. We shared preaching at County Line Baptist Church near Dudleyville, Alabama. He drove and we both visited the congregation after a meal with a member of the church. The tragedy that shattered Joe and affected me was when his girlfriend, Gayle Hyle, died in an automobile accident when Joe was driving them home from a dinner date.

One Sunday I was visiting members of the congregation, including an attractive and talkative woman. I asked her a question.

"Lorene, why do we never visit the family in that house?" I pointed to a small brick house on a street by itself.

"Preacher, don't bother with them. They're drunks," she spit as she spoke.

A chill ran through me that I later understood was foreshadowing of what was soon to come in my life. The spring term ended two weeks later. So did my quest for becoming a man of the cloth just because my pastor told me to do so. God had other plans.

I refer to the next year of my life as taking a sabbatical. Most people take one of those to advance their career and to get ahead. My time off was nothing more than the time I would trade in self-righteousness for alcoholism.

Someone had said I would make a good lawyer, so I hustled my way into Cabaniss & Johnston, one of the most prestigious corporate law firms in the south, to file briefs and do other tasks the attorneys needed for me to do.

It did not take me long to decide I did not want to be a lawyer. Although these men were brilliant, they were also hobnobbing snobs to the nth degree. But that year-long apprenticeship aided and abetted my path to alcoholism and reckless sinkholes for the next twenty years.

One day I was asked to take divorce papers to a woman staying at the Tutwiler Hotel in downtown Birmingham. I heard a lot of loud music and someone singing off-key when I got to her room. I knocked and the devil opened the door.

There stood a tiny woman with a mound of yellow hair dressed in a see-through peignoir and shaking a charm bracelet that spelled double trouble. She grabbed the divorce papers and stuck a frosty martini glass in my hand and said, "Honey, come on in and help momma celebrate her divorce from the biggest redneck son-of-a-bitch in Hicksville, Alabama."

I'd never had an alcoholic drink in my life. I let her rant and rave and dance and sing. I guzzled five or six martinis just like they were Coca-Colas.

"You're no fun. Let's go down to the Piano Bar and sing with Suzanne. I'll bet there are a lot of drunks waiting to twist and shout to my divorce news." Momma Mona started looking me up and down like I was a race horse and then asked, "Honey, how old are you anyway?"

"Nineteen," I answered.

"You're kinda little and green behind the ears, but let's go tear up that goddamn bar like we're a wrecking crew," she cackled.

We stayed and drank and acted crazy until the bar closed. I never forgot Mona and still remember Suzanne, the piano player.

I woke up the next morning at about six o'clock. I looked to one side, and there was a scary looking woman. I turned over to the other side and there was a beefy man.

"Good morning, sunshine," the mystery lady said as she planted a boozy kiss on my lips.

What happens to drunks shouldn't happen to the nice folks we want everyone to think we are. Too much booze has a way of painting everything rosy after a couple of belts. Sitting in a bar or getting smashed at a cocktail party, all logic is replaced by stinking thinking.

Someone in recovery told me years later that we want people to judge us by our intentions. Instead they nail us by our actions.

I took a job sorting checks at First National Bank. Remember these were the days before technology came along to dupe us into thinking it was here to help make our lives better. Thank God for that job. It kept me afloat, wallowing in booze and overspending.

I enrolled at Birmingham-Southern College in 1959. Never would I have gone to school there but it was up the hill from where we lived. I took a lot of history and psychology courses, and got a minor in Latin and Greek. There was little time for extracurricular activities because I had to work to pay my way through school. I spent one quarter slaving away in the library. That work was boring. I quit.

I took a job where my mother worked, Ribe & Associates, filing tariffs and other documents. Were the monotonous and boring chores for which I had been employed ever going to end?

I was drinking the whole time I was trying to get a college degree. I stayed sober through school hours and work. But then when the sun went down, I drank, and sometimes like a gentleman. That changed with time and frustration with stuck places.

I never know when analyzing my drunkalog how much high octane energy was due to being in a constant state of inebriation or to enthusiasm for a subject or anything else I threw my heart into.

Although I was a Pi Kappa Alpha at Howard College, I did not affiliate at BSC. My den of iniquity was the Sigma Alpha Epsilon fraternity. The brothers were known to live in a bubble of self-importance. In my state of never being sober, that description fit me like a well-tailored suit.

A close friend of mine from my Hunter Street Baptist Church days was John Andrew Martin. He was as smart as he thought he was and president of the Alpha Tau Omega fraternity, rivals of SAE. When he ran for president of the student body, I was an unappointed Campaign Manager for Tom Hearn, who ran against Martin. Hearn won and Martin never seemed to notice my preference for president had been Hearn.

All through my Birmingham-Southern college days, any candidate who ran for president of the student body sought my endorsement. My candidate always won. Perhaps it was a hangover for having lost the election for vice president in high school. I may have grown addicted to all the sucking up the boys in SAE did to court my favor.

I will admit that drinking destroyed any inkling of shyness that I ever had. But I continued to people-please to win applause from anyone who would clap.

The highlight of every day was when a long, tall black woman behind the counter in the cafeteria, Pearl, would dish and deliver with me. When I graduated, I bought her a gift for helping me make it through the oftentimes trance state of higher education. Now that I am sober for a long, long time, I have decided that humor and laugh and the world laughs with you are friends with my normal nature.

One big, exciting event happened in my senior year. One of my close and dear friends was a beautiful blond with an Ipana smile. Pippa was from a small town in southern Alabama, but there was nothing tiny or miniature about her. She was a gifted painter and had a laugh that could have driven Medea off the Argo.

One day a tall and muscular man with black wavy hair asked to speak to me.

"I am Chuck Garner and this is my first quarter at 'Southern. You seem to be quite friendly with someone I want to date, Pippa Patterson," he said.

There was an over-long pause in my retort.

"I hate to be rude but I don't think she'd want to go out with you because we always think muscle men like you are gay," I answered.

Garner was well over six feet. He snarled and fumed at my characterization of him.

Clamping his big wide hands on my shoulder, he spit out his retort. "I am not gay. Where in the name of God did you come up with that notion?" he asked.

This was 1961 and muscle mania had a different reputation then than it does today. We were living in the South where a lot of notions get skewered by false impressions.

"I am sorry that we seemed to have misjudged you by your, eh, size and manner of presenting yourself," I stuttered my apology.

Chuck seemed to decompress from my insinuation.

"It's lunch time. Why don't you and I have lunch? Are you a member of Birmingham Country Club?" I asked.

He nodded in the affirmative.

"Do you have a car here on campus?" I asked.

"Follow me," Garner answered.

We got into a humongous Buick convertible. Trying to play coy and not register my impression of what an amazing car he was driving, he flew across town. Thank God I did not wear a baseball cap in those days or it would have been gone with the wind at the speed he was driving.

He pulled up in front of the Birmingham Country Club. An attendant took the keys and we went into the inner sanctum of the ritzy crowd from "over the mountain," Mountain Brook. My friend Annie used to call MB the tiny kingdom. Some people swear that it even smells better in Mountain Brook, which was built by the rich.

Now here's a tidbit about this enclave. It is harder to become a member here than it is for Snow White to get into Heaven. There are a lot of clubs and organizations reputed to be exclusive, but money talks. Not at Birmingham Country Club. Remember the South lost the war and there are some things money can't buy? A club membership here is one of them. Oh, it costs alright, but these people are more interested in who your family is and how long they have lived on the right side of town. Pedigree is everything. Having said that, I was delighted to sit and have lunch and talk to Chuck Garner.

"The iced tea is a must. I always have a club sandwich with Durkee's dressing and cole slaw," he suggested.

"Whatever you're having is my pleasure," I said.

Before the best meal in town came to our table, I asked Chuck to fill me in and not to leave out how and when he got those muscles.

"I used to go to Washington & Lee before I transferred to Southern. Once I quit school to work on a ship at hard labor. My passion is writing. I have always been a bodybuilder," he told me.

"Charles, may I call you that, instead of Chuck? A famous psychiatrist once said that diminution of someone's name is trying to control the person whose name you are cutting off at the knees. Did you know that? Trivia, the country seems to live by it," I chortled.

I could tell that Mr. Garner was seething beneath visions of champing down on that Durkee's slathered club sandwich.

"Do you think that because you were more arts than labor you wanted to have a buttress, muscles and willingness to work among ordinary folks, to make you appear anything but soft artsy?" I asked.

"What are you, Albert, a shrink? I never think about why I do anything. I just do it if it feels right," he retorted.

Throughout the afternoon I found Charles charming and rather upfront and fearless about himself. As we both had a slice of pie, I threw an olive branch.

"Charles, why don't I set you up with Pippa? I like one of her sorority sisters. We can double date," I proposed.

"I like that idea. So I pass muster?" he asked.

"You and I will return to campus with you having been accepted with flying colors. And thanks for lunch. You had a few good suggestions, all delicious," I said.

He drove me back to school as fast as we made it to his country club.

As I got out of his car, he said, "How about Saturday night? We four can go to the drive-in to see *La Dolce Vita*," he asked me.

La Dolce Vita was one of Federico Fellini's cinéma vérité spoken in Italian with streaming dialogue interpretation in English. I didn't know if the other three of us would enjoy it or not.

"I'll set it up. I'll be at the women's dorm so we can all go see the movie from there," I said.

Fast forward. He was so intense in the movie that the two girls and I were amused. But he was earnest. This movie was his slice of life. Within a year of meeting Pippa they were married. He wrote a number of books and taught in private schools. One of his books was made into a movie. My baby sister Jeannie was an extra in it.

Pippa painted and taught art. They have three grown children and live somewhere exotic and fun, I am sure.

Another bit of trivia: When I was in my mid-30s I confessed that I had introduced more than twenty couples who got married. All but two are still hooked up as far as I know.

I had a major knee surgery six weeks before graduation. Dean Abernathy recommended that I drop out of all my classes.

"Ask your professors and see what they think," he said to me.

I took a course entitled "Napoleon and The French Revolution" from Dr. Evelyn Wiley. Although I was absent for two weeks, I took the final. I made an A.

I asked Dr. Wiley at graduation if she fudged my test results so I could graduate.

"I certainly did not, Albert. You wrote that exam paper as if you had lived the French Revolution. As a matter of fact, so much of what I asked for on the exam came from my notes and not a textbook. Your paper amazed me," she answered.

All my professors allowed me to stay enrolled in their classes and, to their surprise, I made As and Bs.

When I finally got my diploma it seemed as if I would never hold it in my hands. When you take six years to get a four-year degree, it seems as if you are languishing in an alternative universe. I have always lived between worlds and it was only when I finally bottomed out in 1980 that the life I was born to live really got started.

Chapter Three
Acting Out

After graduation in June 1962, I went to work as an assistant field director for the American Red Cross at the Charleston, South Carolina Air Force Base. Our primary purpose on base was to make emergency leave loans for airmen who had a crisis back home. We also oversaw blood bank donations. There was a lot of face-to-face counseling on a myriad of subjects and situations.

The job also gave us officer status so we could join the Officers' Club and drink scotch for ten cents a glass. You could afford to buy drinks all night long for a ten-spot. I felt like I had died and gone to heaven.

As a Pisces ruled by my feet (you got the scoop about the clubfeet), I loved to dance, drunk or sober. There was one beautiful blond named Holly Binke, ravishing but not reckless, every man's fantasy. Her husband was also a looker, but the men never wanted to dance with him. On Friday nights they closed the club drunk as skunks.

And then Shakespeare came to my rescue because I'd had a few turns on the boards before I got to Charleston.

On a dare, I auditioned for the part of Gerald Lyman, a minor role in *The Best Man*, written by controversial writer Gore Vidal, at the Dock Street Theatre. Emmett Robinson was managing director. You know Gore Vidal. He spent a lifetime trying to justify the cruel turn the gods gave him for being born gay. My character Gerald Lyman insinuates that one of the candidates had a questionable relationship with another soldier while on duty.

Robinson was so enamored by my drunken late entrances on stage that he said as much at the cast party.

"Mr. Gaulden you are a great actor on stage when you remember when it's time to enter stage left. You were impossible during rehearsals. As long as I am director I will never cast you again in another play."

I whispered to a lady who was in the play, "Gosh. Emmett really must have loved me to let me stay for a three-week run of show."

I lived on the Isle of Palms as opposed to the BOQ, bachelor officer's quarters. My roommates were members of the famous Blue Angels, an elite flight demonstration squadron, with aviators from the Navy and the Marines. One night carousing and getting into trouble in the Swamp Fox bar at the Francis Marion Hotel in the historic district, I met Simone Turner and Joy Sampson. They would become my mainstays while I lived in Charleston.

Simone was low-key but Joy was a two-fisted drunken hell raiser. In addition, Joy lived in one of the major old historic houses where we got looped most nights. It has been my history to attach myself at hello and stay until the last sad song is sung.

There is a great divide in Charleston, known as "below Broad," the snobby, upper class for monsieurs and madames of high society. Simone and Joy played with some bridge-a-philes in this ritzy bridge enclave. I got invited knowing next to nothing about how a certain player declared trumps, card count, or how many points a hand held in order to bid.

Alexia, the Italian contessa of the neighborhood, was my partner. After a few rubbers Alexia turned to me and asked, "Who taught you to play bridge so badly, Mr. Wonderful?" Needless to say I was never invited back to the exclusive bridge club again.

But Alexia did ask me to a few social dinners and parties.

"I'll go but never refer to me as your 'walker.'"

"What do I call you? My lover?" she asked.

"Alexia, you must be close to 70," I said.

"You're close. I'm a bit more. But the face is 10," she offered.

My history with the American Red Cross started when I was in the first grade. I was selected every year throughout both grammar school and high school to be the homeroom representative. Word got around in national Red Cross Headquarters of my service to the organization. It made a great PR story.

In December 1962, the American Red Cross sent me and a lot of staff to expedite medical supplies for prisoners being held by Cuba from the Bay of Pigs debacle. We did our work in Miami, which turned out to be one of the highlights of what was to be a short-lived career for me at Charleston Air Force Base.

"Laugh, and the world laughs with you; Weep, and you weep alone," were my sentiments entirely. For all of you teetotalers, drunks thrive on being able to motor on to the next bend in the road no matter what we leave behind us. Base Commander Colonel Griffith must have cosigned my insanity because he and I drank together the next night, and many nights afterwards.

Toward the end of my first year on the job at ARC, I was arrested on base for drunk driving. My drinking buddy was Colonel Griffith, and he bailed me out of the brig.

God works in wondrous ways. As we say in recovery, when one door slams shut another opens. In May 1963, Charleston Air

Force American Red Cross Field Director David Cooper called me into his office and told me that my former high school principal, E.E. Sechriest, wanted me to return to Birmingham to teach Latin and Civics at Woodlawn High School. Birmingham Public Schools were forced by the attorney general of the United States to integrate and Woodlawn was chosen as the first school to do so.

"Life always seems to have a plan," Mr. Cooper said. "Within hours of that call from Sechriest, I got a call from national Red Cross Headquarters that they were terminating your employment due to alcohol abuse."

Please sit quietly and ruminate about how God was working in my life. Up to this point I hadn't a plan or a clue where to go to next. Dorothy of Oz had the yellow brick road. I, first had the brig and then was summoned to the halls of ivy.

I called Dr. Sechriest and took the job. September 1963 would be a major turning point in my life. I would not get sober for many years but I did get to work with kids from middle and lower middle class socioeconomic families. President John F. Kennedy was also assassinated on November 22, 1963. Wait'll you read how the students celebrated the loss of our great president.

Have you begun to see how I always depended on geographical changes, new scenery and a whole new group who did not know I was a drunk? If you are asking yourself as you read, "Even a monkey learns. What happened to this guy?" I had no inkling that the potholes and missteps were all planned by the Upper World to try to get me to my bottom.

While driving back to Birmingham, I had an accident outside the Magic City. Trying to drive home, I decided to drive the distance without a pit stop except to buy gas. Whether it was the hangover from all the celebration at the Charleston Air Force Base or just being tired, I woke up just in time to swerve and miss a huge truck. Thankfully I was thrown from my MGB onto a deep pile of hay.

This may be a bit early and premature disclosure, but I know that my karma entitled me to an angel who turned the wheel for me. These kind of things happened all through my drinking career.

Going back to Birmingham could have been the Upper World's way of saying, "Go home. Start over. There is no better place to learn than teaching students. Learn your lesson."

Chapter Four

The Teacher Learns a Lesson

Thank God for Dr. Martin Luther King, the Kennedys – John and Robert – for their tireless work for civil rights, and, of course, for Lyndon Baines Johnson who got civil rights legislation passed in this country. The Birmingham battleground for sit-ins, marches and going to jail for one's beliefs was the agony all of us faced in Birmingham in the 50s and early 60s.

When I was asked to teach at Woodlawn High School in Birmingham, Alabama in 1963, I had no idea that the recent decision by the attorney general of the United States would set every nerve in my body on edge and try my patience to persevere.

On one hand, I had always hated the state of affairs in Alabama with denial of rights to blacks, especially in education. I was rankled for years that the leadership in my state was determined to deny, block, undermine and refuse to give equal rights to all people, regardless of color or religion. And so much of the state is in a sorry state as I write this.

There is an expression that suited me perfectly after my year there: "Had I known then what I know now, I would never have taught at Woodlawn High School in 1964." But I did, and here is what happened.

Teaching at Woodlawn High School was an out-of-body experience because the principal, Ralph Martin, was the biggest buffoon in town. And he was a bigot to the nines. On the first day of school he assembled students and teachers in the auditorium for the beginning of a week of mourning.

"I am declaring this a week of mourning for the unintegrated school we should still enjoy. Plutocrats in Washington have invaded our city and brought nigrahs (sic) into our classrooms. They should stay with their own people.

"As a symbol of mourning we are distributing black arm bands to show disdain for the federal government integrating our great school. Wear this armband as a token of support for the way it was here and around the country," Martin concluded.

Apparently a black armband symbolizes protesting going to war. It can also be used as a form of protest against a social or political issue. U.S. courts revealed that wearing a black armband as a means of freedom of speech is protected under the First Amendment.

When the kids got to my Civics classroom, I introduced myself and then said, "Take off those silly armbands. No one will wear them in my class and that's that," I orated.

"Mr. Martin told us to wear them," some nitwit piped in.

"When you enter this classroom I am in charge. Ralph Martin will never dawn the threshold of the classroom," I emphasized.

I knew that I, this 20-something renegade teacher, was out on a limb but I didn't care. I had abided all the redneck hoopla denying minorities the same rights as whites. It still festers in the Heart of Dixie.

"I'm gonna tell my momma and daddy what you done (sic) today. They gonna git (sic) all over you," said a freckled-faced girl munchkin.

"What is your name, dear one?" I asked.

"Laura Jean Poole, Mister Albert," she answered.

"Laura Jean Poole, tell yo momma and daddy that I will not discuss this matter with them. Better they save their gas money and spare me having to escort them to the FBI for interrogation for their seditiousness," I said with humor in my delivery.

"What is sewishous (sic)?" asked another.

"Each of you must look up SEDITION in the dictionary and write a short essay on what that word means. A hint: I am a constitutionalist, which means I separate ignorance from the true meaning of our country's bible, the Constitution. And the Constitution guarantees the right to worship as one chooses.

"Class dismissed. Now, Laura Jean, make sure you tell your momma and daddy what I said. No crazy parents or Ralph Martin crosses the doorway here in Mister Albert's classroom. Have a nice evening, ya'll," I said as I shut the door after the last kid made his exit.

I never heard a peep from the Pooles or any other student's parents. I did tell them to spell Negro phonetically: Knee Grow. When half the class thought George Wallace was president of the United States I gave them a card with John F. Kennedy's picture and the words president of the United States.

Then Friday, Nov. 22, 1963 happened. Lee Harvey Oswald killed President John F. Kennedy in a motorcade in Dallas at 12:30 in the afternoon Central Standard Time, the same time zone in Birmingham. Or so they say. I was smoking a cigarette off campus with Louise Pope, another teacher.

We hustled back to the school. There was cross-eyed crazy nutty pandemonium. A lot of kids were jumping out of windows. Many were celebrating the death of the president of the United States by whooping and hollering. Chaos reigned at the school all day. Principal Martin announced that the school would close. By 3 p.m., everyone had gone home.

CBS Washington correspondent Roger Mudd summed it up: "It was a death that touched everyone instantly and directly; rare was the person who did not cry that long weekend. In our home, as my wife and I watched the television, her tears caused our five-year-old son, Daniel, to go quietly and switch off of what he thought was the cause of his mother's weeping."

And who will ever forget what Kennedy said at his inauguration speech: "And so, my fellow Americans: ask not what your country can do for you – ask what you can do for your country. My fellow citizens of the world: ask not what America will do for you, but what together we can do for the freedom of man."

That weekend I did what I often do. I talked to no one and said nothing, even to my family that had always lived in the Magic City. Deep resonance of fear and dread filled me. I was confused. Anger paralyzed me. Rage consumed me. I also was mortified that unregulated gun control would soon kill Sen. Robert Kennedy and Rev. Martin Luther King. For those of us who believe in the inclusion of all people, we believed that insanity had been unleashed on our country.

There needs to be an amendment to the Constitution that alters the interpretation of the Second Amendment. It should say the right to bear arms ended with the independence from England. We do not need to have an open-ended right to bear arms.

A few weeks following the assassination of President Kennedy and after national news coverage reported the unthinkable cheering at the death of the president, the students calmed down.

My Latin classes made my teaching enjoyable. In my class was a wonderful young woman named Louise McPherson. She would correct a translation when I was in error.

"Girls and boys – as the intellectual bedrock of this otherwise unwashed and ignorant student body – please thank God for Louise. Had she not signed up for this class you would have learned a half-measure comprehension of Latin. I thank you every day of my life, Miss McPherson, for teaching me more about proper Latin than I ever learned from Dr. Butts at Birmingham Southern," I said to peals of laughter.

I was wont to tell a young girl being groped by her boyfriend in the halls of ivy, "Young lady, slap this ruffian so hard he'll keep his hands to himself." If I saw stragglers loitering in the halls I would interrogate each until they either left school or convinced me they were there on school business.

I drove a brand new white MGB convertible to school every day and parked it in the regular parking lot. One day after I had been teaching half a year, the office summoned me to say that someone called and threatened to bomb my car. The whole school was in an uproar. Police were called. The car was searched. No bomb. Principal Martin suggested I take my car home to defuse the hubbub over the threat.

For a few days one of the teachers picked me up at home and gave me a ride home. After following the routine for a week, I started driving my car into the lot. The incident blew over as quickly as it started.

Toward the end of the school term there was a Favorite Teacher vote to see who the students liked best. There were five teachers chosen for the final accounting. I was one of the five. We spoke in the auditorium at assembly.

"I have no idea why I was voted one of the finalists for Best Teacher. Many of you threatened to have me censured or at least to be confronted by your parents for misconduct. Someone threatened to blow up my car. None of this seems to qualify me to be Favorite Teacher. But this is what I will tell you: I have learned more than I ever taught any of you. This has been an incredible experience for me and it will affect who I am as I grow older.

"Although I have learned a million lessons at Woodlawn High School, I will not be back in September. Today I accepted a fellowship at the University of Alabama to teach Latin.

"And in closing, I have no idea how someone like me can be honored by people like you for just doing my job as best as I can. God bless all of you wherever you go and whatever you do after high school."

To my amazement and to the wonderment of a lot of students, I was selected Favorite Teacher. I gave my trophy to Louise McPherson because she had been my favorite student/teacher.

These years were the rollercoaster up and down and all around of my alcoholic drinking years. The best I can describe it is that I have always been a thrill seeker. Going from one high seeking a higher thrill was how I lived my life. In today's psychobabble it's called ADHD. What I had was active alcoholism, pure and simple.

When I got to the Tuscaloosa campus of the University of Alabama in the summer of 1964, I had been given the opportunity to live with a close friend's younger brother. Reese Hunt was star quarterback for the Crimson Tide.

By the time I had moved in with Reese, he had quit the team because the legendary coach, Bear Bryant, slapped and kicked him. Reese quit the team but not before he told Coach Bryant that no one would ever treat him like that, including the most famous football coach in the history of college football.

One day I was in our apartment when one of Reese's friends who had played football with him at Ramsey High School knocked on the door. His name was Greg Gilbert. Greg had played college ball at Auburn University.

After breakfast, I told Greg that I was going to Birmingham because my sister Margie was modeling for Seventeen Magazine at Loveman's Department Store. He asked if he could go with me.

I have always had an incredible relationship with Margie. I took her to first grade and always seemed to stay in close touch when I moved away from Alabama.

Margie was beautiful with a personality that could make a sourpuss smile. She was Miss Phillips High School, Miss Fire Prevention, president of her sorority and received a lot of other honors. Rarely have I met anyone to measure up to her. As she strutted down the runway I saw that Greg was very interested. We had lunch in Loveman's dining room, made small talk and then I drove back to school.

Someone came up to me on the Alabama campus several months later and told me that Margie had gotten married. I drove up to Birmingham and confronted her about it and she said yes.

"What about going to Auburn?" I asked.

"I am in love. Greg and I got married," she answered.

We talked for a couple of hours and then I went back to school. Soon I came to understand that she and Greg were meant to be together. And in my sensibility, God used me as a way to get to meet her.

Today she is a mother of three boys and grandmother to a slew of grandsons. Unlike most young brides, Margie went to college and got a Bachelor's degree and a Master's degree in psychology.

Graduate school turned out to be anything but where I could afford to be. For starters, I racked up so much debt that I could not stay in school. The real reason I left school was I saw a male student with our history professor in the stacks at the library in what looked like true love or lust. The professor was infamous for having sex with his male students. But you know tenure: kissy-face between consulting adults was no reason to throw the professor out.

Naive me went to the dean of the History Department and reported in detail what I saw.

"I am here to report an atrocity. Joe Blow was kissing Dr. Doolittle in the library. He's making an A for his bedside manner with our professor while I am sweating hours to get the same grade. What are you going to do about it?" I asked.

The History Department dean rubbed his hands together and then delivered his decision.

"Mr. Gaulden, we have enjoyed having you teach Latin to willing students. The Head of the Classics Department, Dr. Caesar, gave you a sterling review.

"Now, about your diatribe about Joe Blow and Dr. Doolittle, I suggest you withdraw from our Master's program as you will never get a degree from the University of Alabama. Do I make myself clear?"

I would liked to have said, "If that's how you feel about the matter, *&^%$ you and the horse you rode in on."

Instead I told him I had loved teaching Latin and perhaps I will learn to tend to my own business.

More of God's will. It is as if the Creator has high master minions tracking each of us on Earth, ready to put our train on that proverbial track of Manifest Destiny. As I left the office of the closed-minded cover-up head of the History Department, an acquaintance saw me loading my car.

"Albert, where are you going? I thought you were in summer school," Josh asked.

"I just quit," I lied. I wanted to say I was thrown out but my bruised alcoholic Ego thought better of it.

"What are you going to do now?" Josh asked.

What does a rambling rose, rudderless boat do when his life in tatters gets another tear?

Meekly I replied, "I have no plans."

"How about you come back to New York and stay with me and my family for awhile. We live on Long Island," Josh asked.

Never one to turn down an offer to get high on life with a little help from Jack Daniels, I excitedly said, "Yes, I'd like to go home with you."

Later in life I would fall in love with that Bette Midler line, "Take me, take me anywhere..." That could have been my theme song throughout life.

The long and winding road to New York was amazing, torturous, heart breaking as well as hitting another bottom – but I did not stop drinking.

Chapter Five
Pretending

Staying with Josh's family was just what Doctor Who ordered. For a few days we had fancy dinners out, played a lot of tennis at his country club, and swam every day at his pool. The two of us had too many calories from alcohol. His mother sucked up the Beefeaters as if she were an ad for overeater drinkers anonymous. His Dad was a teetotaler. Josh had an occasional beer.

One morning at breakfast his Dad and I were eating alone.

"Please pass the sugar. Oh, and by the way, Albert, either get a job or go home," Dad said, giving me notice that my freeloading days were over.

I decided to go into the city to look for work. Dad said that there were two major industries in Manhattan. One was advertising and the other was fashion. My pick was women's fashion but I would one day dabble in advertising.

First off, I have three sisters. I read labels in their shirts and sweaters. In those days with our economic limitations, the girls swapped, loaned, borrowed and bought a few things that were from Villager and Bobbie Brooks.

Secondly, when I was 16 I was in the chorus of a musical, *Best Foot Forward*, at Town and Gown Little Theatre in Birmingham. There was a number called "The Barrel House, the Boogie-Woogie and the Blues," sung by three woman, two of whom went on to be Miss Alabama and runner-up to Miss America. I became close to Lee Thornberry, later Miss Alabama 1958, and Anne Ariail, Miss Alabama 1956.

Through these women I met Polly Cain, fashion director at Loveman's department store in Birmingham. Knowing Polly, I learned a thimble-full about women's styles and fashion.

I had Dad drop me at the preeminent cluster of ladies' ready-to-wear at 1407 Broadway in the heart of Manhattan. I scanned the directory of showrooms in this building, recognizing Bobbie Brooks, Jonathan Logan and The Villager Sportswear from labels either worn by my sisters and their friends or from Polly Cain.

I started with Bobbie Brooks because the name sounded so folksy and not too fancy. Here is how the interview went:

Sonny: "So what brings you to New York?" he asked.

I wanted to say I just got kicked out of school, and I'm dead broke and have become a deadbeat at a friend's parents' house. Not a good ice breaker, so instead I said: "School's out. I always wanted to break into fashion. So here I am," I exaggerated.

"Why Bobbie Brooks? What qualifies you to sell in our show-room?" he asked.

I wondered to myself, "Is this Sonny man what they refer to as *peculiar* in Alabama?" I later found out from an interviewer at Jonathan Logan that Sonny was as gay as Liberace and not as much fun.

"I am told that I am clever, easy to know and I like women more than men," I answered.

"I think you'll do just fine here. But I could pay you more if you moved to Cincinnati, our home office," Sonny said.

I said to myself, "Did you asshole think I came to the Great White Way to go to senseless Cincinnati? And what's with waving those hands around like an Italian in heat?" I could swear Sonny was wearing pancake makeup and eyeliner.

"I'd rather stay in New York," I said.

Sonny pursed his lips and batted his eyes like Rosalind Russell did in *Mame* and said, "Would you like to continue this interview tonight over dinner?"

Not missing a beat I stood up and said as I headed to the door, "I'm late for Jonathan Logan. Thank you for seeing me."

When I got to Jonathan Logan, I was ushered into a tall, dark and handsome man's office. His name was Jonathan. After pleasantries I sat waiting for the interrogation, I mean, interview to start.

"You must be one of the Logans," I said.

"Nope, I just work for them. My last name is Schwartz," he answered.

I repeated the lie that I had always wanted to work in fashion. Alabama was such a drag and New York seemed to be so exciting.

"Two days a week anything goes in Manhattan for a rag salesman. The other five your ass is glued to a showroom waiting on boring people who sometimes are just here to eat the lox and bagels." Jonathan laughed like this was standard for the newcomers.

After a few minutes he interrupted my rehearsed pitch about always wanting to work at 1407 Broadway and said, "Sorry, Albert. Jonathan Logan is not for you. You're a *goy* and we do better with Jewish salesmen."

If it had been today and not 1965 I would have said, "Listen, you asshole, I will sue you for the millions of dollars you've stashed in the Cayman Islands. You cannot hire or refuse to hire someone based on their ethnicity!"

Instead I shook his hand and thanked him for the interview.

On my way to The Villager Sportswear on the twenty-first floor, my guardian angel whispered in my ear. "Go into the showroom and act like you're a buyer shopping the line. Match skirts and sweaters. Refuse any help from a salesperson," the devil on my shoulder said. I did exactly that.

William Shakespeare wrote, "All the world's a stage," so watch me make my entrance.

I walked into the showroom and matched skirts with a pan collar shirt and sweater just like I was a seasoned buyer. This went on for about half an hour.

"Mr. Bigler would like to see you in his office," a blond bombshell said. I followed her offstage.

I went into his office. Mr. Bigler asked me to sit.

"Who in the hell are you and what are you doing in my showroom? I know you're not a buyer from a department or specialty store. How did you get into my showroom?" Bigler asked.

Earl looked like a character out of a Damon Runyon novel. Runyon was best known for his short stories celebrating the world of Broadway in New York City that grew out of the Prohibition era. To New Yorkers of his generation, a "Damon Runyon character" evoked a distinctive social type from the Brooklyn or Midtown demi-monde. Think Nathan Detroit in *Guys and Dolls* and Bigler was a dead-ringer.

"I have run away from home and I am lost," I wanted to say, but the look on Mr. Bigler's face said spill the beans, so I did.

When I was done with my tale of woe in need of a job, he hired me on the spot.

"I will run a make on you and if you're not wanted by the FBI or police in Birmingham, and are as clean as a whistle, you keep the job," Earl said. So that was how I auditioned my way into a job at The Villager Sportswear.

Day one on the job, the buyer from the Federated office brought Lady Bird Johnson and her daughter Lynda into the showroom. It was not uncommon for well-known people like the president's family, celebrities and other hoity-toity types to get clothes for wholesale.

Three things happened while I was in New York that redirected my perception of me and of the life I had lived so far.

The first thing: On Nov. 9, 1965, the lights went out in the northeast. The blackout occurred around 5:27 p.m. My coworkers and I were stranded on the twenty-first floor. The blackout lasted until the next morning.

Betsy, manager of Ladybug, junior division of The Villager, roomed thirty blocks north. She had a three-bedroom that she shared with stewardesses who were all on flights, thus an empty nest this night. We schlepped uptown, all 14 of us.

Norman Rabb, the CEO and President of the company, was in town so he hiked with us. Betsy arranged a game we played to see who slept where and with whom. A few of the crowd found a sofa in someone else's apartment. That left eight of us who needed to bed down at Betsy's.

As the game was played, Mr. Rabb and I were selected to sleep on a queen-sized pull-out sofa bed in the living room.

I guess you're thinking, "How awkward?" Not in the least. Like Scheherazade from the Arabian Nights who saved her life with endless exotic tales to the Sheikh, I got a promotion simply telling Norman who I was, where I had been and what I had done. Throughout the blackout sleepy time Mr. Rabb kept saying, "Is that really true?" "You did what?" "I have never heard anything quite like your life."

The next morning, in the light of day, Mr. Rabb announced that Betsy was leaving the company and Albert Gaulden was the new manager of Ladybug.

You could have heard a faint heartbeat. The news went up and down the elevator shaft like celebrity gossip which went something like, "The only way to get ahead at Villager and Ladybug is to sleep with Norman."

The second thing: I drank at all the happening watering holes in Gotham City. Mike Malkins was my drop-in-stay-all-night pub of choice. Famous barflies were Baby Jane Holzer, Edsel Ford and Huntington Hartford, the scion who looked a lot like Howard Hughes in his last days. Huntington would die at the age of 97 in 2008 with a lot less money than he inherited.

I became known as the head honcho of the posse of great looking girls and boys from Villager. We haunted Harlow's, which was owned by Sybil Burton, Richard's ex-wife. We dropped in and out of Le Club, an upper echelon dive where I met Mark Goodson, who owned quiz shows. He put me on *Match Game*. Florence Henderson was celebrity team captain. We won a ton of money. A small sidebar: Mark was married at the time to a former Miss Alabama, Virginia McDavid.

I'll never forget my favorite, Patsy Drohomer, my closest posse pal from Ormond Beach, Florida, who could drink and throw bon mots at all the hangers-on. She was famous to say to a wannabe getting nosy about who she was and where she worked, "One has to have family fortunes to work at the Villager." Villager paid 75 bucks a week to newbies.

Drinking too much is akin to being homeless, always available to cut and run at the hint of everything turning to *merde*. Alcoholism is an infusion of drinking daily and always seeking someplace, somehow living on the top of all notions and conjectures. When I got sober in 1980, one of my favorite shares in meetings was, "We were so high we could have jumped from the Time & Life Building to see if we would bounce."

Third Thing: After I was a big presence at Village and Ladybug, I brought women to buy wholesale. Out drinking one night, I met Walter Gould, who produced concerts and records for well-known artists and was the husband of Mimi Benzell, the opera singer. He was drinking with his friend Sol Hurok, the legendary impresario who made the impossible breakthrough by bringing the Bolshoi Theatre Ballet to America during the Cuban Missile crisis. Mimi came and bought and was glad that Walter and I met.

I met Jayne Mansfield on several flights and we became instant friends. She was Mensa-brilliant and used her body and beauty to earn a lot of money making movies. She flunked the wholesale test by being too buxom for our clothes.

Vicky Power was Miss Alabama 1965 and runner-up to Miss America. Her chaperone was Byrd Knapp, who turned out to be a master astrologist. Byrd and I had a three-hour lunch during which she explained my birth chart to me. Her knowing that Carl Jung would not see a patient without reviewing their birth chart astonished me.

Not only did she spot my alcoholic drinking but she picked the very year I got sober, 1980. She became my first teacher and I could decipher astrological charts in five weeks.

I was offered a job at rival ready-to-wear house Crazy Horse. They paid so much more than where I was, so I left Villager and Ladybug.

Drinking was costing me a lot more than it used to. Rents were so cheap that three of us had a three-bedroom apartment for around $600 a month. But this also was 1965-66 — more than fifty years ago!

One day I was writing Patsy Drohomer a letter. Email and social media were nowhere on the drawing board. In that letter I said that one of the owners had rotten lox and bagel breath. But the insult that got me fired was that I said that he had gout so bad that some mad dog might run into the building and eat his legs off.

Where do you go when you run out of money and get fired from your job? I ran home to mommy who lived in Birmingham, Alabama. She was not real thrilled to see me. Everybody might turn their backs on you, but not your mother.

Because I had a reference from Villager's ad agency, Braun & Miller in New York, Martin White and Mickwee Advertising Inc. in the Magic City gave me a job as copy chief. I drank, but less, and did a lot of good work there. I went to church at Briarwood Presbyterian and reactivated Jesus and Christianity in my life. There were fun times and I learned to love and adore Barbara Barker, the minister Frank Barker's wife. Compassion overrode her capacity to be preachy.

What lay ahead was getting sober, and with the help of God and Guardian Angels, my life would change for the better.

Chapter Six
Flying High

———

"Keep moving" is the mantra drunks make with life to survive. A lot of this is because in a moment of clarity, we can't stand ourselves. We do not want others to figure out who we really are – phonies full of baloney. In my case, debt was an instigator to seek another job, another place – anywhere but where I was.

I was looking in a newspaper and found an ad that said that Harris & Weinstein on Peachtree in Atlanta was looking for a copy chief. Right down my alley and just far enough from Birmingham that news wouldn't travel that fast.

Another thing about us drunks is that we think we are the center of everybody else's universe. And we are hopeless people-pleasers. The pleasing is all about "don't look too close or ask too many questions."

What a place H&W turned out to be. Immediately Carolyn Harris, the company's vice president, and I became joined at the hip. I was her confidante. She told me everything about everybody and she insisted I tell her every last shred of information unverified, even if it was salacious gossip.

But I loved her a lot. She was another drug for this alcoholic. Oh, yes, dear class, advertising sorts drink like fish. Did you ever watch *Mad Men*? Believe every frame.

I was hired because H&W was going to be fired as the agency for Southern Airways (SA). The CEO of the airline told Carolyn and Abe Weinstein, the company's president, to hire a man to write copy for them. It seemed that the big fish at SA didn't like Carolyn, so here I was. It must be another "God's will thing."

You have to remember (oh, look it up on Wikipedia) that in 1968, Atlanta was a small town. There were no mega-highways or freeways. I lived in Peachtree Battle – tiny in comparison to what it looks like today. I knew where every classy bar or dive was in the first 48 hours. We drunks always like to have one with the classy drinkers but then as the night gets darker and more dangerous, we will find a hole in the wall.

Now for the crux of the reason I was hired – change the advertising to get Southern more business. You have to ask your oldest friends how air travel was in the halcyon days of air travel. Airlines delivered great service and good meals, even in coach. There were no baggage fees, charges to change a reservation, higher rates for certain seats and never, ever add-on fees that are so ridiculous in the twenty-first century.

There were two main thrusts of my tenure at H&W. First, I had to deliver a campaign that Southern Airways would accept and use as their road to higher profits through ticket sales. Second, the account executive of the Southern Airways account was tall, dark and handsome Fred McVickers. Like the head of the airline, Fred and Carolyn were oil and water. He was determined to steal the account and take it to a New York agency. His job before this one was in Gotham City.

No problema, señor y señora. It'll be a piece of cake. No, it was not, in any shade of the fabrication.

As the contest of wills heated up, along came Baba. Her real name was Ruth Noble Golden, who had been a Corolla beauty when we were at the University of Alabama. When I say she jammed traffic and frazzled pacemakers, she was a showstopper.

She seemed to have been between engagements as had I all of my life. Baba was working at an employment agency, the type that got executives jobs for which they may or may not have been qualified. She lived in a so-so building near every fun restaurant and bar in Atlanta. Ruth eventually married Winston Groom, who wrote *Forrest Gump* among other best-sellers. It won a lot of awards as a movie starring Tom Hanks.

Baba and I were fated to meet and have a great time together. She didn't drink like I did, but don't count the drinks, pity the drunks.

I loved to shock her with stories and the typical hillbillies who were all over Atlanta.

One day I met a young traffic cop named Chaz who was keeping people out of a shopping area next door to where Baba lived. He and I got to talking, and I told him I wanted to play a joke on my friend who lived in the building adjacent to this shopping mall.

We planned what he would say. I gave him a $20 bill for playing this silly trick on my friend.

Here's what happened. We went up to her apartment together but I hid behind a wall at the stairwell.

Knock. Knock. Knock.

"Ruth Noble Golden, this is the police. We have a warrant for your arrest for growing marijuana. Open up," the officer demanded.

"Oh, dear God, I don't even smoke that horrible stuff," Baba said behind her closed door.

"Open this door, Miss Golden. This is the Atlanta Police Department with a warrant for a search," Chaz said loudly.

The door flew open and Baba had that deer in the headlights look and pleaded, "Come in and search. I have no drugs."

I popped out and screamed, "April Fool's in March!"

"Albert, I could kill you. Ya'll come in. I assume you two know one another," she blathered.

A few weeks later she and I went to Washington to see Winston Groom. He was a charming and funny man. Why do I, Zacchaeus-like in stature, always have to know and like tall handsome men? Could it be a lesson in humility?

In the dress rehearsal before we went before the Southern Airways executives, Fred McVickers, as account executive, was to approve the presentation. As he walked around looking at each storyboard while rubbing his chin-a-chin, he said at last, "This approach is not hitting me."

I got up from my chair, walked over to a storyboard, picked it up and began hitting Fred over the head while loudly declaring, "Let's see if this hits you!"

"You don't have to get physical just because I disagree with the campaign," Fred said.

The meeting was adjourned until another campaign could be prepared for Southern Airways. By this time Carolyn Harris had managed to take back the responsibility for the Southern Airways account. A few months later I took another job in Mobile, Alabama.

In 1979, Southern merged with Central Airlines to become Republic Airlines. On Oct. 1, 1986, Republic became part of Northwest Airlines, which in turn merged with Delta Air Lines.

I liked all the people at Harris & Weinstein, especially Carolyn. She reminds me of a myriad of women I've worked with or fought with over the years. Every step I take gets me closer to God's will for my life.

If you are beginning to ask yourself, "Why is this man telling us where he's been that too much drinking took him?"

All of us have an Achilles heel so I wanted to weigh in that my weakness was gnarled feet at birth. "The best laid schemes o' mice an' men," a saying adapted from a line in *To a Mouse* by Robert Burns in, "gang aft a-gley." Publicists are in the business of sanitizing one's backstory to create a better image. But not me.

In the life and times of the twenty-first century, so much of what we are experiencing — wars and financial woes — are the consequences of lives we've lived somewhere as someone else before. My purpose for writing *Moments and Windstorms* was to let others know that more is required of us than sweat lodges and tapping and rapping with inspiring sermons from gifted speaks. It is our duty to unwind and relive with soul honesty and to expose the things we've done to create the world we live in.

Chapter Seven
Fantasy

The best and worst thing that ever happened to me was when I decided to move to Los Angeles to sell a movie I wrote, *Mae West is Mother Goose*. The year was 1972 and I had decided to leave the ad agency in Mobile, Alabama.

But before I took off for the Wild West, I agreed to take a meeting with the biggest account we had at the time, a bank. I got to the board room an hour early. Sitting drinking was a man I'd never seen.

"Son, what are you doing here?" he asked.

"I am creative director of this bank's ad agency," I answered.

"I think we are both a bit early," he offered.

"I am always early for a meeting. You know that old saw 'early bird catches the worm?'" I joked.

"How do you know I'm not your competition for the bank's advertising budget?" he asked.

"You might be, but I always go into anything thinking I'm going to win," I answered.

"Have a drink. It'll do you a lot of good for what's coming," he chortled.

The man introduced himself as Richard and I told him who I was. We got into what I would do to help the agency keep the account. Richard confessed he was not the competition. I gave him the complete campaign that the ad agency had turned down, but which I thought was a better pitch for the bank. When he asked me what my ideas were, I told him in five minutes.

In a matter of minutes the room was full of bank employees as well as the president, art director and media buyer for the ad agency. A man who was president of the bank introduced himself, and said that the bank had been unhappy with the advertising agency and that this meeting was to decide whether to keep us or let other agencies make pitches for their business.

"I would like to introduce you to the chairman of the board of the bank, who asked for a review of the agency's work. May I present... Richard." He was the man I had been drinking and gabbing with. Stars fell on Alabama and my heart fell into my shoes.

"I will keep this brief and say that I have decided to stay with the ad agency of record. I spent an hour with Albert, the creative director, before the meeting started. I do not want to see your campaign ideas. Go back to the drawing board and bring me the campaign that Albert and I have been talking about. Meeting adjourned for two weeks. Good luck, fellows."

Then Richard came over to me and shook my hand and said, "Never change who you are. Do not cut the foot to fit the shoe. See you in two weeks. Good luck."

The art director and I agreed on a strategy. I stayed at the agency for several more weeks. We kept the account and I loved what Richard said to me after meeting.

"You told me when we first met that you were going to Los Angeles to try to sell an idea for a movie. Thanks for staying until the agency got your ideas on storyboards. Stay in touch and let me know how things are going," Richard said.

He hugged me goodbye and slipped a business card in my jacket pocket and said, "In case you need me, here's my private number."

Let me be clear about Richard's generosity. I liked him and thought he had big balls to stand up for me when I was the youngest and newest at the agency. I like to say that God will lead us even when we won't let him. The inner compass still pointed to the City of Angels. Four weeks later I left Mobile and never looked back.

I decided to stop in New Orleans to see a couple I'd met there in a bar. New Orleans and Mobile could be sister cities for more drunks per square foot than anywhere else in Dixie. The two of them were drunks to the nth degree. She said, "We never met anybody who could keep up with us drinking until we met you." That night we partied until dawn with some floor flushers that we met.

I left my car on the street parked overnight with the doors unlocked. The next morning all my clothes had been stolen except what I had put in the locked trunk. *Peut-être*, could this be more foreshadowing of my trip out west?

When I got to LA I found the hip bar The Raincheck Room to ask where I could find Mae West. "Ask Rona Barrett," an actor said. "She works at KTLA on Sunset Boulevard."

I hightailed it over to the television station and told the receptionist I had an appointment with Rona Barrett. She called Rona and she said to let me come back.

"Who in the hell are you and why did you tell the receptionist we had an appointment?" Rona asked.

"Tell me, Miss Rona, why did you agree to see me if you didn't know me?" I asked.

There was a pregnant pause.

"Let me guess. You felt that I took a page from your playbook – how to get in the door uninvited," I smiled.

"Sit down, Albert. I like you already. How can I help?" Rona asked.

I told her how I had seen some old Mae West movies and found out she was still alive and working. I had written a skit for the Tri Delta Sorority at the University of Alabama titled *Mae West is Mother Goose*, which was a huge success.

I think I'd better fill you in on a bit more of a backstory. In the mid-60s I was asked to teach Latin at the University of Alabama in Tuscaloosa. I hung out at a fraternity house whose brothers were Tri Delta favorites. I met a one young woman who asked me if I was interested in writing a skit for an annual program that Tri Deltas were signed up for.

She and I went out to dinner that night and I can tell you she was the most aggressive person I had ever met. And she was pretty and Mensa-genius constructed. After the dinner I said I would write the skit, and what I wrote was *Mae West is Mother Goose*. They won skit night.

Now back to LA and Rona Barrett.

I spoke so fast I am surprised Rona could follow my trail. My tale included how I had seen her on television and read one of her books. Without a pause I said I always wanted to live in Los Angeles. Savvy businessmen always told me not to leave one job until you have another, which I did anyway. I did not tell Rona that I was an alcoholic who didn't know who he was or what he wanted to do with his life, but I knew I wanted to drink. I swallowed a lot of hooch in the next eight years. But we discussed my movie project in depth.

"Albert, you remind me of me. I was a Jewish girl from Queens who changed her name to Barrett because Burstein wouldn't get it in Hollywood. You may never get Mae on the phone. She is older than God and they have to shoot her through layers and layers of Vaseline on the lens, just like they did Marlene Dietrich. But I can tell you where she lives: on Rossmore. With your chutzpah you'll probably get in the door," said Rona.

She gave me the address for Mae West on a private "For Your Eyes Only" business card and said, "Good luck. I have a feeling you don't need it."

Mae West lived in the Ravenswood compound in apartment 611 at 570 North Rossmore in Tony Hancock Park. I tipped the doorman twenty bucks. The elevator stopped at her apartment, the only one on that floor.

When the elevator door opened, there was a tall, dark and handsome man in a suit who asked what I wanted. I could see Mae West dressed in an evening décolleté gown under soft flattering light, sitting in a chair across the room.

"What does he want, Roger?" Mae asked.

"He's here to talk to you about starring in a movie he wrote, *Mae West is Mother Goose*," he answered.

"Fuck Mother Goose and Donald Duck. I like my men hung and dumb. Throw him out," she told Roger.

And therein lay the end of the magical magnifying mind about me and Mae West.

The eight years before I got sober were filled with Looney Tunes of my own production. The Raincheck Room became a haven for all us drunks and drug addicts. "I buy, you buy." The next drink was a ritual. If you broke the drunk's code, you were ignored if not banished.

Chapter Eight

Conjuring

———

Although I had done a lot of astrology birth charts in the last four years, I did not know enough people in Los Angeles to work with or to get recommendations. This is called networking. I had no net and no clients who could work me into their social crowd.

Remembering what Josh's Dad said on Long Island, the voice in my head whispered to me, "Get a job or go home." What a concept.

What I never tried nor would I was hustling or begging. I was only 32 at the time – and possibly passable with my looks – but I would never think of prostituting myself.

I found the biggest department store in Beverly Hills was Robinson's. In a matter of days from "Get a job or go home," I applied for a job at the department store. They put me in the sheets and bedding department. I had a ball. The human resources department head was over the moon about my time with The Villager Sportswear and Ladybug.

Retail is always looking for ways to make sales staff outdo one another to make the bottom line of the store sizzle for corporate headquarters or stock holders. This notion probably started with

Jesus and his famous sermon, the Sermon on the Mount. Vendors and others purveyors were making deals all over the hillside.

In a few weeks I was a phenomenon. Keep your cheat sheet on my life updates: I was still drinking. Where do you think I headed the minute the bell rung to let us slaves out the back door? If you said The Raincheck Room, you have a good memory.

This was Beverly Hills so we sold a lot of comforters, duvets and silk sheets to movie star actors, directors, producers and to their wives or majordomos.

After six months I got restless.

What can you do with bedding and linens but sell more of the same? Someone told me that a high-fashion store, I. Magnin, was hiring, so I skedaddled a few blocks down Wilshire to interview. The woman in charge was so officious that I nearly walked out before the interview started. The minute I stood up my name was called.

"I see your background is in women's fashion and advertising. You are presently working at Robinson's Department Store. What made you come to California and why do you want to leave after six months?" the woman said.

By the way, the woman, Mrs. Auschult was no Judy Holiday in *Born Yesterday.* More like Nurse Ratched from *One Flew Over the Cuckoo's Nest.*

"I came to Los Angeles to break into writing for movies. The town is full of wannabes, so I decided that selling was in my blood. As for I. Magnin over Robinson's, I am better at fashion than bedding," I said.

She called me back a couple of days later and offered me a job in Men's Wear on the second floor.

When I was working my last day at Robinson's, a nurse came into the store with a wild-haired redhead in tow. Although the disheveled woman was unrecognizable to most people in the world, I knew it was Margarita Carmen Cansino, better known as Rita Hayworth, one of the biggest movie stars in the world for forty years.

"May I help you?" I asked.

"Don't come near me or I will kill you," Miss Hayworth said as she threw a pile of towels at me.

The nurse calmed her down. She sat Rita in a chair and then quietly said that her client had dementia and often was unable to be in public.

What a way to say ta-ta to Robinson's.

I am attempting to show a pattern of how a Source or Energy was working to help me even though I was still drinking.

I. Magnin had a reputation of being très hoity-toity and impressed with itself that I just threw caution to the wind and made it my fancy playpen. Selling men's clothing was a piece of cake. Men tend to buy, not shop, just like I do.

The store had a policy of salespeople taking turns in a rotation system. I was not interested in abiding by that rule. When someone sashayed into our department, I took him whether it was my turn or not. We were on commission so the dog-eat-dog mentality was rampant. By the way, the commission was so tiny that you could barely find it in your paycheck.

One day, a well-dressed Italian tapped my shoulder and said he wanted to buy a wardrobe. Two hours later he had spent $20,000. The minute he left the department, Miss Jan had me called up to the office to be scolded. When the brouhaha was over, they gave Jan half of the commission. She crowed for eons about how she runs the show in the men's department.

The gentleman turned out to be a gigolo-chef from one of the top retreat spas. His paramour was a rich lady he met and bedded at the spa. She liked him so much she paid him $50,000 for her one-week stay.

He was charming but dangerous. His reputation as a chef was impeccable. Let's call him Marcello. He had so many women that he went to Italy several times a year. When we met he had just published a very successful cookbook.

Several months later I had a fascinating and kind gentle Jewish mensch who came in every two weeks or so. I'll call him Barry. One day he asked me to go on my break with him to have coffee. I told Jan I was going with the gentleman on a long break and she said, "Take your time. Momma is hungry for a big commission."

We went to the curb and a chauffeur opened the door of his Rolls Royce and Barry said, "Let's go to the Beverly Hills Hotel."

I had no idea what was to come.

At table, Barry ordered a magnum of Louis Roederer Cristal and food for an army.

"Don't worry about getting back to I. Magnin today. I called the store manager and said I had business with you. I also told him not to expect you back today," Barry advised me.

We drank and we ate and had a lot of laughs. Barry asked a few questions about my background. I told him everything – except that I had a drinking problem. When we got to the movie I wrote and my going to see Rona Barrett and Mae West, he held up his hand, which I took to mean, "Enough already."

"I have brought you here to offer you a job," he said.

I was dumbfounded and more than curious.

"What kind of job?" I inquired.

"I own a Porsche automobile dealership downtown Los Angeles and I want you to go to work for me selling cars." Barry smiled when he said that sentence.

"Barry, I have no idea why you would offer me a job selling exotic cars. I don't know how many cylinders a car has or whatever else is under the hood. When I take my car in for service, a mechanic fixes it and charges me," I confessed.

"You have sold me a lot of clothes I didn't think I needed. But more than that, you told me when something was not right for me. My wife asked me recently, 'When did you get so good at picking out clothes that look so good on you?' I told her about Albert.

"I let the manager at I. Magnin know that I was going to offer you a job. If you want to work for me. You'll work out a two-week notice. Albert, no one would ever care how many cylinders are in a Porsche or anything technical. You are a natural," he said.

"I work on salary plus commissions at the store. From what I know, car salesmen work on commission only. That might be a deal breaker for me, Barry," I said.

"Albert, I am prepared to give you $5,000 per month for the first six months against any commission you make selling Porsches. If you are not making double or triple that by that time, I will shake hands and wish you well and say goodbye.

"The best incentive for taking my offer is that you will drive a loaner car, a Porsche, as long as you work for me," he finished with that mind-blowing incentive.

"You've got yourself a know-nothing salesman. Thanks for the chance to have a great experience and make a lot more dough," I said.

We finished the magnum. He dropped me back at the lot where my car was parked.

And that, ladies and gentlemen of the jury, is how the Source got me on track and driving a Porsche.

So much of my life has looked like a movie, you know, where they rewrite the story line to death, stop and start and re-shoot until the director gets a movie that he thinks the public will buy.

One rainy Saturday night I decided to drink the night away in a dive off Sunset Boulevard. I got there after eleven o'clock and the bar closed at 2 a.m. It is obvious that most of these rats in a cage were looking for a warm body to go home with. You know, the ones that won't remember your name if you ever run into them again.

I was gulping a couple of double scotches and leaning against a wall when a man poked my arm.

"Baby, sit down before you fall down," he said, pulling me into the banquette where he was drinking with a few other men.

I sat there as quiet as Mallymkun the Dormouse from *Alice's Adventures in Wonderland* by Lewis Carroll. Maybe I dozed off or nodded to any silly sally thing any of the men said.

The man whispered in my ear, "What I love is a man who shuts the fuck up. He wants you to think he's drunk, not stupid."

At that I chuckled. For some off reason I liked my nanny rescuer on this dreary night.

When the bar closed he asked me to breakfast at one of those all-night diners down the street. He and I talked for a long time. As do most drunks, I spilled the beans about coming to Tinseltown to do *Mae West is Mother Goose* and how soon I will sell Porsches.

As we parted on the street he kissed me on the forehead and hugged me tight.

"You are one of the bright lights of my life, Albert. Who knows, maybe one day soon I'll write about you and me and the dark night of the soul," Tennessee Williams said.

He went one direction and I headed back to my car. I never saw him again. Tennessee, who was born on March 26, 1911 – an Aries – died on Feb. 25, 1983.

Just like my encounter with Tennessee Williams, I met a young actress sitting at the bar in the Polo Lounge at the Beverly Hills Hotel. In "getting to know you, getting to know all about you,"

I told her that I worked time to time with birth charts using the modality of Dr. Carl Jung.

"Are you like a traveling therapist?" Gaia asked me.

"Yes and no. I'm actually starting a new job selling Porsches tomorrow. But I have also rebooted my desire to do therapy with people as they find me,' I answered.

We talked for an hour. She gave me her birth date. I got her some input.

"This is both creepy and so accurate what you are saying about me. Could we go to my house and continue these insights? I am at a turning point in my personal and business life," she said.

She lived in a big beautiful house behind gates in Bel Air. I recorded our session on her tape machine. Gaia and I were together for several hours. Around one o'clock in the morning, I stood up to leave.

"Can we set up some regular appointments?" she asked. "I have been in therapy for three years and we got more done in three hours than I have with her."

We decided that I would book her some appointments on my days off. She handed me an envelope.

"I hope that this takes care of your time with me," she said as we hugged goodbye.

In the car I opened the envelope and there was $2,000 with a note that said, "Here is your fee. However, you and what we did are priceless."

And that's how I started an active therapy practice with a stranger at a bar. The next day I began my rollercoaster job at Barry's Porsche dealership.

Through both Barry and Gaia, word spread up and down Sunset Boulevard and throughout the Hollywood Hills. They came in droves from Beverly Hills, Bel Air and Santa Monica to see how the intuitive man could help them through the tough times of their lives.

My practice had a home in 1982 when I started the Sedona Intensive, a 12-step based alternative program to guide clients to higher ground. We never walked on coals, there was no hocus-pocus and the endgame was always to save someone from his or her dark side.

But there was a lot more flip, flop and fly away whenever the opportunity presented itself.

Once I was drinking with friends and a woman with dyed red hair and too much make-up blurted out, "Let's fly to Puerto Vallarta right now. No clothes but what we have on our backs. Can you think of anything better to do?" Cindy boisterously cried out.

My former sober self might have explained: "Last minute plane tickets are atrociously expensive." Or the little conscience on my shoulder might have piped in, "Albert, your mortgage is due in two days and you won't be able to pay it if you go to Mexico." And momma Maggie would surely have scolded, "Albert, straighten up and fly right!"

So what did we do?

When the four of us got to LAX the ticket agent wouldn't sell us tickets. His shrill voice blurted out, "You all are too drunk to fly. Go home and sober up and come back another day. Now move along and let me help the lady behind you."

The next day, on a Sunday afternoon, I worked at the Porsche dealership from three o'clock until closing. The manager of the dealership was a very gangly, mean-looking man named Heinz. He emitted guttural staccato expressions in German. He was not nice. And he obviously hated that someone like me had been hired.

"You won't make it here one week if I have anything to say about it," he blurted out upon meeting me. I swear I thought he made the raised arm and said, "Heil, Hitler!"

While he was in the back watching television with the door shut and locked, I was brushing up on my Shakespeare, er, I mean all that I would ever know about Porsche but soon forget.

Since this was November, day lights turned off at 5:30 in the afternoon. Almost on the dot with no light in the sky, a bedraggled black man in overalls walked in and headed straight to a beautiful chocolate 911 Porsche turbo Carrera convertible on the showroom floor.

"Man I've had my eye on the car for weeks. Can you tell me how much it is? There is no suggested price sticker on the car," he asked.

"My name is Albert and I am brand new at this. Let me check my records," I said.

I found some suggested retail prices in a book. I scanned the document very hurriedly and went back to the customer.

"I didn't catch your name," I said.

"My name is Benny, Benny Haynes. Did you find the price?" he asked.

"Eighty-thousand," I stuttered.

There was stone silence. I thought I must have read the price list wrong.

"Albert, I'll take it. Can we go for a ride?" he asked.

This was downtown Los Angeles, one of the most dangerous hoods in all of southern California. USC was right around the corner but I am sure they have gun-toting marshals seeing over them.

"Sure. Let me get the key," I said.

Heinz was probably deep into his soap operas. I was sure of it. There was neither a peep nor a care out of him about the greenhorn in the front of the showroom on a dark and dreary Sunday night.

Automobile showrooms have folding doors that allow for one to drive a car right off the showroom floor. And that is exactly what Benny Haynes did. Benny was a good driver but he definitely treated the car like the made-for-fast-driving car that it was. He didn't say a word but smiled and laughed and acted like a kid in the proverbial candy store.

When we got back to the showroom Benny said, "Albert, I will be here to pick up the car at three o'clock on the dot. Have it ready for me to drive it home," Benny said.

"How will you be paying for the car, Mr. Haynes?" I asked.

"I'll pay in cash. I'll bring the money in large sacks," he said.

We small-talked for a few minutes and as he turned to go he turned back around and said, "Albert, thanks for showing me respect. Tell that &^%$ German Heinz that I wouldn't buy this car from him at half the price. When I was in few weeks ago as I left the showroom, I heard him mutter, 'Shvartzer' under his breath."

At exactly three the next afternoon Benny came to pick up the car. He brought so many sacks of cash that the man who wrote up the deal had three people help him count and secure the money. Because there was no bank loan on the purchase, the whole transaction took about an hour.

Barry happened to be in the dealership that day. Benny said to him on his way out: "Albert is a treasure. I knew without him telling me that he knew nothing about Porsches but he knew everything about how to treat a black man. You be good to Albert or I will come back and gitchya (sic)."

Barry took me in the back and sat me down and said, "Albert, you read the price list wrong. The car with taxes and dealer profit should have been closer to $70,000."

"Jeez. Should I call Benny and give him a refund?" I asked.

"The new cars will be here in a few days and they'll be closer to $80,000," Barry advised.

I sat in my chair, stunned.

"I am going to give Benny a lifetime warranty on the car. We keep the deal as written."Because there is a $10,000 profit we are going to give you 50 percent of the cash deal, which comes to $5,000. On top of that, you get your $5,000 guarantee. Let's go pick out your new loaner, Mr. Gaulden," Barry told me as he hugged me.

I don't think that God loves me anymore than He/She/It does anyone else. What I know to be true for me is that man looketh on the outside and God in the inner world. All of the Adventures of Albert have a plan to what otherwise looks like willy-nilly rudderless living. Not true. What you'll read is what and who finally got me to my bottom.

Chapter Nine
John Travolta and Me

In 1978 I lived in Hancock Park, California. At a certain age I was going to be older than I was the year before. What a drag. But I decided that at such a milestone I would celebrate getting older in Italia. Touring Italy in a Rolls Royce with a couple of rich royals seemed like a brilliant idea. What else should a social climbing sycophantic sot do?

In those days you had to have all kinds of annoying immunizations to get a Visa to go anywhere in the world. My archaeological doctor found that I had alcoholic hepatitis. Who'd a thought? *Il dottore* told me to jump in bed and cover my head until the bilirubin levels dropped. If you knew me better, even back then, you would bet against all odds that I would never stay in bed and I definitely would not stop drinking.

My best friend at the time, Bill Randa, owned Ahead Realty, a real estate agency in Sherman Oaks that sold houses to almost all the actors, directors and writers in Hollywood.

"Albert, with all of this downtime in sick bay, why don't you learn how to sell real estate?" Dumping a couple of books at my feet, he added, "Besides, you work with all those famous

Hollywood types. Don't just heal these Hollywood boys and girls – sell them paradise in Bel Air or Beverly Hills. For the gay blades there's always the Hollywood Hills."

When Bill was a young actor looking for roles in movies, he was Clint Eastwood's roommate. That year Clint was playing Philo Beddoe for Warner Brothers in *Every Which Way but Loose* with his soon-to-be wife, Sondra Locke. Bill's salespeople were schlepping the 3 Bs – Brentwood, Bel Air and Beverly Hills – to sell overpriced houses that would more than likely slide down the hill the next time Southern California had six months of rain.

"Bill, this is a great idea. I should have thought of it myself," I lied.

I called Bill's office and told one of the smart alecks I could not unravel the whys and wherefores of real estate.

"Stop where you are," said Florence Nightingale. "I have your solution. I will bring it to you when I go out to lunch."

Her name was Rosalie. She had been an instructor at Anthony School of Real Estate. When she saw her roommate's check for selling two houses, she called Randa and asked for a job selling instead of teaching real estate.

She dropped a not so big book of solutions on my bed.

"Memorize the anecdotes and take the quiz after every section. When you get out of sick bed, sign up at Anthony's, take the course, and ace the exam which you'll pass with flying colors."

I did as I was told. Two months later I took the exam and got my license.

Life is nothing if not a series of open doors or blind alleys or brick walls. From the moment I became a licensed salesperson, every door that could fly open – did. A good friend was photographing a huge estate above Santa Barbara, El Adobe de Tajiguas. It abutted the ranch of soon-to-be President Ronald Reagan. The day I got my license, he took me to look at the property on 35 acres. There was a main house with five bedrooms, each with its own fireplace, and five bathrooms.

There was a house for staff and a gardener's cottage. El Adobe had a hippodrome and stables for eight horses. There were tennis courts. A white fence wrapped around the entire property. And it had a six-car garage.

When I got home I watched *The Merv Griffin Show*. A young actor who had just starred in a blockbuster movie was his guest. The actor said he was looking for a big house within a 100-mile radius of Los Angeles.

"But it must have at least a six-car garage."

Real Estate broker Mary Collins – Randa's sister – was a decorator for clients like O.J. Simpson. She called to see how I was faring. Mary was hip and into everything alternative.

"I know this great psychic who can show you the trailer of what's to come after your near-death experience from being a drunk," she laughed as she told me all about Bill Corrado and how to contact him.

I called and he took me immediately.

"You have been sick because you drink too much. You will get better but you will not get sober for two more years." Corrado opened the session with a bang.

"You have many creative gifts. Soon you will sell a big estate near Santa Barbara to an actor with the initials J.T., who has an office at the Burbank Studios. There will be many problems with the sale. But it will be successful."

I was stunned. I was amazed. But didn't believe a word he said about selling the property. It was too far out there. *But* the actor's initials were J.T. So a niggling, unsettling, indescribable voice whispered to me, 'What if he is right?'

"One of the teachers named Hugh is conducting a two day-seminar starting tomorrow. Its purpose is to help you create something that is your heart's desire. Each of us knows how to do this but we have forgotten. This class will help you to remember."

What startled me was the language he used. I am wont to say to anyone starting on the path to renunciation of his past, "You never learn anything. You remember."

I paid for the reading and a few hundred dollars for the class and left. The next day I went to the seminar at The Corrado Academy of Perception. The most valuable lesson from this experience in a room full of desperate seekers occurred in the last session in an altered state of meditation. Using a non-invasive form of hypnosis, our facilitator took us deep inside ourselves.

"Release, relax and let go of the outside world." He started the process of leading us into our inner sanctum. He told us to decorate our private meditative space in order to want to return to our inner sanctum daily.

All of this would soon prove to be a powerful and workable auto-suggestion.

"Visualize an elevator in your room. I want you to think of someone you need to have a conversation with. It can be a spouse. Or someone at work with whom you have had a disagreement. It can be someone you don't know but with whom you would like to discuss an idea or a project. When the elevator door opens, bring that person in the elevator to come sit with you."

I chose the young actor I had seen on television. When he tried to speak I said, "Shhh. I've got too much to share to waste time."

When the specter on the elevator who looked just like J.T heard all about the estate, he practically peed in his pants. Before long, his eyes were bulging and his mouth was watering. When I said, "Six-car garage," he hollered, "Sold."

Okay, okay, I'm making this part up. But I did see the actor's presence and we did have the conversation. I am not a twinkie or a foo-foo kind of man. The underpinning of this exercise was to create a clean and conscious atmosphere, a space for you to influence another person when you encounter them in the real world.

When we came back to a conscious state, the instructor said, "You have just learned how to create anything in an altered state that you want to happen in the future."

The very next day I was sitting *en plein air* at Joe Allen's on Third Street to meet a client to show her a small boxlike house on Fairfax. I knew everybody on Gawkers' Row. Before my doctor-imposed sobriety, Sunday nights always found me at my table eating and drinking and reading *The New York Times*.

The next year on April 2, I was sitting alone with a fish dish and Soave Bolla, my vino of choice. A raucous crowd of five people stormed into the restaurant and sat across from me in a large table.

The one I recognized was Oscar-winner Maggie Smith of *The Prime of Miss Jean Brodie* — recently the centerpiece of *Downton Abbey,* whom I always thought was the cat's pajamas top and bottom. She was so great. I sent over a bottle of good wine and went back to fish and *The New York Times*.

"May I ask what you are doing having supper by yourself," Maggie Smith asked as she stood next to my table.

Rising to my feet I told Ms. Smith, who would one day be Dame Maggie Smith, "It may come as a surprise to you, but I happen to like the pleasure of my own company."

Picking up my plate and glass of wine she said, "Let's see if I do," and we headed to join her rowdy friends.

Actually, the whole group was delightful. Embarrassed that I had not seen *California Suite*, for which Maggie Smith had been nominated as Best Supporting Actress that year, I was caught off guard when she asked if she would win.

Admitting I had not seen *California Suite*, but that *The Prime of Miss Jean Brody* was my all-time favorite movie, I said, "You won't win but you will, and you will but you won't."

Everybody laughed because the next night she did win. The role was playing an actress who loses the Oscar to another actress in a different movie.

I was brought back to the present moment when the waiter paged me to say my prospective buyer was unable to keep her appointment. Being a Type A+ personality (Mars in Aries conjunct the Mid-Heaven of my astrological birth chart), I ordered a bottle of Soave Bolla.

"Screw it. This booze might kill me. What a way to go," I said to myself.

Since college days I have worked crossword puzzles and always have them with me when I am forced to eat alone or to wait for a tardy narcissistic egomaniac. Remember I unravel and retool actors of both genders and rich men and women on Wall Street. While I am crosswording and drinking and people-watching out of the corner of my eye, I have inadvertently stuck my feet in the passageway between tables. The next thing I know a young man has stumbled over my feet and fallen into my table.

"Oh, sir, I am so sorry for being so clumsy. I see I've knocked over your bottle of wine," he said.

Oh my God. This is my young actor. The one I brought down on the elevator in my meditation.

"Oh, please accept my apologies. It was my fault. Please sit down. I've been expecting you. My name is Albert," I muttered.

John Travolta and I sat chatting for half an hour while the whole crowd drooled and oohed and aahed. Thank God this was long before cameras on cell phones. When his entourage came in, they asked him who he was sitting with and why. The ringleader was so indignant that a stranger would ask him to sit down and was more incredulous that he did.

"Get up, John. We have a private table inside," the man said.

Turning to me as the mob scene dispersed, the man, who was John's assistant, said, "I am John's personal assistant. Who do you think you are asking John to sit with you?"

"I am going to sell him a beautiful property that I just told him all about," I replied.

The puffed-up toady huffed off and I started making my plans.

You are probably saying to yourselves, "Albert's made all of this up. Movie stars don't sit down with strangers and talk about real estate. "

Well you can chalk it all up to my having drunk a bottle of wine for the first time in several months. And you may be thinking that this was God's joke on me for going to that weekend with the wizard who helped me turn fantasy into reality.

Oh, to hell with it. I've decided to fuck the short cut and tell you the ins and outs of what happened with the whole truth and nothing but the truth, so help me God, as Marlene Dietrich and Tyrone Power swore to do in *Witness for the Prosecution*, 1957, United Artists Studios, directed by Billy Wilder.

The next day I found out what gate would get me into Travolta Productions. It was Gate 2 on Olive Street. When I got there, the guard dialed Travolta Production Company and spoke to Kate Edwards. She had heard of my sit-down with John and we chatted. She said he was not in. I asked her birth sign and she said it was Capricorn. We schmoozed and then she told the guard to give me directions to their offices.

Presto, I'm on the Lot. Calm down Albert. This is only Step One.

Kate was as gracious as the English always are. She was blond and adorable. Miss Kate had that Ipana smile. I loved the accent. I went on and on and on about Capricorn. She told me about a boyfriend. He was an actor. Ya-di-ya-di-ya. John didn't come in like I'd hoped. But somebody else did

"Hello, mum, this is Albert," Kate said. "Albert, meet my mother, Joan. She is John's assistant."

"It's so nice to meet you, darling. John told me he met you yesterday at Joe Allen's. Something about real estate," Joan said.

"Well I guess I need to get going. He's not here," I moaned.

"He's in the loo. He'll be right in."

And just at that moment, John came walking through the door.

"Hi, Albert, how did you get on the Lot?" he asked.

Step Two, John and I are face-to-face again without his henchman.

We talk. I show him old photographs of the property. He says that he's due to leave for London the next weekend for the London premiere of his new film for the Queen of England. I guess that's the end of the line for getting John to see the property.

Not on your life.

Get a load of Step Three.

I called Joan at home. Can you believe that she gave me her private number after "hello?" This was a Wednesday. I called on Thursday.

"Darling, John won't commit." And again I dialed Joan on Friday.

"Darling, not today," Joan said. "I'm so sorry."

Then I hatched a scheme that worked.

John had recently gotten his pilot's license. He was buying his own sky ride. So I went to our real estate office, broke into Bill Randa's desk and stole his credit card.

"Hello, Joan. This is Albert. I decided to rent a Lear Jet and fly John and his posse to and from the Santa Barbara Airport. We'll limos at each end to go to and from El Adobe de Tajiguas. Is he in or is he out?" I asked.

She called back and John agreed to delay his flight to London by one day. So using the broker's credit card, I rented a Lear and limos to get his majesty, rising superstar John, to his new pad near Gaviota Beach.

Oh, so you think he's not going to bite and buy heaven on Earth? Your logic tells you that this is a probate sale and that me and my agency may not get a dime even if he does buy the property? And does your Mensa mind convince you that the hocus-pocus in that seminar put me under a self-deluding trance?

Keep reading.

Joan did not go. Kate did not go. The henchman stayed home as well. John and three others and I fly on that Sunday to see the glorious mansion on 35 acres.

I won't bore you with the oohs and aahs, or how God painted the sky azure blue with puffy white exhaled clouds — or how every minute of the flight and drive was 20th Century Fox picture-perfect. But it's true.

After the tour we sat under the proverbial spreading chestnut tree for a picnic of pasta, Caesar salad, and brownies, all of John's favorites. Those were the days when he could eat half a dozen brownies and not gain an ounce.

"When are you going to ask me if I want to buy this place?" John asked.

"You don't think I stole the broker's credit card and rented a jet and limos to bring you up here if you weren't going to buy it, did you?" I replied.

"Albert, you ought to be in show business with your chutzpah," he said.

"John, we're all in show business. Now, how do you want to pay for the magic kingdom?" I asked.

"I do want to buy it. But I want the seller to throw in all the furniture or there won't be a deal," he preened.

I went inside to talk with the seller, Mrs. Barbara Hubshman.

"Who is that young man?" she asked.

"That's John, you know, John Travolta. Did you see his latest movie?"

"Yes I did. God I didn't recognize him," she said.

I didn't say so, but she ought to see some of the women in movies out of makeup and wigs. Not a pretty sight.

"John wants to buy El Adobe at full price. But there's a catch. He wants all the furniture, dishes and flatware. He says you can take your clothes and personal pictures, but everything stays," I exhaled.

Barbara went to an antique armoire and pulled out a stack of papers ten inches thick and dropped them on her eighteenth century secrétaire.

"I have a decorator's license so I buy wholesale. To furnish this house, the gardener's cottage and the staff house cost me a lot of dough. If he pays asking price with no hassles and no laundry list of more stuff he wants, *mi casa es su casa*," she said.

I brought John into the study and here's what I said to them both.

"John, Mrs. Hubshman agrees to sell you El Adobe de Tajiguas for full asking price, which includes all furnishings. Barbara, John knows there are not to be to any contingencies or interferences from anyone about anything," I said as I took a gulp of Soave Bolla to steel my nerves.

If you are wondering how much this crown jewel cost Travolta it must remain a secret. We promised that our lips were sealed. Today it is worth ten times what he paid almost forty years ago

"This is a probate sale. When all inspections have been done and after John's accounting firm tours the estate, at a date to be determined all parties, we will appear in the Santa Barbara court-house so that the sale can be finalized," I said breathlessly.

"I want you both to know that I did not bring a deposit receipt which is protocol and in compliance with the Real Estate Commission of the State of California, but nonetheless, this is a binding oral agreement. And I will hold you both to it. I know some dangerous boys in the hood who can break a leg if you renege." Pause. "Gotchya. Joking! Let's have a drink to toast the selling of El Adobe de Rancheros to John Travolta."

Now we'll fast forward with Cliff Notes. I had lunch and a look-see of the property with a legendary Hollywood financial adviser. What a gentleman. He said, "All looks fine to me." This upstanding and righteous man would lose a ton of money in the Bernard Madoff scandal in 2008. An Earthquake broke every window in the houses. No problemo. They were replaced. Cool. Deal's still purring.

Enter asshole, fancy-pants Beverly Hills schlemiel Frank Graves of the law firm, Graves & Graves. He was a nightmare. When I called to ask him if he wanted to drive up the Coast together he declined. We met at a designated spot on the highway.

When we arrived at the estate, Frank was dismissive of me and walked the grounds and in and out of houses alone with Barbara. When we sat together in the living room of the main house, Graves addressed all remarks to Mrs. Hubshman. As he rose to leave he palavered her and slightly tipped his head to me.

When the offer came in three days later, Mrs. Hubshman called and asked me to see her. Although it was 100 miles I scampered up the 101 and met her for lunch.

"Frank Graves made an offer minus the 6 percent I agreed to pay your real estate firm. He said that Ahead Realty had no business trying to sell a probate property and he wanted to tender his offer with no commission to you and your firm," she told me through clenched teeth

"What did you tell him?" I asked.

"I told him then we had no deal," she replied.

We sat in silence for a few minutes, sipping Margaritas in humongous cha cha stemware.

"Let me make a call," I said.

I went to the pay phone. Remember this was ages before cell phones. It was after two o'clock in the afternoon and I knew these tight asses would be in their office billing tons of client hours.

"Hello, I would like to speak to all the Graves lawyers. This is John Travolta's agent."

One, two, three, four, five seconds later cooing voices were heard on the conference call.

"Bob, it's so good to hear your voice. How are you?"

"This is not Bob Lemond, it's Albert Gaulden, John's real estate agent. Frank Graves is fucking with us, and we are about to pull the plug on his bullshit. My broker, who was roommates with a huge star and director when they were young and dumb, is on the other line with this man as we speak. He is willing to pay full price including the Ahead Realty 6 percent commission. I am about to call John in London to tell him he lost out because Frank is a colossal cocksucker. Good-bye. Fuck all of you and the horses you rode in on."

Joan gave me John's number in London. I dropped a dime on Frank and his rotten stinking shenanigans. John called Frank and told him to offer full price which would cover the commission. "Or I will find myself a new attorney."

I stayed at the San Ysidro Ranch in nearby Montecito babysitting all the things that could go wrong, which sometimes did. This is where Jacqueline and John Kennedy, as well as Laurence Olivier and Vivien Leigh, honeymooned. I have stayed there a lot over the years. It's not unlikely to see Barbara Streisand and her ilk there.

One day at the swimming pool, I spent the day talking to a man vacationing there with his wife. He, at the time, was producing film. Since I had just written a movie called *The World is Waiting*, I talked him into reading it and having me come into his office in Hollywood to discuss the merits of him producing.

The meeting happened a few weeks later. He did not like the idea of a film about reincarnation and two star-crossed lovers.

His name was Steve Tisch of the Loews Corporation, which owns a lot of hotels. I stay at the Regency when I am in New York and we say hello.

On Oct. 15 that year, El Adobe de Tajiguas became the property of John Travolta, who had just become the biggest movie star in the world. Back-to-back blockbuster movies would eventually cement him in the big league of Hollywood movie stars forever.

My reason for this long and winding tale is to let you see how God is working in our lives even when we won't let him. The method God uses to get us where we need to go is magical and golden train tracks along which we move. I never dreamed in a thousand years that when I got well I would get a real estate license. And in eons of time I would never have suspected that I would sell the magical kingdom to one of the biggest movie stars in the world.

My ultimate shock and awe was where all of this ultimately took me. Let's start with drunk driving, one more time. I was finally forced to go to meetings and take that damn drivers' diversion program every Friday for a year, which you couldn't miss, even if your mother died or the world went tilt on its axis.

Chapter Ten
Hitting Bottom

___

You would think that with all the recent successes that I was sitting on top of the world. Alcoholic stinking thinking was still afoot for at least a year or more after all of this hubbub died down.

There was a flurry of activity including a dinner party at my house for John and all the people involved with the sale of El Adobe de Tajiguas. I had 18-karat gold coins made for each of his inner group at the dinner. The designer engraved El Adobe de Travolta arched over an etching of the house and grounds. When dinner was over each guest turned over their coffee cup and there was his or her coin. On the back of John's was Brother John, and Kate had Sister Kate. Years later, knowing I had hocked mine, Kate gave me John's – for whatever reason he had given it to her. She said she had given hers to him and vice versa.

There was also an intimate fête that Bill Randa's sister, Mary Collins, gave to celebrate the star real estate adventure. It was at that party that I met O.J. Simpson, who had just started dating Nicole Brown. Mary was the one who made the introduction to Bill Corrado, the psychic who had predicted the Travolta affair.

Within weeks of getting our money from the sale, one of my acquaintances who owned an exotic car dealership on Sunset Boulevard – not my former boss Barry – talked Bill Randa and me into buying a 1962 Silver Cloud II Rolls Royce. The backstory was that a drug dealer was about to be arrested. He needed cash that day to make his getaway.

We went to Bill's bank in Beverly Hills and got $25,000 in cash to give the seller. The car was worth at least $60,000. Bill said that he was doing this because he knew I was a drunk and would have none of the Travolta sale money left in no time. I also had a two-car garage to house it in and an apartment over the garage that an actor/driver could live in rent-free to chauffeur me.

The one thing I knew was that I was a drunk. As a matter of fact, as of this time in 1978, I'd had three drunk driving citations. There was no way I was going to drive the Rolls Royce. Never say, "Never."

One Sunday I decided to drive the car to Santa Barbara to have lunch alone at the El Encanto Hotel. They had a terraced restaurant – I always loved to dine outside, but only here overlooking the Pacific Ocean, or in Italy or the South of France.

At the next table I saw and heard a gentleman speaking in the most beautiful English – London English, please – and dining alone. I walked over to his table and asked if he were eating alone and he said he was.

"My name is Albert Gaulden and I was wondering if you would like to join me at my table?"

"Yes," he said. "My name is Peter Fudakowski and I'd be delighted to lunch with you."

Peter was 24 and on holiday, as the Europeans like to say. He worked at First National Bank of Chicago in the London office.

"My real interest is in writing, directing and producing films. In my job at the bank as a loan officer we furnish the last 10 percent of an approved film's budget," Peter explained.

"Interestingly, I just wrote a film, *The World is Waiting*. I moved to Los Angeles several years ago with a project, *Mae West is Mother Goose*, but it never got off the ground," I said.

Peter was riding buses around California on holiday, so I asked if he would like to go to Los Angeles with me in my car. He was thrilled not to take a bus. I offered to let him stay at my house.

"You as a burgeoning maker of films ought to go to the Polo Lounge with me tonight and see the stars that might one day star in your movies," I said.

We went, dinner at 8, in a centerpiece table right in front of Elizabeth Taylor holding court surrounded by Roddy McDowell, her then-husband Sen. John Warner and a number of self-important people hovering. Milton Berle was having dinner with his wife. The room was mobbed. Peter was eating it up. One day he would direct big stars in movies he either wrote or directed.

He read my movie when he got back to my house. He offered to have me come to London to see if anyone at Pinewood Studio might be interested in producing *The World is Waiting*. I went over in May.

Now I want to get to the nitty-gritty of the trip to London. Peter took me to Pinewood Studio to meet with Elliott Kastner, who had been married to Joan Collins and who had produced a lot of movies with big stars.

Peter introduced us and then left Mr. Kastner's office.

From the outset, Mr. Kastner could not stay off the phone. In the middle of my pitch for *The World is Waiting,* he would answer the phone. After the third or fourth call I got up and slammed my hand on the dial to disconnect him.

"I flew all the way over here from Los Angeles to see if you are interested in producing my movie. Stop taking phone calls. It's so rude," I said.

He was laughing and of course smoking a round, long cigar.

"You're a bold one, Albert. I have never had anyone hang up a phone when I was talking to an important potential client," Elliott warned me.

"It's about time someone taught you some Southern manners," I said.

"You're no Golding (*Lord of the Flies*) or Goldman (*Marathon Man* and *Butch Cassidy and the Sundance Kid*) but I kinda like *The World is Waiting*. The problem is, to put it bluntly, you're a nobody. It takes years and years of who you know to get ahead in this business.

"But I tell you what I will do. I'll package your film with seven others but I'll only pay you $25,000 for the rights to it – you will never see any more money even if it is a big hit. That's not very likely. What do you say, baby?" he asked as he made loud sucking on that damn cigar.

I stood up and said, "First thing, never call me baby. Second, stop sucking cigars. It's a nasty habit. And lastly, I would never sell the rights for you to package with other scripts for all the tea in China," I said as I exited stage left.

When Peter asked, "How did the meeting go?" I answered, "If you don't ask I won't tell!"

Something good came out of the trip. Peter had just started dating a woman named (Henrietta) Minette Williams who was as calm as I have ever seen an Aries. We got along famously. I straight-out told Peter to marry her after doing her astrology birth chart. He did and they have been married 37 years, and they have two amazing children and grandchildren.

His dream to be in the movie industry came true in 2006 when *Tsotsi,* a movie he produced, won Best Foreign Film. Minette has written a beautiful film that I am sure you will soon see on the screen.

The week I was in London I got on the Tube and went to see stage shows. One night I started talking to a nice man as we were reading the information in a framed publicity announcement about *Ain't Misbehavin'* starring Nell Carter, who of all things, was from Birmingham, my hometown. The gentleman was Billy Dee Williams, a great actor, and he and I went backstage to see and compliment Nell on her performance. Then we had a few drinks close by.

When I got home in early June, things were getting tight financially. One night I was out having drinks with my friend Jim Bob Winfrey at Dan Tana's Restaurant on Santa Monica in Hollywood. The waitress said the manager wanted to see me in her office.

"Albert, I am sorry, but American Express said to take your card. I have known you for years and I hate to do this. I will comp dinner but your Amex stays with me," she explained.

Bob offered to give me a few hundred dollars but I said I didn't need it. I told him I would settle with American Express the next week.

Little did I know that there were going to be a lot of pressing issues besides a credit card that would require all my time and attention.

The one thing about alcoholics is that we always have two sides. The face to show up at fancy parties and plaster all over church was mild and mannered with a live and let live attitude. The dark side was after a few drinks and we could wake the dead and curse and damn anybody's Lord. It's sort of like the mask of the actor, two sides of the same person.

Chapter Eleven
Tough Love

———

When I moved back to California in November 1979 I asked my friend Darrell's aunt and uncle, Val and Howard, if I could stay with them in Belmont Shore in Long Beach. They seemed happy to accommodate me. They were big drinkers and I still loved the life with a belly full of hooch. Christmas was a riot. New Year's Eve was more craziness and too much to drink.

On Feb. 9 I was driving the wrong way on the Long Beach Freeway and got hauled to jail. One more time I was full of remorse.

Sitting in the jail I had an epiphany. I heard a voice and was struck sober at the same time. The voice that no one but me could hear said, "Surrender bird brain. You are at the end of the line with drinking alcohol."

My first 12-step meeting was on Feb. 18, 1980. I walked into the Monday night Bowling Green meeting and sat in the front row, just as I did when I went to church every Sunday.

I was looking around to make sure no one recognized me.

"What would people think?" my butterflies and bees' brain blabbed in my ear.

The leader of the meeting was a man about six-foot-four, dressed in a vested suit. My conjuring mind told me he was a "plant," probably a preacher man.

"My name is Ernie and today makes 365 days free of alcohol and drugs," he crowed.

There was loud applause all around the room.

"Liar, liar, pants on fire," I said to myself. There is no way anyone can go that long without a drink. Mind you, I had been sentenced to these meetings by the Long Beach court system for a year, but since this was my first meeting, my mind was running the show.

There was an archway that led in and out of the meeting. Later I would discover a well-known saying of the founder of 12-step consciousness: *We will construct a new and triumphant arch through which we passed to freedom.*

The beginning days were fraught with hopefulness as well as despair. When I was five months sober, Val and Howard uninvited me to stay in their house. Val put my suitcases on the front lawn.

"Good luck, Albert. You have overstayed your welcome," she said.

I called a cab and went to a motel on the beach and paid for a month in advance. Its residents were hookers, stoners, drifters and a host of others running from the law.

I still had a job that Howard gave me. He managed a large shopping center in a nearby town. Since he was paying me "under the table," I made a lousy $1,200 a month. Instead of riding into work with him, I caught the bus.

The position had previously been held by someone making $50,000 a year. But when you are homeless with no automobile, beggars can't be choosers, as my granny used to say.

Strangely, I loved working there. One day I met a young woman who was a model and actress. She and I put together a fashion show in the mall traffic area. It was wildly successful.

"I heard you have written a movie," Talia said.

"Yes. It is titled *The World is Waiting*, a story about star-crossed lovers who come back to Earth to do a great work together," I told her.

"It sounds amazing. If you would like I'll introduce you to a producer named George Reeves," she said.

The introduction was made because I sold John Travolta a large estate a year-and-a-half before. John had agreed to take a meeting about starring in *The World is Waiting*. George evidently took it as a *fait accompli*. He said he would produce this film "if it is the last thing I ever do." John dropped out and I never heard a word from George again.

Hollywood is a playground I will never get lured back into again.

My sponsor, Fil, told me to get out of the motel from hell. Since I was used to living in other peoples' houses, I moved in with a couple I met in the meetings. She was a rose with few thorns. He was prickly and a snake with a lot of venom. After a few weeks Fil decided I needed to live alone.

I had little money. When I lived in Hancock Park, a ritzy section of Los Angeles, for two years I had a Rolls Royce and all the credit line American Express allowed. That ended and by the time I moved back to California I was broke and homeless.

D-Day, getting my own place, was torturous. Fil had started a small company and I was hired to man the phones and do some typing. I was miserable but they paid exactly what I was making at the shopping center.

I scanned "To Rent" ads in the *Long Beach Press-Telegram*. After knocking on doors and putting in an application for an apartment, I would sit in my car and cry tears of despair.

I drove Fil's car back to his house. He said a woman I met on my apartment hunt had called back and rented me the apartment.

"It's a duplex on Bay Shore with its own boat slip," he said. "Oh, and I put a used car on hold from someone in the program whose husband just died. She is selling his car. She said you could pay her $100 a month until it's paid off."

I flopped down in a chair and decompressed. I now had an apartment and a car in one fell swoop. Amazing. Unbelievable. There is a God.

I learned so much in my first year sober that it baffles me that I was open to the info. The ones who taught me the most were off skid row and smelled bad and on the surface had nothing to offer.

At a noon meeting, a longshoreman who walked into the room looked in my direction.

"God, do not let that riffraff sit by me," I prayed.

Guess where he sat? He plopped down in a chair right next to me. Here is what he said, and it was one of the most compelling life-changing shares I ever heard.

"God created me to be one thing and I was determined to be something else."

I remember a preacher saying to me one day, "You never know when you'll meet God in the strangest places."

I went to coffee with Tex and I did not smell a thing nor was I put off by his raggedy beard and missing teeth. He was my Eskimo that date. I never forgot him, never, ever.

I learned how to tend to my own business. If someone was acting up or acting out I would report in with someone who had a few years.

"Can you believe that so-and-so is having sex with a lot of women in the meeting at Sunset Beach?" I gossiped.

"Tend to your 7*&*^ business," sober sister scolded me.

I found out we were sick getting well, and not necessarily bad getting good.

When I was sixty days sober I was asked to speak in a 12-step meeting in a psych ward. If you ran over your time limit, the chair for the night would hit a huge gong.

I hadn't even gotten sober in my pitch and the chair gonged me so loud that I was shaking visibly.

On the way home I asked my sponsor if that was the rudest thing he had ever seen on a 12-step meeting.

"Can you believe that nut-case gonged me?" I huffed and puffed.

"I can. You ran over," he answered.

"But I hadn't even gotten to the part when I get sober," I muttered.

"So what did that teach you?" Fil asked.

I didn't say anything for several minutes as we barreled down the 405 Freeway toward home.

"I think it was my Ego," I started to open up. "Maybe I was trying to brag about my drunk-a-log and how great I was," I finished.

Fil agreed and said that we could stop at Hoff's Hut, a restaurant we referred to as the pie place, for a slice of pecan pie. I came into the program weighing 140. With donuts and sweets at all the meetings I gained 20 pounds my first year.

One Thursday night I was a greeter at the Sunset Beach meeting when a beautiful blond in a mink stole sat down beside me. She wore a humongous diamond wedding ring and a couple of rare gem bracelets.

"May I get you a cup of coffee?" I asked.

"I'd love a cup," she purred.

She said her name was Lula Belle from Arkansas, and she was living in Belmont Shore.

"Would you like cream in your coffee?" I asked.

With her puffy Paris lips she muttered, "Yes, Angel."

"Do you care for a little sugar for your decaf coffee?" I asked.

"Stir it with your finger," she exhaled showing cleavage.

I forgot to mention she was bathed in Chloe perfume, just the fragrance I love on a woman. Throughout the meeting she kept leaning toward me.

After the meeting we talked. I introduced her to a few people.

"Would you like to come over to my house for an early breakfast in the morning?" she asked.

"You do not want anything to do with this man, he will steal you blind," my sponsor Fil said to Lula Belle.

With that news flash she skedaddled as fast as her spike pumps would take her.

A week later Fil showed me the Long Beach paper with a headline that said, "Doctor's Wife and Man She Met in a Meeting Arrested for Trying to Kill Husband."

And there in plain sight was the Lula Belle I met in the meeting a couple of weeks before. Evidently she met the hit man in a 12-step meeting in Long Beach.

"The next time a manizer sits beside you smelling to high heaven, change seats," Fil advised.

In my first year I made coffee and cleaned ashtrays. Can you believe even in the dark ages, sobering men and women smoked cigarettes, including little ol' me?

"Hail Mary full of Grace..."

I also took the phones one night a week when Central Office closed. Once I got up at three o'clock in the morning to give a caller $20 because he was hungry and wanted to stop drinking.

When I knocked he opened the door, grabbed the $20 and slammed the door in my face.

I pouted about the nerve of this asshole until Fil told me I was an enabler.

"He was just doing what an user and abuser does – he fleeced you."

Fil educated me on not getting up in the middle of the night to give money to a drunk.

I probably went to 100 meetings in 90 days. Meetings became as addictive as scotch ever was. Sleep was fitful for months. The most inexplicable part of getting sober was that the obsession to drink was lifted from me from day one. Some people take years to stay sober. God was doing for me what I couldn't do for myself.

At sixty days sober, Dr. Paul, a man whose story is in the Big Book, asked me to help him start a new meeting at Long Beach General Hospital. He was the nicest person I had ever met anywhere. But I questioned everything.

"Dr. Paul, If you wanted someone to help you start a new 12-step meeting, why me?"

"Albert, I saw you in your first meeting. You are a real asset for sobriety," he said.

The meetings were real eye-openers for the newcomers.

My sponsor was cagey and as insightful as all the smarty-pants I had ever known. My first sober Christmas, Fil and Val threw a big bash at their house on the bay. He invited more than sixty people. The Christmas tree was floor to ceiling and looked like it could have come straight from the Tiffany holiday display window on Fifth Avenue in New York. There were mounds of presents.

From my fourth step inventory, Fil knew that I had always tried to outdo all the people I exchanged gifts with. He read my mind: "No one ever gives me as good a present as I give them."

As everyone was drinking hot cider and scarfing loads of cookies and slices of cake, he pulled me aside.

"Albert, here is a Santa Claus hat. I want you to give out the gifts from under the tree," he said.

When I was a newcomer I turned from Johnny-on-the-Spot with clever answers and ha-ha repartee into someone open and willing to learn anything I could to anchor, lock and seal my sobriety.

I did what I was told to do.

As I sat on the floor beneath the tree I picked up the first present.

I read the first greeting and to whom it was given: "To Albert from Anne. Congratulations on your first sober Christmas. I know this is something you can use every day."

I opened the gift. It was a five-pound tin of coffee.

I wept. I laughed and cried. Everyone clapped and hooted merriment.

Every present under the tree had my name on it. When I finished I stood up, bawling like an infant. I blubbered thanks to all. Everyone in the room hugged and kissed me. It was surreal.

God speaks through all of us to each other. The healing was complete. I never had another Christmas with the hangover of trying to outgive those in my life.

Fil was tall, dark-headed, had an oilman's belly and wore those Texas pointed-toe boots. But that night he was my Eskimo, leading me away from the dark nights of Christmases past.

My sponsor had a few things that he insisted I do besides not drinking.

"The first thing is never go to lunch or dinner with anyone without having the money to buy your own hamburger. Secondly, stay out of meetings in Beverly Hills or Bel Air. (His reasoning was that I was attracted to glamour and Hollywood). And the third thing is if you ever borrow a cent from anyone, repay the debt before you buy food or shelter," Fil said stomping his feet hard for emphasis.

All the people I got sober with are dead. He would be proud of me that I have no credit card debt, owe no one a cent and that my car has been paid off for years.

Chapter Twelve
Starting Over

——————

I moved to Sedona, Arizona in 1982 after I had been sober only two years. It is my understanding when you break with the past and all the misinformation, dogma and dicta foisted upon you, you are able to swim in God's stream. I liken it to being pulled by an unseeable magnetic force onto train-like tracks to get to where God is leading you.

When I was sobering up I was cautioned to spend the first year in meetings, working steps and definitely not doing anything that could throw me back into bad-boy behavior. I admit that staying sober was not nearly as hard as quitting smoking cigarettes or weaning me from sugar blues. In all the meetings I attended there were donuts and cookies.

I will never forget standing before Judge Sheila Pokras in the Long Beach courtroom in 1980. This was my fourth drunk driving offense in less than eight years.

When my case was called, I walked up to the judge's bench. When Judge Pokras asked how I pleaded, a man waved from the back of the room and asked to speak with the judge. He told her that the district attorney was going to offer two lane changes in place of the drunk-driving offense.

"Mr. Gaulden, do you accept the lane change charges in lieu of the drunk driving offense?" the judge asked me.

"No, ma'am, I plead guilty to driving under the influence. If I don't I will die drunk. I need to accept the plea and stop drinking," I answered the judge.

"For the offense of driving under charges (she read the song and verse of the statute), I sentence you to two years in the state penitentiary (pause, pause, just like in the movies) – suspended. Your fine is $74. You will attend SB38 program for one year and go to Alcoholics Anonymous meetings three days a week for a year. If I ever see you in this court again you will do hard time. Good Luck to you, Mr. Gaulden." Judge Pokras had rendered her verdict.

For the first five years of my sobriety, I sent Judge Pokras an anniversary greeting card denoting another year I had stayed sober. She will always be one of God's flashcards for me.

There had been extenuating circumstances when I was arrested. The arresting officers never gave the clerk at the jail the money and antique cross I was wearing. A friend advised that I file a claim, and I did. The district attorney's office asked me to take a lie detector test. I did and I passed. The officers refused to take the lie detector test, so the City of Long Beach settled several thousand dollars for my losses.

I have always said the first two years of my sobriety were the best years of my life. Tough love came to live with me. When I said that this man or that woman should be kicked out of the 12-step program for some self-righteous reason, my sponsor would say, "Tend to your own business." I thought, 'How rude. Does he know who he's talking to?'

We had meetings on the beach. A group of us would take a meeting into a jail or a mental ward. Every time the cell door clanged shut, I shuddered. There were National Conventions. Although I had lived just forty miles away when I did my most deadly drinking, I was told not to talk to any old drinking buddies. It was three years before I talked to my family in Alabama.

On my sixty-fifth day sober, an elegant black man spoke to our Tuesday night meeting. He looked like he had been dressed by Paul Stuart, a well-known upscale men's clothier in New York. One of the things he said riveted me into action.

"If there is anyone in your life who you owe an amends to, step out of the step you're working and make an amends to that person," he advised.

That night I wrote a letter to my father who was living in Alabama. He had been married to his fourth or fifth wife for a few years. A week later he called me and we talked for hours. He gave me his view of our life together and then the years apart. I slept like a baby that night. My sister called the next morning to say our father had died in his sleep. God spoke to me through that sober man. I believe that is how God works in our lives if we pay attention.

I was sober 16 years when my brother called to say our mother had slipped into a coma. James Redfield (*Celestine Prophecy* author) and his wife Salle Merrill were visiting in Sedona. They called and made reservations for me to go home to Birmingham with them as they were already booked. Salle went to St. Joseph's Hospital with me.

A wonderful black woman at the front desk in ICU told me, "Honey I'm glad you're here. Your momma is not ever gonna wake up. One of those sistahs in her room shakes her all the time and says, 'Marguerite, wake up.' She'll be gone by Saturday."

In the wee hours on Saturday alone in the room with her, I put one finger in her clenched fist and asked her questions.

"Momma, squeeze yes to any question." I asked, "and nothing if the answer is no."

For one hour I asked her a zillion questions and it was the most cathartic experience I ever had since my father and I talked on the phone. We cleared up so many misconceptions I had about her and me. She verified that she now understood me more and the journey my life took. My mother told me she had been in the waiting room of heaven, which I know was the Upper World.

One day in early April 1983, I was sitting at my drawing board plotting someone's astrological birth chart when the phone rang. It turned out to be Shirley Hudson, host of the popular *Northwest Today* television show.

"How did you find me? I have been getting sober the last two years and nobody knew how to reach me. At least I *thought* no one did," I said.

"We have our ways. I would like for you to do my birth chart. Can you do this later today?"

I called her back and gave her my insights. When I was finished with the session, I asked if she related to the information I gave her.

"You are as good as Joann, your client from years ago, says you are," she answered. "What do I owe you?" Shirley asked.

"No charge. It was my pleasure," I told her.

"I would like for you to be a guest on *Northwest Today,* a television show I co-host, this Thursday," she asked.

"I'd love to," I answered.

"Good, we'll book you a room at the University Hotel. A car will pick you up at 7:45," she stated matter-of-factly.

Wow! This was Tuesday afternoon. I had maybe fifty bucks to my name. As with most of us getting sober, I had lost everything and lived on meager earnings from chart sessions. My client base was gone and I depended on one client telling another to try to build back my counseling career.

"Who else will be on the show?" I asked.

"You will be on with the Beach Boys and ice skating champion Rosalyn Sumners and my co-host Clint and me," Shirley said.

We got off the phone and I shook and sat numb and dumb. Where was I going to get the money to fly to Seattle, Washington? I was stuttering to myself as I fell into bed, covered my head and fell asleep.

The phone rang. I looked at the bedside clock. It was six in the morning.

"Hey A, it's M. I need you to do some projections for me," she said.

M was a stock broker and because we were on the West Coast, the market opened in New York three hours earlier.

"I've got your chart right here on my artist easel drawing board," I said, jumping up and going into the living room to get her chart.

We talked for twenty minutes and then came the big beg for financial help to get to Seattle. I told her my dilemma and here is what she said.

"A, you have been such a huge help for me with all the ups and downs in the stock market. How much do you need? We'll take it out in trade as the hooker said to her John." And M laughed.

M offered to call the hotel and secure the room. She gave me $5,000 to cover the hotel and other things I'd need. It boggled my mind to try to figure out how many appointments I would owe her. Never mind. The thought impression danced in my head that this was that proverbial moving finger of God.

I was hyperventilating as I stood backstage waiting for my entrance. The Beach Boys went on first. They sang a tune and then sat down for the soft grilling that celebrities endure. Then there was a station break. Rosalyn Sumners came on and talked about her upcoming trip to the World Skating Competition in Sarajevo, Yugoslavia. A few months later she won the silver, missing gold by 1/100 of a percentage point. She was 18 and Miss America-cute.

When I came on set, Shirley Hudson interrogated me as if I were Nostradamus. What do you see for the Beach Boys? How well will Rosalyn do at Worlds? Cliff—anything? When she asked me about herself I told her I thought she would move to Washington to work on Reagan's reelection campaign. That came true within weeks of the broadcast. The audience was enrapt and the viewers kept me in Seattle for two weeks giving private sessions.

It is my firm belief that the out of the blue call from Shirley Hudson was God's handiwork. No one knew where I was (that's what happens when you are getting sober – shame blinds you into hiding from family and friends), but she found me and invited me to what turned out to be a bellwether appearance on a show that reached several states in the Northwest. And most of all, all these years later, I credit *Northwest Today* for giving me my career back.

One of the calls from my appearance on *Northwest Today* was from a woman named Marjorie Beale. She owned a meta-physical bookstore in Phoenix, Arizona. She was visiting her sis-ter in Seattle and saw the show. Marjorie asked me to speak to a group in her bookstore the next week. She quoted a price and I accepted.

"No one in Phoenix knows you but I was impressed with your appearance on *Northwest Today*. I am putting your headshot in the window so let's see what turnout we have," she advised.

The lecture was set for two o'clock in the afternoon. When I walked into the bookstore it was jam-packed. Marjorie said there were more than 100 people.

"It must have been your picture in the window or the Great White Brotherhood was working for you," she said.

She and I decided I would speak on The Shadow.

"Does Jung insinuate that if the shadow self is paramount to overwhelming that you're probably gay?"

"Why have I never heard about Carl Jung and the concept of the Shadow?"

"You gave a Meditation that aids in integrating my Shadow. Can I buy one, and where can I find one?"

"You seem to believe that until you see your Shadow as an active part of you that you might keep picking the wrong lover."

All of these were great questions. The event spilled over into a nearby restaurant that put a large circle of chairs and tables to accommodate more than thirty people.

"Albert, you said you could stay in town to accommodate private sessions with attendees," said Marjorie.

I nodded in agreement.

"That's great because I signed up more than forty clients for you. You can have sessions in the back room," she said.

"Wow, that's wild," I said.

God gets his way with us even when we haven't a clue where we're going or why.

That was my first job on the small stage, but after all the humble days and months of sobriety, I was glad to be there.

Remember, this was a few years before Shirley MacLaine (who was in a group with Patrick Flanagan – Father of Pyramid Power – and me and 24 other people in the Great Pyramid of Cheops for a power alignment in the constellation Pleiades or known to others as the Seven Sisters in November 1983) who singlehandedly revolutionized the concept of spirituality. Shirley held conferences across the country, charging $300: $100 for the mind, $100 for the body and $100 for the spirit. There was no

Deepak Chopra. Marianne Williamson was still speaking to AIDS victims in small groups in Los Angeles. James Redfield's runaway best-seller, *The Celestine Prophecy,* was not published until 1994.

A gentleman from the bookstore made an important introduction for me in Sedona – a gifted painter named Delmary. We stopped by the Masters Gallery to meet her. There was a tall and imposing man named Randy Richmond, who today is a brilliant expositor of an amazing analysis of your character based upon your birth data called Human Design. A Human Design Chart or BodyGraph is a precise map and user guide that gives you access to how we are genetically designed to engage with the world. We clicked when he intuited that I was newly sober. He had me come to his house to meet his wife. I did their charts. Six weeks later they invited me back as a house guest.

It was another of those synchronistic God shots. Beirne Richmond had been married before and had two sons. Sadly, the boys died exactly one year apart – on my birthday, March 6. When I moved to Sedona later that year she and Randy gave a huge birthday party in the gallery.

"I will never again be sad on March 6. Knowing you changed the sadness to gladness," she said. She and Randy and I remained dear friends. She died in 2005. He is a part of my Sedona Intensive support staff.

I am a member of the American Federation of Astrologers. Another God connection, the AFA was born May 4, 1938, the year I was born and the date coincides exactly with the degree in the sign of Taurus or my natal Moon.

I do not consider myself a traditional astrologist. Like Human Design, my utility of astrology is in concert with my intuition as well as the classic lines of Carl Jung and how he used the Shadow to rescue his patients from their frustrations, emotional distresses and protocols of human nature that differed from the currency in the world. As in Jung's time and more widespread even today is the undue influence of politics and religion on how one is often-times out of step with these two institutions. I feel that one yearns to know who he or she is, separate from politics and religion and the confusions these engender.

It is not my intent to convert newcomers to the world views that I am espousing but rather, to make readers think and go to any length to untie the knots of thought impressions in order to find out who they are and what they are to do with their lives. It was a God shot when Shirley Hudson from *Northwest Today* found me, especially given that we drunks always cut ties with the past out of both embarrassment and not wanting anyone one like the IRS or bill collectors to find us.

Most people who do what I do are dependent on some-one with whom they've worked to tell someone else about you. References. It is like a coterie of like souls on assignment to sup-port your practice. I went to Egypt as the guest of Patrick Flanagan when I was down and out in Sedona. A man and his wife I met in Egypt brought me to Montecchìa di Crosara at their expense for seven weeks. A man on the Egypt trip took me to Singapore for work he had because he needed my mysticism. This same man's sister brought me to Dallas, Texas in 1984 and it is still one of my busiest cities. At one time I worked there four times a year for two weeks at a time.

Later, I would travel across the country on book tours where I met lifelong clients and friends. I went to Milan, Italy to promote *Clearing for the Millennium,* which was published in Italian, and later to Barcelona, Spain to promote *Signs and Wonders*. A few years ago Fundana, a charity in Venezuela that provided homes for more than 12,000 children who had been victims of sexual abuse, negligence and abandonment, brought me there to help them raise money for their charity. When I did the Oprah Winfrey

Show in 1985, a woman I met from Birmingham, Alabama set up a workshop there at the Lodestar Bookstore. I have worked there off and on for more than thirty years.

I guess you can go home again, Thomas Wolfe.

Chapter Thirteen
Creating

When I was in the start-up days of sobriety in Long Beach someone introduced me to Pat Teal, who turned out to be a literary agent. She was fun and insisted that if I could write like I talked, she could sell the book.

"Albert, you have a fun, savvy way of putting things. Sit down and start writing," Pat advised.

Let me be quite frank about something. If you cannot commit to sitting hours at a computer (nobody writes long-hand anymore — those were the bygone days of Tennessee Williams and Flannery O'Connor) for days on end, hour after hour, don't think about writing a book. Self-publishing has wasted more peoples' money because they will print and sell anything anyone can write.

I moved to Sedona in the early 80s, and although Pat lived in Ramona, California, she dogged me relentlessly, "Sit down. Write whether you want to or not. You have a lot to say about what you do and who you do it with." She never stopped badgering me.

I've said that author James Redfield — you know, he wrote *The Celestine Prophecy* which came out in 1994 and became the biggest best-selling title in the world between 1996 and 1999

– became one of my favorite clients and a close friend. We met when I was lecturing on Soul Mates at the Lodestar Book Store in Birmingham in 1988. He came the next day for a private session with me. James decided to come to Sedona to go through the Sedona Intensive that same year.

He and I are both Pisces – commonality – and he and I both grew up in the Deep South. Same frequency and similar challenges. When he wanted to self-publish he sent me a copy of the manuscript and asked if I wanted to invest.

"Jim, I love the book and wish you well. I have only been sober a few years and am still rehabbing my finances," I told him.

Everyone by now knows the success story of this amazing book. It's hard to find anyone who hasn't read it, even overseas. It's been published in more than thirty languages.

In the early 90s, when James was lecturing in Boulder, Colorado, someone who worked at Warner Books bought a self-published copy of *The Celestine Prophecy*. She gave the book to editor Joann Davis, who bought the book for a song. (It's on record for being just under $1 million – with millions of copies being sold so quickly, Davis and Warner Books got a sweetheart deal!)

Soon after his runaway success, I was driving through the switchbacks from the Village of Oak Creek into town when the voice of intuition spoke to me.

"Write a book."

I called Pat Teal and told her that I was ready to write.

"Good luck, Mr. Ants-in-Your-Yants. Writing is arduous and takes a major commitment," Pat told me on the phone.

"What do I write about?" I asked.

"Write what you know. All the people you've worked with, including some members of my family, love how you counsel. I advise you to write a book proposal. Publishers want to know what they are buying into. Get a copy of *Write the Perfect Book Proposal*. It is the best manual to sell a book," she signed off.

I did and I did and I did more. Enter James Redfield and his gorgeous brilliant wife, Salle Merrill.

They were in Sedona in December 1994. He and I talked about a book I was writing. He offered to send the book proposal to Joann at Warner Books. She got the proposal a few days before Christmas. She had actually already left the city for the holidays, but when she got the call from her office about Jim sending her a friend's book proposal, her driver took her back to the Warner Books offices.

After Christmas, Joann called and asked me if I could come to New York the first week in January to talk about the book.

Let me be frank about how I live my life as a sober man. I have met billionaires, royalty and rock stars. I've had movies stars and athletes sit across from me. I wouldn't trade places with one of them for all their money. After steering them through their crazy mucked up lives, more times than not, there's a rainbow at the end of the malaise. When they walk in to work with me, no matter who is in the hot seat, I am nonplussed. But then I got that call from Joann Davis and I was over the moon.

I put together an outline with a couple of sample chapters and explained why this book would sell like hotcakes, just like *Write the Perfect Book Proposal* said. There was one person I trusted to read it: Former actress Sagan Lewis, who unfortunately for the planet made her transition earlier this year. She made a few tweaks and then I put it together and headed for New York.

I've confessed to everybody but Pope Francis and the CIA that I never fly coach. Have you been in the back lately? Spare me.

Sitting in 3C, I was rereading the proposal a zillionth time when the woman seated next to me asked what I was reading so furtively.

"I am on my way to New York to try to sell this book proposal idea to an editor," I responded.

"May I see it?" she asked.

She read it. "It's not my kind of book but you write well. The chapters are very clean."

We chatted for a couple of hours. In the chatter she told me what fee to ask for the book.

"If you have an agent, ask for more to cover her fee," she advised.

Until the very end of the flight I had no clue to the identity of this woman. I had a light bulb moment deplaning. She was Gloria Steinem.

The next morning I met with Joann Davis at the Hotel Carlyle.

As a side note, I want to give a shout-out to the finest hotel in Gotham City. I would still be staying there if a former manager had not doubled the rent on a room the week after 9/11 happened. But the Regency Hotel is fine with me.

I prepared Joann's astrological birth chart. She wanted to get a handle on how I worked with clients.

"I do a complimentary Evaluation Session on the phone. If the two of us are a good match we select a date for their Intensive to start," I said to Joann before we started.

What I like most about her is that she is smarter than a gaggle of Mensa minds. Her manner is fresh and engaging.

When I finished, I asked if she could relate and if she had any questions. She didn't request anything.

"Well, I have a question. When do I start groveling and tap dancing to see if you want to buy the book?" I asked.

"I already knew I wanted to publish it. But I wanted to meet you because James wrote so glowingly about you in the Foreword to *Clearing for the Millennium*," she said.

We chatted for a few more minutes and then she told me to have my agent Pat Teal call her about the offer and pub date for the book.

By the way, Gloria Steinem was on the money. Warner Books paid exactly to the dollar what Ms. Steinem said to ask.

PART TWO

Chapter Fourteen
Correcting

——

I am reminded of the jump from being a drunk to sitting in a room with others like me who were sober. There was a tall, scrawny man named "Singing Sam" sitting in those early meetings. He could raise the dead with his sobriety pitch. In my newcomer days, I waited impatiently for Sam to share.

"You think you're having a bad day because somebody looks at you cross-wise? Your Ego wants you to blame God because you're 45 years old and dead broke. I guess being a beauty at 25 and a washed-up broad at 50 with no takers makes you want to kill yourself," he shared.

He'd stand up for drama and emphasis and bellow, "When men were fighting in the trenches in World War II, their dependence on a Higher Power got them through the knee-deep mud and sweat and gut-wrenching fear. Nothing can get you out of the pit of despair from a life of booze to a reprieve to live a better life like a God that was there for you always. You turned your back on him. He never went anywhere. You did."

One day after a meeting, Singing Sam asked me to go to a local restaurant for some abalone. He always talked about peace and quiet on the dock while fishing for this delicacy. You would have thought Johnny from the *Price is Right* had hollered, "Albert G., come on down!" The power plug in my 12-step meeting had asked me to lunch. Wow!

We sat at Hof's Hut eating fried abalone steaks and fresh fruit. Sam said very little. Fish in his mouth was where he was heart and soul.

"I guess you're wondering why I asked you to have lunch with me today," he said.

"You bet I am. Sam, I admire you more than anyone I ever met. And not just in 12-steps," I answered.

"First off, don't get too much into that admiration stuff. We are just attractions to stay sober for one other. There are no big shots in here and no one is better than the other. That pecking order got left behind where we drank to believe such bullshit," he said.

Then we both ate in silence. This was the best tasting fish I ever ate. And I usually never order anything but a medium rare filet with French fries. Today it's abalone with my friend.

"The reason I asked you to eat with me today was I see myself in you. You are eager, you are so glad to be sober that you want to reach out to other newcomers. Being new and all, your humility shines like the sun breaking through dark clouds. Your hand is always extended to anybody who walks through the door.

"My opinion is you will never be a circuit speaker, like Chuck C. or Clancy or even your sponsor, Fil V. Your road to service will be to help one person at a time walk the steps to freedom from the bondage of self and others, one day at a time," he ended the talk.

We ordered lemon meringue pie and coffee and laughed for the rest of our time together.

"Never take yourself too seriously. And every time I see you, Albert, make me laugh," he said. We walked out of the restaurant, me floating on a pink cloud. I have never forgotten Singing Sam. Sam walked the talk.

Everyone I've ever met who writes about his life's work always finds the first sentence of his exposition rather foreboding.

At the suggestion of a friend, I watched *Kumaré*, a film about a young man from India living in New York who pretends to be a guru and sets about attracting followers. At the end of the film he confesses that his name is Vikram Gandhi.

"I am no one's guru but my own," he said.

In a dramatic denouement to the film, he shaves and comes out into a room of followers to tell the truth. It was so compelling that I was weeping by the credits. Several of his former followers refused to speak to him. They had invested too much in their need to find what they were looking for in someone else.

That story is a good place for me to start because I need to confess to readers that in this book, I share what happened to me and it may not be their story. However, over more than forty years, my clients have said my story has so many points of light that they connected.

"Your story is my story," many of them said to me.

In today's world, there is too much fragmentation and anger. The Blame Game is afoot. In the words of Helen Keller, "I would rather light one candle than to curse the darkness." The purpose of these pages is to try to light the way to freedom from oneself and others.

In spite of alarm and discontent from so many sectors, these are joyous times to be alive. Yet these are the most compelling times to right the World Order by activating inside persuasions through rigorously honest inventory. As a student of history, the challenges we face today have templates from the past that require the same courage and fortitude today.

We will be looking at the individual, not class struggles. Our focus will have our personal choices under the lens of what needs to change and how. Many of us make a critical mistake when we get too caught up in the landscape around us rather than make critical corrections in our own internal disorder.

Throughout my career, my suggestion has been that to change the world that you touch, you must change you. Each of us is 1/7,000,000,000th+ of the total population in the world. Impossible to reach, but the ripple effect can do wonders for the individual to impact the whole.

The Lower World reached critical mass in 1953 with the advent of the computer. The Free Press Dictionary defines the computer as a programmable electronic device designed for performing prescribed operations on data at high speed, especially one housed with or linked to other devices for inputting, storing, retrieving and displaying the data.

What the Free Press does not tell you is the dangerous aspects of this phenomenon. This technology, faster than the speed of light, also gave us social media laden with what came to be called Fake News in 2016, half truths, cut from whole cloth, as well as criminal invasion through hacking and scamming.

Thomas L. Friedman is a three-time recipient of the Pulitzer Prize for his work with *The New York Times*. He's the author of six best-selling books, including *The World Is Flat*.

His most recent book is *Thank You for Being Late*. Here is how his website describes the amazing world of speed-up: "Thomas L. Friedman shows that we have entered an age of dizzying acceleration and explains how to live in it. Due to an exponential increase in computing power, climbers atop Mount Everest enjoy excellent cell-phone service and self-driving cars are taking to the roads.

"A parallel explosion of economic interdependency has created new riches as well as spiraling debt burdens. Meanwhile, Mother Nature is also seeing dramatic changes as carbon levels rise and species go extinct, with compounding results.

"As a result, so many aspects of our societies, workplaces, and geopolitics are being reshaped and need to be re-imagined. He references the impact of social media."

In my part of the forest, I predicted the meltdown in the housing market, banks and the general reversals of fortunes that occurred in January 2008 when Pluto entered Capricorn. Much of what Friedman references were facets of what caused the economic reversals that terrified the world. He demarks the amalgamation of all the parts of the mechanism that resulted in global rethink.

Friedman and I are writing from different points of view. He sees that the runaway development in technology has a downside through acceleration. My window looks out at all the ways in which we are distracted from assessing where we are in terms of our inner life. My view is the speed-up is a negative force for those of us trying to evaluate who we are and what we are doing on Earth.

In fair and balanced terms, the internet and social media also connected people in meaningful ways. We authors depend on this invention to spread the word about our books. Millions of people get news in a nanosecond. My position is to expose the underbelly of this marvel twentieth century invention.

No matter the benefits of the computer, we must always look at the control that it holds over us, particularly for young people.

Levi Felix, who championed the virtues of unplugging from smart phones and other technology, co-founded Digital Detox, which sponsored retreats and camps to help people reconnect in real life. He died of a brain tumor in January 2017. Mr. Felix sought to bring balance to people's lives by disconnecting them for stretches of time from the clutches of their phones and from social media. He knew the hazards firsthand.

"I'm a geek, I'm not a Luddite," Mr. Felix told *The New York Times* in 2012. "I love that technology connects us and is taking our civilization to the next level, but we have to learn how to use it, and not have it use us."

"Squeeze your siblings," he wrote. "Tell everyone that you love them."

My assessment is that most seekers are looking for whatever they think is waiting in the magical world of informational opportunity: fulfillment. They will never find it. Computer binging is as addictive as overeating or the disease of mindless shopping. My clarion call used to be: "Take me anywhere but where I am."

Looking in the rearview mirror I can declare that all that I was looking for was for my curiosity to take me inside myself.

The codependency on the pleasure chest of Supra Ego kicked into high gear with the creation of the credit card in 1959. Runaway spending rose like a tsunami. Credit card debt created an illusion of what one could pay for within his financial means. So many people are paying for overspending with another credit card. It is the penultimate pyramid scheme. When I finally paid off all credit card debt through the strong arm of my business partner Scott, I was living two years ahead of my red ink.

Fear oftentimes determines why we do the things we do or don't do. It is scary places that drive us away from getting to the cause of fright. Shrinks tell us if the pressure leads to depression, take a pill. If one is not enough, take some more.

I start here because you have read the rocky roads I took to get to where I ended up.

Except where I went and what I did got me to this place of dependency on my relationship with a Higher Power. My sermon to you is to beware the false doctrines you have adopted because the glittering messages from newspapers, magazines and television tell you to do so. From here on out you will read what I did and still do to take orders from the Upper World and not from the misleading advertisements I read. The outer world is a dangerous place unless your inner world is in alignment with your God.

One of the most heinous hypnotic trances from popular culture is the need to be known and to be "somebody." Waiting to be lifted up in the eyes of the world is another device of Supra Ego. Fame is something very alluring, and it's more debilitating than satisfying to the soul.

I often work with movie stars and actors who are just getting started. Writers, directors and producers call and come to listen to what I have to say. When we get to the root cause of their discontent, fame (or lack of it) is always in the mix of the miasma of their misery.

As we explore the life plan I am going to share with you, read between the lines when I write about 12-step recovery. Our fellowship has a set of traditions that we adhere to regarding our anonymity, which I honor throughout this book. Google "12-steps" and you can become part of an incredible program that saved my life and gave me a new life.

My backstory is the collective pile-up that was my life when I started drinking. As you found out, I was a 24-karat-gold drunk from my first drink. It was if someone had freed me to be a free-range clucker with no regard for ethics or sanity. More than that, I was able to erase the blackboard of everything that I had been taught that did not work for me. Becoming a drunk allowed me to tear my life to shreds. As Pema Chödrön wrote in her book, *When Things Fall Apart*, my life had really begun to fall into place.

There is an advantage to alcoholism if you have the courage to get sober and change your life with the help of the paradigms of recovery. Friendship and fellowship are tantamount to getting free of alcoholic behavior and its destructive nature.

All of us have had a cross to bear. It's called karmic overload. I wrote this book to give you insight into how to escape what may have never worked in your life. And most of all, to let you know that the God you seek is within you.

When I asked a close friend why no one ever gave me the real scoop on life and higher consciousness, the friend said: "Nobody knew. We have to go to a lot of dark places in order to reactivate the God within us."

That may sound like Southern jive talk but it worked for me when I came to understand that parents and teachers and friends in church didn't have a clue. They just told you what had been told to them.

Breaking the chains that bind us to how we were raised takes a humongous leap of faith. It is hard work to get free of what was not your course for life. Our parents didn't know about Higher Consciousness so they raised and ruled us like their parents did them. It is through the tough stuff – life's harsh lessons – that we pray the greatest prayer, "God help me." More than likely God muses to himself, "There's another one who wants to come home." And we do after having tried everything in our Ego's bag of tricks, which I refer to as his pleasure chest, to make us happy.

When you have been where I have been and done the things I have done and are able to connect the dots, what I know to be true today has both gravitas and grace.

The New York Times says that the nature of the USA is that politicians and constituents have been at each other's throats for millennia. I still stand by my thesis that what flipped me and caused me to drink myself onto a stage was the combination of religion and politics.

Remember that loopy lady who gave me my first martini? God used madwoman Mona to get me to what would one day take me through a door of freedom. Some of us want the church doctrine to run the state of affairs. Not on my watch, preacher man.

George P. Lakoff is an American cognitive linguist and author of *Moral Politics: How Liberals and Conservatives Think*. Lakoff is best known for his thesis, "that lives of individuals are significantly influenced by the central metaphors they use to explain complex phenomena." He also believes that we do not have absolute free will.

Lakoff contends that, "We are trapped by what the neural systems of our brains have accumulated. We can only see what our brains allow us to understand."

His hypothesis is that each of us has the ultimate "strict father," who cannot allow any of his family or inner circle to betray trust. Another archetype is the "nurturant parent" who feels that love and caring is better. For my money, mama is a lot better for the kid than daddy, if it is one or the other. Most of us who are in the search and rescue business find "strict father" to be dysfunctional, politics be damned.

But the overlay message was that Republicans try to change polls and Democrats follow the polls. Interesting but I did not get stuck by Elmer's glue with his premise.

I am giving Signore Lakoff space in *Moments and Windstorms* because of his researched notion that "strict father" morality says, "It is your concern that what matters is re-teaching individual duty." This means obligation to you and not social responsibility.

I don't care if the next trap for man's vote is self-interest. A large part of my recovery was caring about other people. Life is all about all of us, not just us singly. Put that in your pipes and smoke it, "strict fathers."

Most interesting, Lakoff said, "Poor conservatives vote against their own material interest; rather they vote for the Worldview. And the reason for their Worldview is that it teaches them who they are."

What hammered home the insanity of elections was that people believe what they hear over and over again. You know, like in advertising overloads. This is the rotten floor that most of us built our identities on and it was totally a lie.

My final word on the subject of politics is that from the Garden of Eden, through all purported civilizations and supposed world governments, malfeasance and deception have been the logos of their lying. The purpose of this book is not to get you to live off the grid and never read another newspaper or cast another vote. Get well for yourself. Face down all demons and addictions and compulsions and live and eventually die as who you were born to be.

The pejorative notion that we as Lower World people are in an unbreakable trance state to deceptive politics is unacceptable to me. There is no question that our true soul identity has been skewered from all the travel back and forth from Upper to Lower World. We can find our true identity but only when we disconnect from the untruths and outright lies foisted on us by our Ego. The trick to breaking through the manipulation of false promises is to take back your power. You no longer want to act or react to what authorities try to get you to do.

Chapter Fifteen
God is Everywhere and in All Things

———

Bhagavad-Gita: The Song of God is a 700-verse Hindu scripture in Sanskrit that is part of the Hindu epic *Mahabharata*. The *Gita* is set in a narrative framework of a dialogue between prince Arjuna and his charioteer Lord Krishna.

As a Hindu Vedantist myself, the *Gita* is one of the most powerful expositions of man's duty in his return to Earth: to face, admit and seek forgiveness from God for our past misdeeds.

My sensibility says that the *Gita* also represents two sides of our nature: 1) Our inner world is in conflict because of all the lives we have lived on Earth and we collect how we have gained or failed in our journey to selfhood to be who we were originally meant to be from first incarnation. 2) Our outer world is how we legislate life in returning to an egocentric world. As God is the ruler and Supreme Being in the Upper World, the Ego created by the Archangel's desire to be God has dominion of the Lower World.

As when reading a book, watching a film or stage play, each of us concludes what we are watching and what it means to us. So my interpretation of the *Bhagavad-Gita* is that we are Arjuna and Krishna is God. We need to understand that the wars we fight in the outer world are reflections of the struggles we engage inside ourselves. Hence, most of us who have studied the *Gita* agree that the barest bone analysis of it is that the war is always inside ourselves.

My contribution to this masterpiece is that the never-ending battle is between our Ego and our connection to God.

No one – either genius or ordinary – can explain God to me. I don't care whether it's the Big Bang Theory or a resonance at the deepest wells of my being. I know that there is a silent Power Source that rescued me from all the craziness that the big pieces of stuff hammered into my head because they said so.

I confess to twenty years of alcoholism and bad-boy behavior. Such insanity trapped me in a life not worth living. God was leading me even when I did not let him. But in an odd and counterintuitive way, drinking brought me to where I am today.

God gives me peace and no contempt for anything or anybody, and it makes life worth living. God created me to be one thing and I was determined to be something else. The Higher Power gives and that Source takes away. God speaks through us even when we slam the door shut. There are people who see colors and say they can give you all the answers to all the unknowable inquiries. My experience has been that more people see everything as either black or white and ask over and over again, "What was the question?"

The next step for me after having disavowed all that did not resonate was to create a method of talking directly to God. Prayer and meditation is the main stream for my connection to the God within me. The Vedanta Society published the best primer for me about the Higher Power, *How to Know God.*

I cracked the egg of truth when I was open to Upper World guidance. In a book I wrote more than twenty years ago, *Clearing for the Millennium,* I talked about my High Self Guide Paul, who actually is a part of me. Just like I did when I got sober in 1980, I still go to meetings to learn to listen and listen to learn. My sponsor taught me that lesson. Paul became like an emissary to the God within me.

Paul taught me that oftentimes religion excluded the notion of internal inspiration and trust. Religion was in conflict with what my past wanted me to remember. Religion made me think that it knew better than I did; what I should believe and that there was a narrow path to that knowledge. This schism that happened within me was the route to freedom from what had been rote instruction rather than the self-acknowledged wisdom that I unearthed to save me.

I want to share how this High Self came into my life in 1985. I had just finished a talk at Lodestar Books and Gifts bookstore in Birmingham. I went back to my room and that essence of my higher self got my attention as follows.

In a matter of minutes I was totally oblivious of the room as I had stopped my busy mind.

Soon my breathing became deep and even. My lips tingled. A voice struggled to speak through. I seemed to free fall, then nod awake, which silenced the sound. Exhausted, I gave way and spiraled toward darkness and intermittent bright light. I focused on a pulsating white pyramid with a golden aura. This image first began to appear in my dreams when I was about six years old. A powerful presence spoke.

Hello, Albert. Why did it take you so long to talk with us?

"What? Who are you? Leave me alone!" I lashed out. I was startled awake and sat up on the edge of the bed. For years I had heard that some of my friends communicated with spook spirits. I wanted no part of communication with ETs, if that's who this man was.

An overwhelming magnetism drew me back to where the voice was. I lay down and relaxed into deep meditation.

Just relax. Continue to breathe slowly and you will gradually let go of fear. We have been monitoring you. Your actions and thoughts indicate that you are ready for your assignment.

The communication was telepathic, not audible. I couldn't move. I wasn't scared, even though I was being held by a very strong and commanding energy that seemed to scan my intelligence.

He spoke to me with ease and authority.

We have been trying to talk to you for more than ten years.

I was suspended – between floors – in time and space. Ordinarily, I would suspect invasion and harm. At this moment I was at peace and connected to an energy I innately trusted.

I answered mind to mind.

"Who are you? What do you want with me?" I asked to test whether this uninvited guest heard me.

I am Paul, your guide and teacher from the Great White Brotherhood of Light in the Upper World. I am here to help you clear to return to the light.

"Are you an alien or extraterrestrial? Have you come to abduct me?" I asked.

Albert, I am not alien to you. I am an aspect of your higher self. I have no need to abduct you. Talking to you will do. You and I are one. Think of us as spiritual twins.

Paul went on to explain that all of us have such guidance, that I am neither special nor privileged. Everyone has his own connection to the Upper World through their High Self, who is an aspect of oneself. Relationship and family counselors would liken the Albert/Paul connection to an inner child/inner parent relationship. He further stated that each of us can get this help from within so as not to be so attached to control outside ourselves.

Paul advised that one must have cleared enough to be able to listen to the voice of inspiration and high-self guidance. Without eliminating family of origin issues, addictions and resentments, one is never open and free enough to hear the voice when it speaks.

There are those who purport to communicate with disincarnate spirits who have separate identities. J.Z. Knight, former guru of Hollywood celebrities Shirley MacLaine and Linda Evans, has an entity named Ramtha who speaks through her and says that he is a five-million-year-old being who teaches through Ms. Knight. Paul is not such a being. He has stated through the years that he is inspiration and a more informed guide.

Paul uses my mind and my reservoir of life experiences from many lives and he often speaks in my native Alabama vernacular.

When I asked him why he only spoke to me in meditation, he said that I and all mankind are too busy and scattered in everyday life to be able to listen to guidance. Meditation is where the mind is still and the will is receptive. With time, and the clearer we become, we will be able to think, act and speak with inspiration and intuition, without conscious telepathic communication with high-self guidance.

One specific question I asked answered any doubts I had about being able to trust him, or myself, enough to listen to him.

"Paul, if you and I are the same, why do we need to talk and discuss who I am and what I am to do? Why wouldn't I just do what I am supposed to do?"

There was a moment of silence. I began to breathe with smoother rhythm. When I am anxious in prayer and meditation, my breathing becomes faster and more uneven.

You are living on Earth and attached to material illusion and false perceptions that are devices of your Ego. You are not clear. When you still the mind and are quiet, you and I – your high and all-knowing self – can communicate and I can guide you to a clearer understanding of who you are and where you need to go.

I live within you and yet I am that aspect of you that is a part of universal consciousness that is limitless and without boundaries and has no consideration of time and space. As you are within the limitations of your body and function using contaminated knowledge and information, you cannot be free to roam the spectrum of all worlds and all galaxies. Your karma is set up for you to feel and experience certain people, places and things to free you for eventual return to the universe.

You can only be where you are, except for moments at a time. Meditation is a place where you can be free of attachment and enmeshment. I can be there and I am that part of you that can be everywhere. Soon you will learn about soul progression that will lead you and others back to God.

Paul continued.

The stars which you chart for people activate a timing device within you to let you know when you must do certain things. All of you on Earth work off karma from past lives by being in service to others. When a life is ended, to love and to serve are the only two tasks that will count in assessing the life spiritually.

It became time for you to serve others, as you have satisfied conditions of karma from the seventy past lives that created it.

"Seventy lives? Are you sure that I have lived seventy lives?" I asked with disbelief.

You and many millions of human beings have each been reborn more than 4,000 times. The seventy lives that affected the karma for you this life span have been reborn over more than 3,000 years.

I did not question Paul further about past lives. I knew intuitively that we all have lived thousands of lives, and in different galaxies and dimensions.

"Is this assignment exclusive to me? Am I the only one to lead others to the light?"

No, Albert, you are not. Many will be called to clear and then to lead. You were eventually able to hear our contact and to respond. You are simply to bring a message. Others will hear and clear and lead by listening to the voice within them.

I have not come to abduct you. All communication will occur when you meditate or are quiet and reflective. You will remember soon who to trust when you are in your world of inspiration and creativity.

I learned of the Great White Brotherhood of Light more than forty years ago when I attended the Spiritualist Church in Los Angeles. Like one who needs years of education before he can teach graduate school, members of the Great White Brotherhood are master souls at the pinnacle of universal knowledge.

They have gone to reform school, learned from past life mistakes, made amends and are soul-ready to teach and guide others from the spirit world, or "the other side of life," as Spiritualism refers to the silent and invisible domain. Many seekers and aspirants want to know where "there" is, but there has never been a definitive answer. Being there and communicating from here is one of the spiritual assumptions of trust through faith.

It is important for you to know that I was sober when Paul spoke to me. He had been trying for years but I did not want anyone or anything to interfere with my drinking. Make-believe and floorless fantasy is only when I was soused and ready to grab the golden ring that my Ego kept telling me to reach for.

Paul still talks to me daily when I am willing to listen. I recommend to all with whom I work that there is that nature within them. I learned from Kabbalah to tell everyone, "Don't believe a word I say unless it rings true for you."

When I was in college I got a minor in the Classics, Latin and Greek, both of which used mythology to wake up students to hidden truths. I liken this to master metaphysician, William Shakespeare, who taught parables and axioms of expositions of how to know what is true in his plays. The most well-known literary devise, the aphorism, appears on sobriety coins as a daily remembrance: "This above all: to thine own self be true, and it must follow, as the night the day, thou canst not then be false to any man."

I teach that in the School of Life there are stages and degrees of letting go and letting God in. In the first grade, we learn our ABCs and how to count, if I remember correctly, to 10. We go to school within a certain neighborhood. In larger cities, like New York and Chicago, schools are more integrated along racial lines. Every year thereafter the curriculum changes and the lessons get tougher. The same is true in the School of Life.

More people than ever are focused on the outer world. Pop culture changes so rapidly that young people wait in the wings for the latest hip or hop. Social media is a form of hypnosis. A smarter friend than me calls it a drug. Our politics have turned into a jungle without a machete to get out of the miasma of deception and false promises.

The only person you can change is you. There is a consciousness movement afoot that portends what lays in waiting for all of us. You get to where you need to go one day at a time and oftentimes your Higher Self wants to double promote you. That's when remembering gets exciting for those of us who are yearning to return to the God that our Ego wanted us to forget.

Chapter Sixteen
Men and Women are the Same

When I sobered up I read books by mythologist Joseph Campbell. Campbell introduced me to the concept of the Upper World, which was what Christians call Heaven.

His magical fable is as follows:

One day the Head Archangel in the Upper World went to God and said that he wanted to be God.

"'I want everyone to bow down and worship me. I like the spa tub and the white dress with gold trim. What do you say, O High Holy One?'"

God spoke emphatically, "Don't let the door hit you in the tuches on the way out. And take your minions with you."

The story of Fallen Angels has confounded Christians and ultra-conservatives. They are in a trance state to their beliefs from infancy. I found that same religious system bred intolerance. The Campbell myth opened me up to what I had always known but had forgotten. My High Self Paul told me that we never learn anything. We remember.

God did not throw the Archangel and his followers out of the Upper World because he was mean-spirited. Quite the contrary. He allowed choice between Right and Wrong, Light and Dark, and Peace and War. The Archangel came to be known for millennia as Lucifer. And by Natural Law, Lucifer has been given dominion over the Lower World. It operates under the nickname Ego. God the Creator is the lord of the Upper World.

Beware who you follow. Question all that you hear. Follow no one but what rings true. Stay away from bowing before any teacher or his teachings.

The brilliance of the Campbell story is that we have to keep recycling, being reborn, until our contamination is cleared away enough to allow us to remain in the Upper World.

Many scholars ask questions in their pursuit of who God is.

"Does He really exist?" "What purpose was served in his dismissal of those who rebelled against him?"

Campbell saw the Upper World as our personal genesis. The Lower World is where we remember our true progeny by breaking through the deceptions of our own Ego. It is what the broad strokes of Consciousness are trying to teach us. Although I am a Vedantist and not a traditional Christian, the Holy Bible helps us ultimately break through the betrayals of our own dark side.

In the Revolt in the Upper World, as each of us prepared to leave the Perfect Place, God implanted a remembering chip in us as a homing device that allows us Fallen Angels to return to God when we've had enough of Ego lying and entrapment. And to show his compassion, the Light Source created the Earth, the Lower World, so we would not be homeless.

What makes the Campbell myth powerfully realistic is that so much of these admonitions and cautions appeared in ancient Latin and Greek legends. What I loved about studying Latin was all the possibilities that are available to us. If we take these stories and folklores to heart, we could shift and become who we have always been but couldn't remember through the fog of deceit.

But in spite of the knowledge of these stories and myths and legends with a moral, why do we not want to return from whence we came? It is because all the lure and enticements of our Ego are too overpowering. His treasure chest overflows with temptations: money, alcohol, drugs, sex, power, manipulation, control and most of all because we have forgotten that we are a precious child of God.

Because we began our first life as perfect as the God who created us, when we embraced the nature of Lucifer, we obscured God's light from our consciousness and souls. Thus in the Upper World, we were perfect. When we left the Upper World, Lucifer's dark nature became ours.

Another advantage Supra Ego or Lucifer (call it what you will) had when we returned to Earth was the battle of the sexes. Man against woman.

Dr. Carl Gustav Jung was a Swiss psychiatrist and psychoanalyst who founded analytical psychology. His work has been influential not only in psychiatry but also in anthropology, archaeology, literature, philosophy and religious studies. The work I have done for more than forty years is to take Jung's premise, "You can be neither healthy nor happy until you individuate," and help the client to become true to himself. Jung went on to say that you are not your religion, the culture to which you were born. That life's journey is one of discovery – finding out who you are without referencing what other people and institutions have instilled in you about your true self.

Among the central concepts of analytical psychology is individuation – the lifelong psychological process of differentiation of the self out of each individual's conscious and unconscious elements.

There is a very eye-opening section from *The Portable Jung* as translated and expressed by the Master of Mythology, Joseph

Campbell, that offers insight to both a woman's and a man's dilemma. "It is often tragic to see how blatantly a man bungles his own life, and the lives of others, yet remains totally incapable of seeing how much the whole tragedy originates in him, and how he continually feeds it and keeps it going. Not consciously, of course – for consciously he is engaged in bewailing and cursing a faithless world that recedes further and further into the distance. Rather, it is an unconscious factor which spins the illusions that veil his world. And what is being spun is a cocoon, which in the end will completely envelop him."

In 1992 John Gray's book *Men are from Mars Women are from Venus* was published and sold more than 50 million copies. It was the most successful non-fiction book in the 1990s. Those 200-plus pages were a prime example that when you give false information that revs up the gender split, the great unwashed will lap it up like it's the cocktail *du jour*. With all due respect to Gray and the times in which he wrote about how different men and women are, as an astro-intuitive I can tell you that Mars and Venus are in everyone's chart. This insinuates that we are both male and female.

The Ego and the Shadow are the same. Both need to be converted. The Ego manipulates the division between men and women until the Shadow is integrated into the personality of each of us.

When we understand that the Shadow is our other side, the man within the woman and the woman within the man, the Shadow becomes our partner that makes us whole.

The Shadow is an area of darkness created when a source of light is blocked. The shadow, said celebrated Carl Jung, is "the unknown dark side of our personality." It is dark both because it tends to consist predominantly of the primitive, negative, socially or religiously depreciated human emotions and impulses like sexual lust, power strivings, selfishness, greed, envy, anger or rage, and due to its unenlightened nature, completely obscured from consciousness.

Neither Ego nor Shadow is our enemy. That essence, invisible and silent though it is, can become your best friend and the most powerful force in making your life whole and complete.

In order to wrap your mind and open your heart to what is Ego, I need to present a quick overview of how and where the concept of the Ego got its start – and it was not just in this life you are living.

My defining moment for the Ego is a distortion of one's identity based upon who and what a person should be based upon a skewered culture into which one is born.

One of my favorite stories from the Good Book is the Prodigal Son, which in our political environment today should have included the Prodigal Daughter. Preachers make something else of it but I know it to be a dramatization of how the lost soul returns to Paradise, or the Upper World.

At issue with the conception of the Ego is where did the misconception of a man or woman's identity become a breaking point? It was in Genesis – when we left the Upper World with the Fallen Angel. We start over with each rebirth but we carry with us the karma from before.

Let's define Karma. Biblically, we are told that we reap what we sow without letting us know where and when we scattered those seeds. Hindus and Buddhists believe it is the cosmic principle according to which each person is rewarded or punished in one incarnation based on that person's deeds in the previous incarnation.

These Robert's Rules of Order from the Upper World provide common procedures for getting all returnees on the same footing and speaking the same language. Our endgame is to become whole again. In doing so we must feel how others abided our bad behavior. Thus we return to Earth and change roles in the play we cast ourselves into. In one life we are the abuser and then in a subsequent one we are the abused.

If you ever want to become authentic as God created you to be, you must face compulsions and addictions.

On a global landscape as well as in our personal lives, the war is between our legs. The conundrum of why we do what we do, especially in our personal relationships, is wrapped in dissociative identity.

Gay and straight is the same thing, an illusion that hides true feelings. This unraveled mystery of identity explains why many loathe and denigrate homosexuals. It is not gays or lesbians they hate. Rather, it's their refusal to accept the Shadow nature within themselves that is the problem. Oftentimes a man is overwhelmed by his *anima*, or Shadow. The same is true for women, seduced by their male essence, their *animus*, or Shadow.

I once worked with Rob, a 40-year-old man from the great state of Texas. From hello he wanted to convince me he was all man and a super stud. However, when I factored in his third wife, I also zeroed in on the negative affect that ignoring his Shadow had caused the rift in his marriages. He got roaring mad.

"Listen, Albert, I admitted that I'm an alcoholic and in your vocabulary I might be a narcissist, but I will dang well tell you that I ain't no fruit-cake. To each his own, but I am not queer," he scolded as he spoke.

What Rob was revealing to me was that, because he could not immediately accept his Shadow presence, the fear of latent homosexuality was festering inside him. This is often the case. The absence of integration of one's Shadow has the effect of one's Shadow becoming unsettling and a disturber of the peace within.

Some are sicker than others and new information that may heal them takes a whole lot of time to embrace. To his credit, Rob did some dialoguing with his Shadow and he cracked the door of willingness to change by being more open-minded.

Carl Jung explored how a misunderstanding and ignorance of the Shadow causes conflicts in marriages and even problems in relationships at work. His case studies show that difficulty with a husband with his wife or a female executive with her male subordinates was an inability to integrate one's Shadow as if that nature were a real person.

In actuality that is Jung's hypothesis. He said you can be neither healthy nor happy until you individuate, i.e., finding within yourself what you have longed for in a partner. And recognizing and becoming friends with your Shadow improves the relationship you can have with yourself.

Let's be clear about one thing: We are all in varying degrees at different levels of awareness in the School of Life on Earth. Those who return to the Lower World as gurus or master teachers come back to be of service to those who still struggle. My guru, Swami Swahananda, was totally detached from the followers of Ramakrishna, our chosen ideal, just as Jesus is for Christians. Allah is the Arabic word for the God of Abrahamic religions.

Detachment is a fascinating concept that few of us can embrace. Since the sexual wars seem to start when we are mere children, their intensity is fueled by church leaders and even our parents to find a life partner and cling to that partner as if the church leaders and parents' lives and dogma depended on it.

If I may be so bold, some who detach from people, places and things may have finally reconnected to their personal God. The wisest among us would say that the purpose of our earthly return is to break the chains of attachment to our own Ego. That Ego is the progenitor of addictions like alcoholism, drug addictions, and never staying connected to a liberating thought for more than a nanosecond. I refer to Ego as a charlatan and liar, on assignment to keep us trapped in delusion.

How can marriages serve a holy purpose or working under others in a job with peace and harmony be in alignment with the endgame of our return to Earth, the Lower World? It is a matter of integrating one's Shadow, being able to be in a marriage or in a workable environment in one's career without controlling or being controlled by the partner or work supervisor?

I have a confession to make. With all my years and being sober and having integrated my Shadow with who I am, the Ego within can still cause trouble. I know no one who has an absolute solution to never let the Ego run the show.

Chapter Seventeen
Sober and Straighter

I will be ever grateful to Rabbi Yehuda Grundman of the Beverly Hills Kabbalah Center who gave me a copy of *The Power of Kabbalah*. When I read "get out of the blame game," I almost keeled over. As I attempt to be a guide to myself and to others about the skewered Worldview, blaming does not become an element of the search and rescue. It's not so much that most of us want to find something or someone who led us astray. Rather we are trying to find the route out of the self-created maze of absurdity.

In my analysis I uncovered the notions of excess, greed, bullying, shaming, lying, secrets, jealousy and blind allegiance to religions and politics as pitfalls in thinking and doing. I may or may not believe in the allegory of Original Sin as depicted in the King James Version of the Holy Bible, but I do know that the follies and foolishnesses from the beginning of time still plague us.

Part of the continuing theatre of the absurd is the computer that birthed social media. Anyone dead for a mere thirty years would be shocked at what they find on websites and blogs. Remember the woman who posted a frontal nude selfie of herself on Instagram? Has she no shame? No, like many news media sources, it was all about ratings. (Have you noticed that on reality television shows like *Housewives* it is de rigueur to show a lot of a woman's breast?)

Can you imagine the uproar from the male-dominated producers if women stood in tandem demanding penis exposure? Don't make me laugh. Women get big, bigger and biggest breast implants. Can you imagine cock implants to make an actor more appealing?

I have been an intuitive Jungian therapist for quite awhile. College anchored me with psychotherapist Carl Gustav Jung's concept of the Shadow. I knelt in reverence when he wrote about individuation.

At that moment the light switched on. The emergence of the real me, who I was born to be, would turn out to be a contretemps, a clash with how I was raised. I was asked to uncover who I am, separate from the beliefs and standards that identified me from birth onward.

Truth be told, I had always been, done and said what others told me to be, do and say. What was never in the Cliff Notes was that nobody knew which way to turn and the way of the Upper World was to let us meet our lessons (karma) and find the path to redemption or die trying.

For years I read everything Jung ever wrote about his work and what causes mental illness. Before I could become an authentic Jungian practitioner, I had to conquer alcoholism. I am now sober 37 years. In my soul I knew I was meant to work with dissociative lost souls looking for answers to their problems.

But first I had to heal myself by working steps and going to a lot of meetings. There needed to be atonement. The rigorous honesty about what I had done to hurt others as well as myself was the linchpin of healing from the disease of alcoholism. A couple of the best sponsors were tantamount to my getting well, as well as a ton of dry-drunk episodes.

I would drive the freeway to San Diego and back, not drinking, just scrambled-brain conjuring: "When will I get my career back, would I ever get out of debt or get my credit cards back or would I be stuck in this teeny-tiny apartment and have to live in meetings to stay sober?"

These were wrong questions born in my mind by my Ego. What better served me were inquiries like, "God, what would you have me to do to become authentic?" "Please remove the fear of financial neediness from me." "Always you are my source and not what others try to nudge me to do and be."

After those long and jittery drives to and from San Diego, I would fall into bed when I got back to my teeny-tiny digs on Bay Shore Drive. It was hard to fall asleep for the first year. I can still hear the words of Judge Sheila Pokras in the Long Beach courtroom: "Sir, if I ever see you in this court again you will regret it for the rest of your life." I could have sworn she mentioned Sing Sing.

When I met the trained astrologist, I mentioned my interest in Carl Jung and Jungian psychology. She said that Carl Jung would not see patients without first erecting their natal astrological chart. Byrd Knapp did my astrology and became my first teacher. Amazingly, I could do charts in a matter of weeks. That innate ability was a gift from a prior life. But until I got sober in 1980 I would not be able to detach from the results of my work with clients.

Once a savvy Brazilian psychic named Lena told me I had been an intuitive astrologer in a former life. "We bring with us not only karmic issues to atone for but we also are able to tap into talents and gifts from previous lives," she told me.

I had never heard much about psychics but she intrigued me. My background was conservative politics and hellfire and damnation religion. From childhood I knew that I was in a prison languishing in false messages and pretense. I knew deep within that I had to be paroled from this madness or I would not survive.

Jung's methodology was integration with what he referred to as "the divided self." His sermon was that within every man is the reflection of a woman, which he called his *anima*, and within every woman there is the reflection of a man, which he named her *animus*.

John A. Sanford, a former Episcopal priest and Jungian analyst, wrote a book to educate the great unwashed about these natures which he called: *The Invisible Partners: How the Male and Female in Each of Us Affects Our Relationships*. It is ignorance of the invisible partner that causes all problems in relationships, whether heterosexual or homosexual.

I draw from thousands of clients I have counseled throughout the years to tell you that most of us have a significant deficiency in our ability to make good relationship choices. The divided self, through ignorance of the Shadow, is a component of our dependency to drink alcoholically, become drug addicts, perpetrators or victims of physical and sexual abuse, gamblers, overspenders – the list goes on and on about what the incomplete self can use as cover-ups to resist facing and integrating the Shadow.

The Shadow is where we hide our dark side, which I often refer to as the assassin. In order to rid ourselves of unwanted qualities such as lying, cheating, shame and low self-esteem, we transfer them onto friends, enemies, partners and even onto our children.

But the most significant doctrine Jung preached is that you cannot have a relationship with somebody else until you have one with yourself. And you can't have one with yourself because you don't know who you are.

In the South where I was raised, men thought they were "all man." Girls believed that they were "Magnolia Blossoms," determined to marry and tame their husbands as Mama Magnolia had done with Daddy.

As we grew up, men married women, except for homosexuals who stayed in the proverbial closet (many gay men marry and have children but they also have affairs with other men). Women did the same thing. They, too, are able to split their natures.

Once I was invited by a woman client to a golf tournament in Dallas, Texas where there were hundreds of gay and straight women who were paired with their closeted lover.

In my work I introduce the client to his or her Shadow. If a client's given name is Paul, Paula might be an appropriate identity for his Shadow. If her name is Marcia, Marcus would be a good acknowledgement her Shadow. My primary purpose is to put the client together with the only relationship that will ever make them whole, and that is their Shadow, or as Sanford named that essence, their Invisible Partner

It has been my experience that sexual confusion can be laid at the feet of denying that the nature of the man is within a woman and that of the woman lives in the man. For my money, Carl Jung gave us an opportunity to heal that which we deny. Who in the name of righteousness ever taught us that we have a partner within ourselves that needed to be acknowledged and enlivened within us?

More importantly, I am honest enough to let you know that these brave souls taught me as much as they learned from me about being true to their soul urges. Not only are you going to read about how Jung was the guiding light for me and my clients, but also that I consider Shakespeare to have been the most helpful metaphysician with his admonition about who we are.

Throughout my life, music played a big part in my staying alive to one day do the things I am writing about and to find holy purpose in my life. Classical music, especially opera, will do more to lift the human spirit than all the hallowed words the Sage writes or speaks.

Every person who comes into our life, for a moment or a lifetime, we have known before. This Lower World is where we work off karma. Some are a balm and others are torturous. If you ignore the lesson, someone else will appear in your life until you learn it and are released from the karmic debt.

There are none blameless among us. We put celebrities and rich people on pedestals and feel they are above or better than the rest of us. Not true. We all come back into this world to amend bad-boy and bad-girl behavior. None of us escapes the onus that the past represents.

Once I went to my guru, Swami Swahananda, and told him that I would love to live in the monastery and let the rest of the world go by.

"Ramapriya, (the spiritual name he gave me at initiation in 1985), you are right where God wants you to be. As for me, love me and revere me if you must, but do not worship me. You told me when you did my astrology chart that 'all the world's a stage and all the men and women merely players.' And I told you if you will play the astrologer I would be your guru," Swami said.

Dead or alive, the people who were born to find you and to help you work through dilemmas will show up as if they had made an appointment. They did. But it was in a different time and another place. And by the way, we never die. We go back to the Upper World, which I am wont to call the Perfect Place. If anything else I've said in this book does not ring true for you, so be it. But you can bet the farm that we live life after life after life. And when we are in the resonance and frequency and vibration of the Upper World, all karma having been satisfied, we will be home to stay.

Chapter Eighteen

You're Not Who You Think You Are

No one is who we think we are. Everything and everybody seems to be wrapped in plain paper or hyperbole. Because I was once centuries older and in other places, my consciousness is going to drop back to when the only concern I have is how I should treat others. Do I walk in their shoes before I make an assumption? And am I still connected to the Will of the Upper World?

I work with so many people who are feeling lost, disoriented and want to end a relationship, many times a marriage. Most people know I am wont to say that relationships don't work unless the two are on the same page of detachment. Since we are living in the glorious days of turning our heart and soul back to God, my optimism insists that the good guys are going to win in this convoluted and fractious world.

But some people came to me wondering who I was. Why was I not better known?

"Why have I never heard of you?" Mrs. Gotrocks asked with pursed lips, her swan neck atilt.

"My granny used to say that fool's names and fool's faces are always seen in public places," I wanted to say, but instead I told her, "I am a member of an anonymous fellowship."

"Oh, really, one that I might know?" she motored on.

It seems that name and fame are more important than substance. However, what I am to clients should never be fighting for the klieg light.

I remember when I was a teenager I started to rewrite my life story while still living it. When I was in college, I worked in a kids' camp in Ouray, Colorado. As I got to know the staff, I shifted my backstory to one more glamorous and richer. The apartment I lived in with my mother and five siblings morphed into a mansion. I am wont to say that *Grimm's Fairy Tales* and *Mother Goose* prepared us to become anyone our imagination could conger. I made it up as I went along.

My alcoholism was driven by my vivid imagination. After a few drinks with strangers in a bar, my drunken state allowed me to tell lies as if they were truths. But it was everything about my life that skewered reality for me. For me it was religion that did not fit. The political climate shocked me. Inside I loved Blanche, a Negro lady who ironed for my family. She was closer to me than my own mother. As I got older and dabbled in past lives I realized I had been black. Because I was drawn to black people more than whites, I must have lived many lives as a Negro.

It is not my intent to sell reincarnation, rather to share what I have learned. I have lived on a golf course for more than 25 years but I've never played the game. I don't care a whit if Alabama ever wins another National Championship although I went there to graduate school. My father played baseball. Games we all play are only interesting to me if the object is exposure and getting out of whatever ties me to what's not true.

The First Amendment of the Bill of Rights guarantees freedom of the press, freedom of speech, freedom of religion, freedom of assembly and right to petition. But not everyone wants to live and let live. What irks me is that this country too often lets religion override what our founding fathers created: The right to worship or not.

A few years ago I did a television show in Birmingham on reincarnation. We all know Alabama, the Heart of Dixie, is in the iron-clad Bible belt. My publicist and I were shocked but pleased that someone cracked the door to this subject. Overall it was a positive experience which I enjoyed.

Later at lunch at Bottega Cafe, one of the best of four restaurants in town, I was at a large table with clients and friends shucking and jiving when a fashionably dressed but overweight woman charged our table like a bull running wild in Pamplona, Spain.

"I saw you on that ridiculous show on reincarnation today. You ought to be ashamed of yourself. You were raised a Christian and you have fallen from grace with that past lives garbage," she spit out her disgust.

All five of us were stunned to have someone come to our table with such rudeness. Say what you will about the South, but most folks there are kind and gracious.

Keeping my seat I turned to her and said, "I never stand for rudeness. Excuse me if I get back to my non-judging friends and red snapper."

She stormed out of the restaurant, her backside knocking over chairs as she flew.

No one said a word about her or her outburst. What I love about me and my friends is that we let others live as they choose and we do the same. Mrs. Pugh Van Samuels had no idea that my guru gave me a mantra that includes Jesus because he knew from hello that I'd had trouble bringing that part of my religious upbringing into my new-found Vedanta faith.

In 1985 I was attending the International Astrologists Convention in Chicago. The doyenne of American astrologers at that time was Katharine de Jersey. She was the most sought-after stargazer all over the world. Her clients were politicians and business moguls as well as Oprah Winfrey.

At the time, Miss Oprah was about to begin her own show under the banner of Harpo Productions, which as you know made her a zillionaire. During the five-day convention, producers of Oprah's show roamed the hotel where attendees were staying. Katharine de Jersey said that she had told them about me and I was invited to be on the show as part of a panel of four, three women and little ol' me.

Let me be as kind as I can about the hour of astrologers dying for their one minute of fame during the show. One woman would not shut up. She talked more about herself and her specialty as a psychic when the program was about astrology. Another woman on the stage sounded like she might be strung out on Zanax. Oprah corralled her like the runaway she turned out to be.

Katharine de Jersey was as cool as a room at 70 degrees. Her manner was understated as if she were talking to a client of hers. My turn was low key as I tried to address someone watching at home.

Miss Oprah moved the most of the hour toward more audience participation. The last half hour sounded like a hootenanny.

Humor is my middle name. There is something to be said for getting older. When you are nearer to the exit door it behooves one to leave nothing unsaid. My Higher Self reminds me to use a laugh to dry tears. To be self-effacing rather than a know-it-all. More people are drawn to sharing experience, strength and hope than crowing and bloviating.

Chapter Nineteen

You Have Been Here Before

"To sleep perchance to dream – ay, there's the rub. For in that sleep of death what dreams may come." Therein lies the rub – or to quote exactly – "there's the rub" means that's where the problem or obstacle is. Hamlet is reflecting on the possibility of suicide as a means to an easy end.

Letting you take a peek behind the curtain to see the bad in me and the good was tantamount to my moving forward with my sober life. I was warned by big pieces of stuff not to reveal anything about me or my journey.

"Never tell anyone you are a recovering alcoholic," one of the most famous and infamous gurus told me. "Tell them what you want them to buy and leave it at that."

And therein lies the rub. We are living in a much fractured culture that begs for rigorous honesty. "Where do I find a job?" "When will I be able to follow a route out of the mess I have made of my life?"

Books have been written by authors who were never able to live by their message. From religious credos to political policies, millions of lost souls are asking for the truth out of the malaise of their lives.

Every morning I work crossword puzzles, just as my mother did. There is a scrambled five-clue box to answer what the pictured drawing suggests. When I am stuck for an answer I silently ask the angels in the Upper World, "Help me." Inevitably I always hear the answer.

What you will read up ahead are the systems and routes to freedom from the bondage of self and others. You will read why I think that marriages as a whole do not work. The latest statistic says that 50 percent of marriages will end in divorce. If my kid came home with a 50 on tests consistently, I would have him change schools.

I've come a long way since the echoed warnings from family, "Never say a word about what goes on behind these four walls." Nothing gave me better perspective than looking back to see how I got to where I am now. Getting sober gave me a life and sustained me through times and trials sober that used to drive me to drink.

But getting sober was not enough for me. I had to retrieve a lot of what sustained me even when I was not ready to stop guzzling the bad stuff.

I did not know astrology existed until I was 26. Baptists don't want to know anything about fate and destiny according to when and where they were born. It was all about Jesus is the way. Period.

There is no mention of Jung's use of astrology with his patients in academic circles. Not one of my teachers or any of his books mentioned astrology. Byrd Knapp from Alabama introduced me to astrology when we met in New York in the mid 60s. She knew Jung and she was a Master Astrologist.

The most life-changing breakthrough I learned after shucking religion for what's true was the notion of reincarnation. Dr.

Gina Cerminara was a pioneer of New Age thought when I met her in 1982. *Many Mansions* was an eye-opener but the value of spending hours with her was the basis of how I put everything together that gave me the life and clients I work with today.

I met Dr. Edith Fiore in 1996 when I called her to schedule an appointment. I had just read her dazzling book *You Have Been Here Before*. Fiore had stumbled onto the notion of past lives when a client took her there through hypnosis. Dr. Edith had always been a traditional psychologist who was taught that a patient would only be counseled about problems she or he was having in this one and only life.

PART THREE

Chapter Twenty

The Protocol of the Sedona Intensive – Take Back Your Power

I believe that each of us has the capacity to follow where God leads. My Ego wanted me to stay connected to its will and way. In the split in the Upper World, God kept dominion over the true energy that permits us to be as he imagined us. When Satan and his followers left the Upper World, God created the Lower World, Earth, so we would not be homeless. Therefore, ruler ship of Earth was given to Satan. God also implanted a remembrance chip that served as a homing device to help us get back home.

In order to make a break from the lure of my Ego, acolyte of the Supra Ego, I had to hit bottom. My twenty-year journey that caused me to tear my world apart through alcoholism led me to turn back to God in order to be who I am today.

Getting sober was not as hard for me as it was for others. Most alcoholics and addicts are never successful at sobriety. The prerequisite for staying sober is reaching a bottom from which there is no return except uncovering what defects of character drove us to drink or drug addictively.

I was in my third year of sobriety when I heard a voice. It was not the voice I hear when someone in the Outer World is speaking to me. My hearing the voice was filtered through my intuition. A lot of shrinks work with people who hear voices that tell them to do harm to themselves, to family members or to strangers. This is not the voice I hear frequently. The famous "voice hearer" was Joan of Arc, who tried to free France. Hollywood did a good job of cementing in our mind what hearing a voice looks like.

I was driving into Sedona – I live in the Village of Oak Creek – in the early 80s when an intuitive thought said, "Bring those who are having difficulties in their lives to Sedona. Help them heal."

In the next few weeks I put together a program that would fit each one who came, no matter what drove them to get into deep trouble and need guidance. Although it is 12-step based, many of our clients do not have an alcohol or drug problem.

As a bit of trivia, hundreds of groups, no matter what the compulsion or addiction, have obtained legal permission from the General Service Office of Alcoholics Anonymous in New York to use the 12-step model for whatever problems they are attempting to solve.

I was also given guidance from the Upper World not to take insurance as a form of payment. Treatment centers have been using patient insurance as a means for patients to go through their program. Insurance not only does not give a person skin in the game, as Mark Cuban would say on the hit television show *Shark Tank,* but the success rate for traditional treatment is very low. I believe that the insurance formula is the reason for their lack of success.

In my sober meetings I began to find the sobriety way to recovery to be a paradox. Ancient Greeks were well aware that a paradox can take us outside our usual way of thinking. The 12-step paradox that got me hook, line and sinker was, "Surrender to win."

And make no mistake that I was being led intuitively by the consciousness of the Upper World even when I was hopelessly mired in alcoholic madness. Our mission on Earth is to forsake all we learned that does not resonate with our highest good.

For me, politics and religion were the two fake parts of my upbringing that I had to renounce. Advertising is a dangerous form of hypnosis. I cannot tell you the number of times I have fallen for some scheme screaming in high decibels on television only to realize after they had processed my credit card I had been taken.

I decided to accept who I am, the age that I am and to accept what does not ring true for me any longer – another aphorism of Kabbalah that removed me from the bondage of self and others.

Soon you will read the protocol of the Sedona Intensive, which plumbs the depths of one's secret hiding places where lies and deceits hunker down. Through exposing these hidden mental illnesses, the former drunk or drug addict, womanizer, manizer, overshopper, gym rat ad nauseam or plastic surgery compulsive by admission and correction can begin to live a life worth living.

I came to recovery through the court system. Many doctors encourage their patients to go to 12-step recovery. Husbands threaten divorce, same for wives whose husbands are floorflushers. However or wherever, they just come to recovery to be free of what drove them to these killer places.

The voice of intuition told me to start finding pockets of people who would help me find clients. When I was on the *Oprah Winfrey Show,* a woman from my hometown – Birmingham, Alabama – told some prospects about me and they booked appointments when I went there. On the first trip, Cathy Friedman became my booking agent. When I was in Egypt in 1983, a man named Thurman told his sister about me and she brought me to Texas. A few months later he took me to Singapore for three weeks to do chart for his meetings to do business with oilmen. That same voice taught me how I was to process these people who came to me for help. By the way, Skype changed the outreach of the Sedona Intensive as did an incredibly inviting website and a complimentary monthly newsletter.

Chapter Twenty-One
Day One – The Backstory

Day One Homework must be done before the client arrives in Sedona. There is a three o'clock orientation meeting on Sunday afternoon. My assistant takes the client around to show where the various therapy offices are.

I am wont to say that "the whole is a sum of its parts." The people the client sees in the five days include a Human Design professional, a meditation yoga instructor, an art journalist, a facilitator of emotional release therapy, massage and reflexology professionals and other modalities are in the line-up of programs for the client. All work is done one-on-one and the therapies are tailored to the need of the patient.

The initial homework exposes the interaction a client has had with his family of origin. The questions are designed to quash deception and untruths about who did what to whom. All of us have problems with how we were raised, but there is a tendency to resist exposing the underbelly where the problems are hidden. A lot of us like to keep the false face we show to the public. Because Shadow integration is not widely accepted or practiced, oftentimes one's mother has more of the characteristics of what society thinks the male role should be. The father is oftentimes more passive and more as we think the traditional mother is: kinder, softer and gentler.

More often the mother is an inactive participant in raising her children. The father can be overwrought with being a bully, too macho, and the children are confused about their own identity through mistaken messages from the parents of either type.

Tell Me about Your Family

The syllabus asks each client to paint a definitive portrait of their mother, father and siblings with words, placing the emphasis on the psychological make-up rather than physical description. They are asked to give birth dates so that I may get to know the astrological family tree.

A big door of discovery opens when they write their impressions of which of their parents was the more dominant. Which parent was more aggressive? They also detail which parent was more parenting, nurturing, cold, indifferent, etc. Which was more loving and caring? They are asked to indicate if the mother served the traditional father role, and vice versa.

We make huge progress when they describe the animus/anima split within them. They have been assigned the book *The Invisible Partners* to enlighten them about the masculine and feminine natures within each of us. This is the piece of recovery that represents denial at the deepest level, i.e., that no man is "all man" nor is any woman "all woman." There is the nature of the woman in the man and the nature of the man in the woman. It is when we integrate the nature of the other that we get honest with ourselves and begin to heal. The Shadow is the savior of each of us.

They write and we talk about addictions and compulsions in the family or with them: alcoholism, drugs, addiction to food, gambling, sex, overspending, etc. A discussion of intimacy or a lack of it in their family exposes a sense of distancing and non-communication within the family circle.

Intimacy is not sexualizing. It's when you can let someone know you. It's when you can let parents and siblings know how you feel violated by their actions or diminished or what you need from them. That is intimacy. The world misses the point of intimacy, thanks in large part to Hollywood. Were you aware of codependency or any enmeshment? Please write a similar narration as with family above for grandparents, if relevant, and aunts, uncles, cousins, etc.

Please rate your childhood on a 1-10 scale, and explain why you rate it thusly. Were you a leader or a follower, aggressive, passive/aggressive or merely passive as a youngster? Were you competitive with siblings? Which did you like/dislike? Flesh out your childhood.

The purpose of family dynamics is to let me know where your difficulties began and why. Everyone is sick somewhere. We are sick getting well, not bad getting good.

All families carry secrets and shame that set up roadblocks to a happy, joyous and free life as an adult. Be rigorously honest and open about the family. None of us is a saint, not even mama or daddy. There is a bit of bad in the best of us and some good in all of us.

Write to me about the three most deadly traits that you have.

For instance, are you narcissistic — selfish to the point that you feel you need to be the center of your universe as well as the center of everyone else's? Do you sense that you are filled with a thousand forms of insecurity?

All alcoholics are ruled by their Ego. Do you understand that 12-step sensibility compels us to deflate our Ego at depth? Talk about your Ego and how it has tried to ruin your life.

Husband/Wife, Ex-Spouse or Lover

If you are divorced, tell me how you met, married — what attracted you in the first place? — and explain the circumstances leading up to your separation and subsequent divorce. Have you had any extra-marital affairs and if so, with whom?

List all lovers from childhood, separating sexual relationships from platonic ones. Are there unresolved financial issues?

If you are in a committed married relationship, talk about what works and what doesn't work and why. Write about how you perceive your relationship with your spouse.

Chronological History: Begin with your birth year and list all years to the present, giving all pertinent data: boyfriends or girlfriends, schooling, parent's divorce, any deaths, employment history. Include any spiritual awakenings that have affected your life. Share whether or not you have had any major mental problems, including any hospitalizations or regular therapy.

Example of procedure: 1938: Born in Monticello, Florida. We moved to Alabama, but I remained in hospital with clubfeet. 1939: Grandfather died and parents separated briefly. I was still in Duke Hospital, etc. It will help if you list the dates in the margin of the legal pad and use as many lines as essential to completing the dossier of your life. This is an important element of The Sedona Clearing. Be complete and diligent.

God

Discuss your relationship with God. Did you go to church as a child? Do you distinguish between religion and spirituality? Do you have an active prayer and meditation life? Are you in therapy? Discuss. Do you attend a 12-step meeting? Discuss. Many people purport to have a God in their lives, but He is abstract and non-essential in day-to-day living. Write me about your God as if I knew nothing about a God.

Sexual Inventory

What was your first recollection of sex, and how old were you? Did you ever walk in on your parents engaged in sex? Did they talk about sex with you as you were growing up? Was there any sex education in school? Did you play doctor and nurse as a child? Talk about your first sexual experience. Who and when? How did you feel? Discuss what you believe is the difference between intimacy and sexual intercourse.

Are you homosexual or heterosexual? Did you ever have a homosexual experience? If homosexual, did you ever have a heterosexual relationship with intercourse? Are you homophobic? If so, discuss. Discuss any same-sex feelings that you had as a child. Include in this section any inappropriate fondling or overt sexual abuse by a parent, an adult or older child when you were growing up.

Discuss your current relationship: Is there any codependency or enmeshment? Is there any alcoholism or physical abuse? On a 1-10 scale, how would you rate it?

When the program is over, many clients in their written review talk about how tough they feel the Sedona Intensive is. Many complain that the questions are invasive and made them uncomfortable.

A woman named Kristine wrote, "In hindsight I felt as if I had a heat wave blast that knocked me off my feet in preparation for the week in Sedona. Having been through three treatment centers unsuccessfully in seven years, none of them ever asked me to expose the conditions in which I was raised. Not one asked if my parents had influenced my alcoholism by the way they treated me. Not one therapist delved into my sexuality. Not one asked me my sexual preference.

"To tell the truth I am still sober a year later. I still go to 12-step meetings. The two months of After Care SI gave me did the trick. I did hear Albert when he said, 'It's not what you're eating, it's what eating you.' When I would try to argue with him about something he said he would reply, 'I am smarter than you on my dumbest day,' which he credited to Judge Judy on her television show."

Speaking of dumb and dumber, I love to tell the story anonymously about the burly man who was supposedly a preacher in Louisiana whose "lady friend" paid for him to go through the Intensive. The preacher I'll call Bubba. Lusty was his wife and Mildred his lover.

Bubba and Lusty were living in a mansion in New Orleans with Mildred and her husband Raymond. Bubba was having a torrid love affair with Mildred. The rich husband traveled all the time. And with Lusty's permission, Bubba had a sexual relationship with Mildred. Some people will go to any lengths for a free ride anywhere, anytime.

Mildred came to see me when I was in Louisiana working. She was slim, smartly dressed but average looking. The moment she sat down, she spilled the beans about her and Bubba.

"What do you think of that?" she asked.

I wanted to tell her that she was the dimmest bulb in the bunch but instead I asked, "What does your husband think?"

"He doesn't know a thing," she replied.

Cheaters always think they are covering their tracks.

"Believe you me, he knows. He may be waiting to drop full disclosure on the table with divorce papers," I told her.

We talked for a couple of hours. As she got ready to leave, she asked me something that my intuition could not have conjured.

"Could I send Bubba to you to go through the Sedona Intensive?" she wanted to know.

Before I could run it by my Higher Self, I told her I would be happy to work with him.

This was ages ago before I started doing Evaluation Sessions on Skype to determine if SI was a good fit for the client and if I thought we could help the seeker.

Bubba came looking like he had been doing hard labor on a chain gang. He had a scruffy beard before Hollywood determined to be a man you must sprout whiskers. The Bayou boy reeked of bathing only on Saturdays and that deodorant was for sissies. Thank God he came in June and I had a garden to sit in for counseling. Granny used to say, "That boy smells like he needs a good hosing."

Bubba did a half-assed job of his written homework. He complained about the other therapists. When he was scheduled at nine o'clock with me, he would arrive more than thirty minutes late.

On the start of Day Three we were to discuss sexuality and integration of Bubba's Shadow.

"Where'd you come up with this shit? I ain't no queer. Every woman I ever had sex with said I was the best she ever had. My dick is so big it would choke a whore in heat," he spittled as he spoke.

I sat among the jonquils and the Gerbera daisies and magnolia bushes wondering what to say next. My darling Leonora Hornblow used to say, "Don't trouble trouble 'til trouble troubles you." Thank God for Darling Hornblow, because this one is triple trouble.

"Bubba, I have worked with sex addicts, sissy actors and butch actresses, millionaires and zillionaires, world-class athletes as well as the haves and have nots. And among that menagerie of lookie lous and distraught seekers, I have never had a Bubba who was beyond my help. As far as I am concerned, this Sedona Intensive is over, done with, dead on arrival, never to be resuscitated," I declared.

We both stood up. He may have been surprised but I had withdrawn my intuitive instincts as a way to get Bubba out of my house and my life.

"I'd like a check for the entire five days since it didn't work," he said.

"Let me call the bank to see if Mildred's check has cleared my bank," I responded.

"Don't bother," he heehawed, "I stopped payment the minute I gave it to you."

"Bubba, that would be criminal had I written you my check and the one you gave me was no good," I replied.

"I gotta make a living somehow," he laughed as he departed, throwing the textbooks and meditation tapes and journal in my trash bin.

I never heard a peep from Mildred or him after that. Someone told me he had been arrested for assault and battery when Mildred and Raymond tried to throw Bubba and Lusty out of their house.

"Gosh, Bubba," I thought to myself, "Those boys in the big house are probably loving to get to know you."

Chapter Twenty-Two
Day Two – The Harm Game

The oldest trick in the world while facing one's past is to transfer one's own bad-girl or bad-boy's behavior onto somebody else. The heavy duty work of the Ego is to lie and deny. Shame is coated with deception and half-truths. It's similar to someone who has committed a murder and then stonewalls with every alibi in the world of vivid imagination.

The drag that one initially tries to bring into sessions to confront the past is like the French reputation for perfuming without bathing.

My technique is always to get the client in session to confess to their malfeasance before they attempt to "out" someone else. Getting those with whom I work to come out from the lying nature of their Ego is the foundation of how they heal. It is no wonder in the world of blame that my clients would try to dump their stuff onto all those people they ever interacted with in their life.

It is not so rare that a man comes and wants to blame his wife for why his life is screwed up. The same goes for a wife throwing her junk onto him.

"Sorry, my friend, but your wife is not here to give her side of the penalty phase. Talk about yourself. If you clear up your past she might want to try to see if this would work for her," I counsel.

Who Have You Harmed and How?

A fearless and moral inventory is the path to clearing up the wreckage of the past. I caution the client to be honest in their appraisal of the harm they've done to others. Forms of harm are: mental, emotional, financial and sexual abuse, character assassination (gossip), dishonesty in relationships (extramarital or being unfaithful to a lover), being unkind with deeds and words in the workplace and with our parents, siblings, spouses, children, friends and enemies. This exercise in cleaning up the past tells me a lot about what triggers my clients emotionally and psychologically.

First, they make a list of those they have harmed. They write a narrative about harms and hurts. I caution them to put themselves in first place on the list. I ask that they write long enough in descriptive narrative to let me know how serious was the harm and to share any mitigating circumstances.

I find that most people who come here want to be honest with themselves about how they have damaged others, from siblings, friends growing up and mainly boyfriends and girlfriends – and especially ex-spouses.

I worked with woman married to a doctor, second marriages for both, who thought her mother was perfect. She rhapsodized about mommy dearest. The butter was dripping from her lips. What she failed to mention was that her mother also never taught her children about restraint of tongue or pen or what her perfect kiddies put in their mouths. They were all overweight.

I cajoled. I drew diagrams. I huffed and puffed. Finally she came into session the next day, crying.

"What's wrong, Brenda?" I asked.

"I went to Dr. Feel-Good and he said I had barricaded myself with pictures of perfection of mama and my brother and daddy. He said that I needed to tear down the false facade that I had built to be able to deal with myself as wellness required," she confessed.

From that moment on she was honest with herself about food being a cover-up for what she was afraid to face. I was so amazed by her that to this day she is one of my favorite clients. I make a point of keeping in touch with her and her husband, who also is a graduate of the Sedona Intensive.

Harm one does to oneself is the most severe harm in the whole program. The culture in which we live today has so many cover-ups and distractions that I am amazed that many still want to change the thing they can – themselves.

Who Has Harmed You and How?

I ask each seeker to make a list of those who have harmed them and to write a narrative about the ways they've been harmed.

I impress upon the need for specificity. Take the outline of ideas from the examples given and explain wrongs done to you. Examples: 1. My brother was physically violent to me throughout my childhood. (Descriptive) 2. My husband ran away with his best friend and left me in debt and brokenhearted. (Write in depth) 3. My boss fired me without cause. (Elucidate) These slights and harms are the basis for the lingering and toxic resentments that keep addictions active and destructive.

What You Like About Yourself

Each of us has qualities that are positive and admirable. Some people have a tendency to overvalue themselves while others who have low self-esteem find being positive about themselves very hard.

List things that build your self-esteem and describe why you believe these attributes are positive. Be descriptive – write in narrative form. Don't merely list attributes.

I point out that this is not either or but both qualities that define them. Also, they are not to write, "I love my hair." "I fall in love with me every time I hear myself speak." We cover narcissism in depth. These exercises are to allow the client to get feedback on how they assess themselves. It's not a vanity exercise and certainly not an opportunity to bash them.

What You Dislike About Yourself

I ask each to be specific about what erodes their self-worth and self-esteem. They need to get to the bottom of what bothers them about themselves. I suggest they write in narrative form.

Chapter Twenty-Three
Day Three – Hidden Deal Breakers

———

Day Three of the Sedona Intensive can be touchy for clients. Treatment centers as a rule never delve into the dangerous waters we do here in Sedona. Some tell us that when it comes to Day Three, we take no prisoners. "Where did you think you were coming, to one of Tony Robbin's Walk on Fire, Cool on Water seminars?" Now there's a big piece of stuff I would like to baptize with fire in the SI.

I am in shock and awe from all the hocus pocus that the great unwashed consider consciousness raising. Better you ask the high holy ones to let you peek behind their curtain to see what they have to do and still do that is not in alignment from the Upper World. The reason the world is teeter-tottering right now is that so many people won't go inward to clean up their false selves. Rather, they are looking for messiahs in politics, religion and the glitz and glamour world of show business to identify them – to make them feel better about themselves. Getting clean and clear takes everything you've got to persevere to reach who you authentically are.

I will never forget Marilee, the hillbilly debutante from Kentucky with holes in her stockings and a scarlet letter in her hair. She had the potty mouth of a "sleeping under the bridge, begging for food" street urchin. Every time she opened her mouth I wanted to see her birth certificate. I needed more proof that she was the daughter of parents who had been so successful in their careers and given so much of themselves to the needy. What's that expression, "The rotten fruit doesn't necessarily belong to the tree it fell from?" By deep diving into her past, she was willing to use God's Clorox to scrub her soul's basement floor.

To her credit, Day Three homework was mind-boggling. Suffice it to say that Marilee was a floozy and a slut, a user and abuser of people, and was amazingly able to throw them away after she had her way with each of them.

In the start-up days of our program, we interviewed parents and partners of seekers for our methodology of getting you well and giving you a how-to follow-up protocol that kept you clear of what drove you here.

Secrets

Everyone who climbs the hill from the airport in Phoenix to Neverland, aka Sedona, must let go of all secrets. Most of them thought they would die before revealing a scintilla of the sexual escapades they've had.

For men, it usually involves an isolated incident, or incidents, of homosexuality. As I said to one former pro-football player, "The more butch one is, the greater the need to climb into the snake pit to see if the rattler's pee-pee was worth the descent into Gooterville." After this secret is laid bare, the client does not ever ask, "What is Gooterville?"

He doesn't realize until I tell him that the sacred fifth step says, "Admitted to God, to yourself and to another human being the exact nature of your wrongs." I let him know he does not have to post this queer event on Facebook, nor does he need to go into a stadium with a million drum beaters (most of all who have done the same thing but will never admit it, no matter how many drums they beat) and throw themselves at the feet of homophobes.

For women it more often involves white lies or whoppers. You are as sick as your secrets. There is a difference between secrecy and privacy.

Example: Who you are dating or sleeping with is privacy. If he/she happens to be married, that's a secret. Also, the seeker is asked to discuss fantasies or tendencies to exaggerate.

As an aside, I sometimes share that I see dead people in my room at night. Once I was abducted and taken to a spaceship. My backstory is amazing but the important connection to make is that one must empty out all the nonsense and insidious traps of one's Ego to be able to live authentically.

Dishonesty Issues

Most of us rationalize and justify bad behavior and inappropriate actions. An example of dishonesty is someone taking credit for something he didn't do. Stealing or embezzling is obvious dishonesty, but the bigger killers are staying in a relationship that doesn't want you and you know it, or putting up with a marriage that died years ago, or pretending to be sober and straight and yet using alcohol and drugs recreationally and abusively. All of these are examples of fooling oneself and being dishonest. Bottom line? Being dishonest with yourself is as detrimental as being untrue with someone else.

Gossip

This is character assassination and is one of the biggest sins of all defects of character. Give examples of who you have talked about destructively and how. What were the results? Are you prepared to make amends for this behavior?

Indolence vs. Workaholism

One of the most unheralded diseases is someone who is afflicted with the inability to do what he is paid to do when he is paid to do it. Working a 16-hour day is not company loyalty. It is abuse of time – your own! Others of us never do an honest day's work for an honest day's pay. Be rigorously honest about this section of the inventory.

Meditate and Journal

Chapter Twenty-Four
Day Four – Anger and Rage Letters

All of us have people and situations that have been stirring and smoldering inside us for years. Homicide occurs more because of pent-up anger and rage than for any other reason. It is appropriate in The Sedona Five-Day Intensive to get in touch with all those issues from slights to catastrophic events in our lives.

Because this is a one-on-one program, we ask the client to feel free to be as rageful and angry as necessary. Because we never claimed to be goody two-shoes and pursed-lips perfect, I personally suggest that they be profane and as mean and as mad as they need to be on paper.

Day Four is the even the time to swear and to let the dark side free them from trying to put a happy face on hatred and loathing. This is one of the most important assignments of the entire Intensive week.

Anger and rage letters should be written to all the people that the client believes has harmed him. We urge the client not to leave anyone out, including himself or herself.

You have harmed yourself more than anyone else has.

Insights into How to Write Anger and Rage Letters

Within each of us is a mother lode of unresolved anger at those in our lives, from childhood onward – perceived enemies – who have caused us great grief and pain. We feel that they have harmed us, caused us to do things that we wouldn't have – brought out the worst in us. Oftentimes we have lashed out inappropriately, randomly and at will, at anyone in the path of our emotional breakdown – causing them to fear us and to recoil from us. But many times we have stuffed our feelings of outrage – leading to depression – or we have chosen partners who we believed could take away the pain. Just as damaging to our psyche and as toxic to our mental, emotional and spiritual development is suppression of our feelings and emotions – being unable to connect with someone on a deep intimate level, letting them know us up close and personal, or letting them nurture us. This results in a split in our personalities. We oftentimes disconnect with who we really are. It was as if someone separate from us was living inside of us.

It became obvious that as good as our parents tried to be, or teachers and friends, spouses and family members tried to be, they sowed the seeds of discontent that grew into oaks of anger and rage.

The truth is that we attract people and circumstances that teach us what we need to change in ourselves. We are not victims – we are volunteers to experience the good and bad in our lives. We get what we deserve in life. However, as a technique to face the past and diminish the effects of these silent and invisible ghosts of discomfort, we must rage at these sources of our spiritual madness. And always remember that there is a bit of good in the worst of us and a bit of bad in the best of us.

If you have insulated yourself by denying that you are angry or need to rage at someone, there is a greater need for this process. The silent and invisible worlds are armed and dangerous to our well being.

Let's begin the rage letter writing process by listing our perceived enemies or ones who caused us great anguish. This list is an exercise to break through walled off negative emotions so we can be happy, joyous and free.

Some people are ripping and tearing themselves and others apart in their life. Oftentimes it is painful to read what some of them wrote.

Anson came to work with us because others in his lineage had done so. He was early 30s and already married to his second wife. Having met her, I was convinced that she would rather be with another woman than a husband. It would be up to him to confess that notion if he had one. Some of us prefer to stay anywhere but in the sunshine of the spirit or the dark night of the soul.

"I am having problems with this anger and rage assignment," Anson said.

"How so? What's going on with you with this day of homework?" I asked him.

"I can't rage at my mother. She is a saint," he replied.

Oh, God, not another sainted mother. When a client takes an either/or stance and doesn't know where the middle is, I moan and groan and get very direct.

"No one among us is perfect. And more than that, only a handful of us mere mortals are ever declared a saint. And I certainly have my doubts with the pope on that one.

"I would like for you to sit in my garden and rewrite all your rage letters. Remember all of us are fallible or worse toward ourselves and others. In the format I gave you it says that "there is a bit of good in the worst of us and a bit of bad in the best of us." Consider that when you do your rewrites," I instructed.

Anson went outdoors and I fiddled while Rome burned. No, I didn't. Instead I reviewed the latest newsletter I was editing. I took a couple of phone calls. Two hours later Anson emerged from wherever this assignment had taken him.

I read aloud his anger and rage letters. They were measurably better, especially to his ex-wife and himself. Here is the letter he wrote the "saintly" mother. Shut your eyes and ears and close your agape mouth if you do choose to hear and read what he wrote about mama.

"Dear Bitch from Hell:

"You have been the worst mother a kid could ever have. You are manipulative and controlling. Just because we are `First Family' as Albert is wont to call us, we are as f*&#* up as any family could ever be. I remember you insisted on bathing me and my brother when we were at least eight or nine years old. You said it was because you wanted to teach us not to feel guilty about masturbation so you tried to get our penis erect by stimulation.

"My shrink never listened to me when I tried to tell him about you and your sexual abuse. Yes, mama dearest, you abused me and Hank, which was criminal behavior. The reason I could never talk about this to Dr. Weasel was he always breathed hard when we talk about anything sexual.

"*&^%$* you and the horse you rode in on. Stick a pogo up you and jump up and down until you drop dead with pleasure.

"I never want to see you again.

"Your former son, Anson"

His forgiveness letters were even better. These letters allowed him to confront his wife in my presence about her lesbianism. In a matter of months they were divorced. He found three small houses that she bought to house the clothes she bought from salesgirls who she was attracted to from Bendel's and Neiman Marcus and Saks Fifth Avenue.

Anson married a third wife several years ago. They are still married. Surprisingly she had more money than Anson did when they married. That may have something to do with a union that will last.

Chapter Twenty-Five
Day Five – Forgiveness Letters

___

When I did my own inventory of those who had harmed me and those I had abused, it was seeking forgiveness from everyone on my list that cleared away the wreckage of my past. To make amends means to make things better. You are going to write letters to the people you have harmed and at whom you have raged during the Sedona Intensive.

The rage list and forgiveness list is the same. Whenever you're disturbed about people, places and things, the problem is always with you. This exercise is to free you from the bondage of self and others once and for all.

In order to structure how the act of forgiveness accomplish its end, we give the clients a form letter for each of their forgiveness letters. They individuate each one by writing their comments to each person they need to ask for forgiveness.

Often clients will ask why they have to forgive people who have done them harm. Here is my answer. Everyone who comes into our life, family, or friend or enemy – the whole kit and caboodle – are mirroring our transgressions: hurt, harm and bad deeds from some time, some place in space.

"If a person is in your life it is the Upper World's way of letting you know that you have done the things to others that are now being done to you. You are asking for God's forgiveness through asking forgiveness of those you feel have harmed you. It is also a way of thanking them for showing you the life lesson that started in some other life." I explain.

The rite of passage – cleansing yourself of how the "imposter you" overlaid the precious child of God – comes to a crescendo, like in a symphony. It is the ceremony of forgiveness.

Hopi-Egyptian Letter Burning Ceremony of Forgiveness

I am in Sedona going through the Sedona Intensive, and as part of the program I have to write Forgiveness or Amends letters to those I've harmed or injured, including myself.

I cannot write "I'm sorry" or that "I apologize" in my letters. I've been using those empty words for a long time without seeing any change in my behavior. "I'm sorry" and "I apologize" are passive-aggressive ploys to get the heat off me.

To make amends means changing my behavior and my attitude so that I can repair relationships with myself and others. I also cannot write that I forgive you. This is my amends. This is my opportunity to clean up my side of the street. If you ever seek forgiveness from those you've harmed, it is your business, not mine. I must seek forgiveness from you because I've played a big part in the bad blood between us.

When I open my heart and sincerely ask God to forgive me, He will and my life will change forever. Forgiveness _is_ the path to clearing.

Without a shred of doubt this is the part of the five days that transforms clients.

Jason was a very tall and handsome man from Chicago. He was an investment banker. He had been married with a daughter and divorced. He married a man when he was 41. When I got him he was 50.

Although likeable and determined to be kinder, softer, gentler and more honest about his life, forgiving his mother was a deal breaker.

"My grandmother raised me because my mother was busy marrying rich, richer and finally richest. My mother had no time for me until I came out gay and subsequently married my partner, James.

"'You are despicable. Get out of my sight. I never want to see you again as long as I live,' my mother screamed at me the last time we met.

"When my grandmother died, the security barred me from my grandmother's house for the viewing. I was also prohibited from the funeral service," Jason shared.

"'No goddamned fag son of mine is ever going to come into my house again. When I die he will be legally barred from coming to my funeral,'" Jason quoted the words she spoke to her attorney.

Two years ago his mother died and left him one dollar and the balance of the estate to her daughter and stepdaughter.

"What do you think is the purpose of these forgiveness letters?" I asked.

"To realize that I am forgiving the part of me that each of these people represents," he answered.

"Jason, that is such a genius response I could cry with delight. Go into the woods and let God lead you out of darkness into the light," I said.

He left and I read while sitting close to the gardenias.

He returned in about three hours. Jason was crying while resting his head atop my gate post.

"Albert, I love my mother," he sobbed.

While Jason and I were talking, the tears turned to laughter. He said that after he finished the letters, his mother "spoke" to him. They spent an hour talking aloud. She made amends to him. In his sensibility, she said that when she got back to "Upstairs" she was reprimanded for her behavior toward a lot of people.

"I love you Jason. Please forgive me because I want you to know that things change in a big way after death," she advised him.

Clients go out into the sacred lands around Sedona and read their forgiveness letters, shred them and bury them and make the graves with a twig and three small pebbles at the base of the stick.

They meditate before and after reading their letters. Beneath the shredded forgiveness letters they burn and bury all the homework they have written throughout the week.

Symbolically, the clients are letting go of their past and all its painful interrelationships. This frees them from the people, places and things that kept them stuck in resentments and blaming.

If you do not unravel the mystery of resentments and blame, you will carry these stigmas to your grave. And whatever you did not face will await you when you return to the Lower World.

PART FOUR

Chapter Twenty-Six
Switching Over

A lot of my newbies come from clients who send someone in need of our services. The man you are about to meet was such a piece of work that I nearly turned him down. But that still, small voice I hear told me to open the door of receptivity to his deep dark dilemmas and lacquers of shame.

Roger swaggered into my office in a bombardier jacket and designer jeans. There were blond high-lights in his shaggy hair and he was grinning like a Cheshire cat. We greeted one another and after he sat down in a chair opposite me, he asked, "Where do we start?"

It is Roger's nature, having been born under the birth sign of Aries, to cut to the chase about everything he does.

"I always say that the whole kit and caboodle begins and ends with honesty. The first step of this process is humility. Be honest. Stick to the facts. Don't embellish. Our work together will take the wind out of your sails. You will be looking at things that have been eating away at you. We'll find your hiding places – your secret hideouts where you keep things that make you look bad," I said.

I have always seen my brand of therapy as being like a train leaving the station. We begin in fits and starts. We chug along slowly but soon pick up steam. It never really matters where we start, but it's the bee's knees how we end up.

"Humility is not my long and strong suit. I can be arrogant. Perhaps I am prideful. What area of my life do you want us to talk about first?" Roger asked.

"Start by telling me your three biggest problems. Do we have a deal, Roger?"

"Deal," he replied. Then the verbal volleys started.

Albert: "What is your No. 1 problem?"

Roger: "Booze. I drink too much."

He had talked about his problem with alcohol in our phone interview.

Albert: "What kind of trouble does boozing get you into?"

Roger: "When I drink too much I forget appointments, I stay out late and don't remember where I've been or what I have been doing. I waste time when I have a hangover."

Albert: "What's the No. 2 problem?"

Roger: "Weed. I think I am superman when I am high."

Albert: "No. 3?"

Roger: "I wish I were single again."

Albert: "Have you ever been arrested for possession of weed or drunk driving?"

Roger: "When I was sixteen I got busted in a raid at a beach party for being drunk and disorderly and possession of marijuana."

Albert: "Any problems with drinking and driving as an adult?"

Roger: "Twice in the last five years, but my mom is a lawyer so I beat the charges," he said.

Albert: "You didn't beat anything, Roger. Drugs and drink are beating you."

I was purposely turning it up a notch because Roger was a bit too smug for an addict and alcoholic.

"You could kill yourself or somebody else under the influence. It is confession time. Roger, you're a 24-karat gold drunk with a drug habit. You need to stop both. There is no middle ground with either one of these diseases. This is not `Rational Recovery,' where you are taught to drink like a gentleman.

"You are an Aries, an all or nothing kind of guy. We have to look at the underbelly of these bad-boy habits to see what drives them. And I haven't forgotten about your wanting to be single. That may be where the real villain lives."

"I can tell you something else about me: I won't put up with a lot of bullshit," Roger declared.

"The only bullshit you'll hear in this room will be yours. I want to make sure you understand I'm sitting on this side of the table and you're in the 'I need help' seat. There are no calendars or clocks for sobering up or getting off drugs and I can't wave a magic wand and make you a bachelor again," I said.

"Wow, no holds barred! Albert, are you sure you can't find a way for me to have one drink and one hit instead of stopping cold turkey?" He saw the look of "I don't believe this guy" written all over my face when he added, "Just joking," and he started to laugh.

"There are no jokes, Roger. Alcoholism and drug addictions are a loser's game."

After a bit more chit-chat and small talk, I shut the door and started peeling back the layers, looking for Roger's secret hiding places – why he was afflicted with these diseases.

As I suspected Roger, was all revved up for anything but what I had to say to him. The Cheshire grin was a cover-up for part narcissism and more scared little boy. Clinically narcissism is a mask for low self-esteem. He copped a plea to being full of creative real estate ideas – most ahead of their time – and throwing the "go" switch early in the morning until he parked in his garage late at night.

Because he had already admitted what his problems were, my job was to find out what drove them. Beneath all addictions there are the usual suspects, a family of alcoholics and/or drug addicts, parents who didn't know how to love their children, or self-imposed isolation or different forms of abuse. The two most lethal overlays are politics and religion.

When I find the cancerous nature of Roger's upbringing, I'll know where to tear down and rebuild. Love and trust, or lack of them, are big factors in what kind of adults we become. I only had a few days to find the vulnerability he needed to admit to, and then, for him to be open to change.

Soon you will discover that his can of worms was very different indeed. Although he was married, he never mentioned his wife. He said he felt marriage was a problem for him. There was no conversation about his parents. Never once did he bring up a close friend. Roger seemed to live in a world of one and liked it that way.

Any time I would try to lead the conversation to other people in his life he would shrug his shoulders and change the subject. Everything we discussed was all about him. He was very defensive and resentful if I poked at his sore spots. I had to pry it out of him. When I brought up his wife and how he never talked about her, he blurted out, "She had a miscarriage two weeks ago and nearly died."

"Losing a baby is serious business, Roger. Why do you think you never mentioned it?" I asked.

"Because the minute the doctor told me we had lost the baby I thought to myself, 'Why couldn't that have happened to me? Why couldn't my mother have miscarried and then I would have been spared the insanity and the crap that I have been going through since I was born?" he answered.

I have learned through years of experience when to sit without comment. I had the sense that Roger was drowning in emotional overload from his childhood. He closed his eyes and breathed heavily. I softened how I said my next words.

"You are still here because you are meant to be here. You are still here because you are worth what it takes to face and reeducate the demons that have been chasing you. We are doing this work so you can be free of your past to live happier in your present and future. I see a lot of good in you. Together we have a lot of harsh and painful history to get through.

"It's time to take a break. Let's reconvene at two o'clock this afternoon. Eat lunch and hike Well Rock. The exercise will do you a lot of good."

Roger left. I meditated in my office. No phones and no mind chatter – just silence and emptying out all thoughts.

When we got back into session, Roger talked a couple of hours about how bad he felt about dismissing the pain and suffering his wife had endured with the miscarriage. He asked if he could call her to make amends for having shut down emotionally during the loss of their baby. I allowed it in this instance. His amend was long overdue. Ordinarily clients are asked not to send emails or call anyone – no communication with the outside world.

His birth chart coupled with my gut reaction told me that Roger was a closet homosexual. The pain around his wife's miscarriage was primarily because he knew that he never wanted to be married to her at all.

My job was to break through the defense lines of his Ego. I ask questions in a proactive manner. Many of my clients tell me their psychologist and shrink never tell them anything – they wait for the client to tell them what their problems are. I once told a client that when I was drinking, none of my therapists got me to admit I was a drunk. The squad car that took me to the hoosegow did. The judge who court-ordered me to 12-step meetings was the real wake-up call.

I decided to end his Ramblin' Rose speeches with some direct inquisition.

"Roger, did you ever fool around sexually with boys when you were in mid-school or high school?" I asked.

The grin was gone. He had come into the session this particular day dressed in shorts and a torn tank top. He definitely was not in the mood to impress. He had his head bent low in his hands.

"Albert, believe it or not, I never had a sexual experience in grammar school or high school or even in college with a guy. You asked in my life history whether I had ever played doctor and nurse as a kid, and the answer is no."

I often hear stories from clients that they played doctor and nurse or were curious about a playmate's genitals or engaged in touching another youngster. I refer to this as discovery and a normal part of growing up.

I knew he was not telling the truth. His birth chart clearly indicated he had started fooling around sexually with young boys when he was seven or eight years-old. The nature of an Aries is like someone living parallel lives, or as the old chestnut goes, "Don't let the left hand know what the right hand is doing." All my instincts told me that he was still having sex with men and I would have to confront him head-on.

"Roger, you're not telling me the truth. I think you started playing around with little boys when you were just a kid and you are messing around with men now. Your dirty little secret is gay sex and we need to talk about it."

Roger sat silently in his chair fiddling with his fingers. Reluctantly, he continued. "You're wrong, Albert. It started when I began to make a lot of money in real estate about five years ago. With so much more free time on my hands, there was this overwhelming urge to get it on with a man. I guess my daredevil drove me into uncharted waters, but ones which have had a strong pull on me always."

Roger was sweating and kept drinking water and wiggling in his chair. In barely a whisper he said, "Sexual contact with a man started with a body worker who used to massage me and my wife. I later found out he was getting it on with both of us."

I didn't say anything. I sat in silence.

Roger began to spill his guts about how he had never considered his behavior to be gay because he thought he was happily married, basically straight and never went to gay bars or surfed gay porn websites on the internet. When I asked him where he met these sex partners, he said, "At the beach or in the men's shower at my athletic club. I would just 'start up' with a man and then both of us would climax and that was it. No words and no affection and never, ever any kissing. And I still don't consider myself gay. I'm not a pansy or a fruitcake. I'm as butch as they come. It's just a novel new turn-on for me."

"How do you define gay?"

"He is either a sissy hairdresser or a swishy decorator. You know the type," Roger said.

"Roger, I hate to be the one to burst your misinformed bubble, but a man who has sex with another man is homosexual."

I could tell his volcano was about to spew.

"But I don't *want* to be one of those guys. I'm not one of them. Okay, so I'm not in love with my wife and to tell you the truth, I have never felt loved by another single soul, not by my parents or my brother or sister, no one, ever. See how screwed up I am? I am 29 years old and married to an intelligent and beautiful woman and yet I want a man. God, I hate myself."

Stoic and sunshiny Roger started to cry. In a few moments he was bawling. He reached for a tissue and then another, laughing through his tears that he would probably use up all of the Kleenex in the pop-up box.

"Roger, let it all out. This is tough and it's only going to get harder to talk about all the things that happened to you, particularly since you cannot accept being gay. But you are no longer alone with your secrets. When you remove these phantoms of fear you will find self-love and be a lot happier."

"Don't you think I might be bisexual and not homosexual?" he asked, like a drowning man looking around for a life raft.

"Your actions indicate you're gay. You've been having sex with males since you were a child. I feel you use marriage as a smoke screen to hide your secret affairs."

"Do you think I was born gay or became gay because of what I did?" Roger asked.

"Your choice of sex partners is not the real issue we are dealing with here. It's `I'm married and yet I have sex with men.' Marriage is your face for the world to see – but you have hidden liaisons with men. These secret trysts are killing you slowly every day and they are at the foundation of your addictions.

"By the way, Roger, this explains the unconscious reason you never wanted to have a baby. You knew you wouldn't be around to raise the child," I answered him.

Roger was letting not wanting to be gay drive him to despair. He needed to look at how affected he had been by the absence of love, covering his feelings with a veneer of "I'm doing great— I'm happy as a lark" and needing to be the center of attention with everyone he met. My job was to get him to accept his past, who he really was and to live authentically as his true self in present time.

There has been a lot of controversy as to what makes someone gay – genetics or environment. In an article in the June 2007 issue of *Discover Magazine*, "The Real Story on Gay Genes," Michael Abrams, adjunct professor at Seminole College of Florida said, "The environment a child grows up in has nothing to do with what makes most gay men gay. Two of the most convincing studies have proved conclusively that sexual orientation in men has a genetic cause."

Roger did not need any more prodding and probing for today. He needed to decompress.

"We're done for the day," I said. "Write in your journal. Go to the Spa and sit in the Jacuzzi. Meditate. Pray. Order room service. Make some notes on our session. Let me know what you heard that clicked with you. It took a lot of courage for you to come out."

We embraced and I walked him to his car.

"Thanks for today, Albert. I know I played the artful dodger when we started but I want to stop tap-dancing around this stuff."

"Roger, be open and honest and accept what we find. We're at the point in therapy where you have to take off the mask and tell me what you have been hiding."

When Roger came back the next morning he was more playful; he had a sense of relief about the session the day before.

"Albert, I got the best sleep I've had in years. I wrote in my journal. I discovered that I *have* been living in the closet. I have been fooling myself that what I was doing was natural and normal. From the time I was a little boy, I felt my mother was too busy to show me much attention and my Dad was very passive. She wore the pants in the house.

"But here is my confession. I have always been drawn to boys. I had sleep-overs with a number of boys as a kid where we touched each other and masturbated. I would fantasize that each one of them loved me. I was on the soccer team in high school and my favorite part of the game was the shower afterwards. I remember when I was in college that I had sex with a fraternity brother who said that it was the `hush-hush secret initiation' of the house."

"Remember yesterday. Roger, when you said, 'Believe it or not, Albert?' I thought you said that you had never had sex with another boy," I said.

"I lied. In AA they say if a drunk's lips are moving, he's lying. I've been lying about who I am all my life."

"Now I think we are going to get somewhere. Read me what you wrote last night in your journal."

He opened his notebook, took a long, deep breath and began to read.

"What is so amazing to me is that I had laughed at Joe and Hayley when they told me about you and your method of counseling. I told them I might drink a little too much and smoke a little weed, but I would never spill the beans, tell my deepest, darkest secrets to a stranger. Now here I am letting you know that I believe I have always been a closet gay. That I married Crystal because she was smart and beautiful and had a good-paying job, and if I am real honest, she was the perfect `beard' for my acting out with men. I cannot do this anymore and I want some guidance on how to accept being gay, how to tell Crystal, how to learn to love myself and someone else, especially how to have a man in my life that I can be true to and love with all my being."

"You may be asking yourself, 'Will I ever meet a man who is perfect for me?' And the answer is: Only God knows," I said.

What really shook my timbers was how relaxed Roger was talking about sex with boys and men. I learned a long time ago that what we resist oftentimes persists. And I came to know that once the floodgates of truth were opened, there was a tsunami of revelation. Roger told me over the next few hours how much he cared for each boy and why.

Next we examined his relationships with his family. His mother was a lawyer and the major breadwinner. His father was a research chemist who could relate to his lab specimens but was lousy at communicating with his children.

His mother worked long hours and when she talked at late night dinners, she lectured. Roger said she talked like she was pleading a case to a jury. His father always sat stone-faced and silent. He never tossed the baseball with his boys, never went to father-son scout retreats and never came to one of the kid's soccer or baseball games. It was as if he did not exist.

A live-in combination cook, housekeeper, nanny and nursemaid helped Roger and his siblings with homework. Maria drove them to school when they were young kids. She was the one who went to the PTA meetings or watched his and his brother's ball games and went to see his sister in school plays.

Clues for many of Roger's difficulties, i.e., feeling unloved and unwanted, lay at the feet of the attachment theory. The lack of connection with both parents exacerbated his sense of isolation and abandonment.

Psychologist John Bowlby was the first attachment theorist, describing attachment as a "lasting psychological connectedness between human beings." The central theme of attachment theory is that mothers who are available and responsive to their infant's needs establish a sense of security. The infant knows that the caregiver is dependable, which creates a secure base for the child to explore the world. Roger did not have this bond and its attendant sense of security. His mother had gone back to work when he was several months old and he was left in the care of a nanny who also cared for his brother and sister. Nannies are not mother love.

In her 1970s research, Canadian behavioral psychologist Mary Ainsworth expanded greatly upon Bowlby's original work. Her groundbreaking *Strange Situation* study observed children between the ages of 12 and 18 months as they responded to a situation in which they were briefly left alone and then reunited with their mothers. Comparison of disrupted mother-child bonds to a normal mother-child relationship showed that a child's lack of a mother figure leads to "adverse development effects."

We spent several days investigating how the lack of feeling loved and wanted by his mother had adversely affected him. One of his explanations rang true for me. He felt that a lot of his sexual acting out was trying to satisfy a primal need, to be touched, held, hugged and made to feel that someone cared about him. But he never blamed his lack of love from his mother or father for being gay. He said that no matter what one's sexual preference is, all of us deserve to be loved as children.

"But without someone to show me how to get in touch with all this stuff, it's as if I've been trying to get somewhere without the roadmap," he said.

And then out of frustration with not being able to contain his upset, Roger began to scream and then he'd sit quietly. He would scream again and then nothing. He had four or five outbursts and then stopped.

"I don't know why but I feel better, less suffocated."

In the 70s, primal therapy, a trauma-based psychotherapy created by psychologist Dr. Arthur Janov, argued that neurosis is caused by the repressed pain of childhood trauma. He wrote in his best-selling book *Primal Scream* that repressed emotional distress pain and its purported long-lasting psychological effects can be sequentially brought to conscious awareness and resolved through re-experiencing the incident and fully expressing the resulting pain during therapy.

Janov criticized the "talking therapies" as they deal primarily with the cerebral cortex, which plays a key role in memory, atten-tion, perceptual awareness, thought language, consciousness and higher reasoning areas, and do not access the source of pain within the more basic parts of the central nervous system.

I beg to differ with him as clients I have worked with are able to make great strides in facing and removing deep scar tissue from traumas from their childhood by talking about them and analyzing what we find.

"My upbringing from the outside looked like the average family but behind closed doors it was a topsy-turvy zoo," Roger explained. "I didn't know what to expect but I know I never felt loved by any of them. I would go over to my friends' houses where their parents really loved their kids. Their mothers would give us treats and would cook us dinner. Their fathers would take us to ballgames or to the YMCA. My mother was being a lawyer until late at night and my Dad never did anything with us."

It was time to play "Let's Pretend." I asked Roger if he had ever played that game as a child. He said that he had. He recounted what he had pretended as a young boy, which relaxed him for how the game was about to change in my therapy model.

"Roger, I want you to pretend – you don't have to believe anything, just pretend – that you have lived many lives. Yes, I want you to pretend that you believe in reincarnation – just pretend, mind you. And in those lives you have been all of the people who have harmed you in this life. You have been a mother who chose work over making a child feel loved like your mother did to you this time around. In some life or lives you were like your father is now –, cold and distant and you never played with your children. Widen the game to pretend that all of the people who have harmed you, you have wronged in the same way somewhere, sometime. Can you do that?" I asked.

"Yes, I can pretend anything that will let me get rid of all of this pain."

We went through all the major players in his life, youngsters and adults, whom he felt had done him harm. I think this technique worked because it took the focus off of the harm-causers that had been fulminating in his unconscious and drew the attention to Roger. He saw himself in his harm-causers. This allowed him to understand that they were in his life to mirror the lessons he had to learn.

"Roger, now pretend that you have to feel every single thing you have ever afflicted on anyone anywhere in any life. This is what I refer to as `let's pretend' meets supra-conscious rectification of all your transgressions."

We continued with "let's pretend" to conjure *why* he had been born into his family. We covered *why* he began to act out sexually with young boys, and *why* he had married his wife and *why* he continued to act out sexually with men. Most of all he came to understand that he had to drink and drug in order to live in his own skin until he healed. When these pile drivers were no longer in his life, he could stop his addictive behavior.

"If the law of attraction is the make-believe theorem of `let's pretend,' its corollary is we get what we deserve," I said.

"Roger, let's widen the 'let's pretend' borders. The sexual encounters as a young boy foreshadowed what you would have to rectify when you were grown. You married your wife because you would have to decide whether you were gay or straight. You began to have sex with men your own age because it was the issue of sexuality, i.e., your judgment of others for being gay in previous lives that made you have to accept that part of yourself you had previously condemned in others. It's the last piece of the puzzle you would have to solve.

"So Roger, having played the "let's pretend" game, what do you think you were looking for in sexual encounters?" I asked.

"I want someone to love me. But I always felt dirty when the touching and masturbation ended. I still feel repelled by me and my anonymous sex partners," he offered.

Roger was highly intelligent. He was charismatic and people were obviously drawn to him. But he came to accept that his "show dog" persona, trying to get love from people, was a sham. He thought that if he were a good athlete and later a successful realtor, he would be fulfilled. He wanted love and affection from his parents and siblings but he decided that none of them knew how to give love or how to receive it. The way he was able to come to terms with the hurt feelings of non-love from his family was to accept them as having done the best they could with who and what they were.

"If your parents were here right now, what would you say to them?"

"'Mom, did you ever really want me?' 'Dad, did you ever think I might have wanted some time with you?' I would ask them why were they hands-off as parents and why they threw all the responsibility for looking after us kids to Maria. And I would ask them if... if... they ever loved me." And with the last inquiry he broke down uncontrollably. He had found his last piece of the human condition puzzle: love. He needed to be loved and to learn to love others.

I put my arms around his shoulders and we walked out into the private garden at the back of the office and sat down by the fountain. He and I were quiet for several minutes.

"Roger, do you see the connection between how you were looking for love but you also needed to love your parents and friends in a way that made you feel whole? In time things will get better, a whole lot better. The more you hang out with people who don't drink and drug and stay out of slippery places like gym showers and stop trolling for men on beaches, you will heal. To be honest, there is an `X factor' in healing – the unspeakable and unknowable but reliance upon God to do for you what you can't do for yourself.

"Tonight you have to write rage letters to those who harmed you. The letters will get all this pent-up anger out of your system," I said.

"Before I go, let me tell you about my soccer coach. When I was in sixth grade I was picked to play soccer. My coach Brad was 23 years old and he seemed to like me a lot. Because I had no relationship with my Dad I told Brad things – what I wanted to be when I grew up, how I felt unhappy at home, how I wished he were my Dad, and he seemed to care about me. With my parents being detached and remote with all us kids, it was natural to care about Brad. Every time he tousled my hair or put his arms around my shoulders, I shivered inside. I loved him and I fantasized that he loved me back. And he was not married so I told myself I could live with Brad," Roger explained.

"Did you ever have sex with Brad?"

"Brad was straight and dated a great looking girl who came to all our games. This was in my make-believe world, Albert. I was letting my needy imagination run wild with me. I needed to know someone loved me"

I wanted to process this information because I needed to explore how Roger met and married Crystal. I know there are a lot of married homosexuals, but I was working with this man and I needed to know how he had the sexual background in the beginning and shifted into dating women and getting married.

"How did you start dating women when your early interest was with boys and Brad?"

"I know a lot about closet homosexuality. Most of my sex partners have been married. They are very straight-looking and very macho. I read somewhere that one of the most obvious attempts we closeted gays make to kill the urge is by dating women or getting married.

"You haven't asked, but I have had sex with a number of women successfully and I can guarantee you that Crystal has no complaints about me as a lover. I have been living a double life that never meets in the middle. She and I like the same things, Italian and French restaurants and books of fiction and we love to travel. By the way, I go to antique shops and buy small treasures for our house.

"This double life has a secret that we are bringing out into the open. I live every minute of every day with the dread that I am going to hit on an uncover cop and get arrested for solicitation or run into one of these clandestine `tricks' at a business meeting. This stuff tortures me," Roger said.

"Although you don't want to be gay, you are, and you need help with acceptance. Did I say that right?"

"I couldn't have expressed it better. I believe you wrote in one of your books, `gay and straight is the same thing, illusions that hide true feelings.' That makes perfect sense to me. From all the books I've read by leading authorities, no one knows why any of us are who we are sexually. I need to go home and end my marriage and stay celibate and single for awhile, without booze or drugs. If I ever meet a good man, or if I stay single for the rest of my life, is none of my business. It's God's business."

"Coming to terms with your sexuality is a process, not a quick fix," I said. "Change playgrounds and playmates. You have got to make a conscious effort to stay away from slippery places. And when you go to the gym, clean up at home."

Roger came back into session the next day with great rage letters. He understood that he would not send these letters to anyone. This is an exercise in letting go of all the hurt, guilt and shame that they represented. This is a two-step process of putting the past behind and living in the conscious present tense. The most impacting rage letter that he wrote was to himself.

In the process of our days in therapy, Roger came to terms with a lot of why he did the things he did and why he needed to blame someone else. His rage letters were the finishing touches of his life inventory.

That night he had to write forgiveness letters to all of the people to whom he wrote rage letters. If he had silent scorn and repressed rage against his own behavior that had manifested in others, he needed to seek forgiveness from each of them in a letter in order to forgive himself.

I took him into one of the powerful vortices for him to go through a Hopi/Egyptian letter burning ceremony of forgiveness. He meditated at a site chosen by him and I left him alone to read the letters and then burn them and bury the ashes in their respective graves, marked with a rock and sticks as markers for his rite of passage.

When he was finished, we sat quietly on the mountaintop with our thoughts and feelings of thanks for having this time together.

On his last day, Roger came into the session with a surprise.

"Last night I Googled 'famous homosexuals' and man there were some great men and women throughout history who were gay. I honeymooned in Rome and Florence. The statues by Michelangelo were beautiful and sensual. Like me, he was Catholic. I don't know whether they had a Rainbow Coalition in the sixteenth century, I doubt it, but Michelangelo was a homosexual. I cried myself to sleep thinking about all the greats who were gay. Can you believe that I am almost at the place of accepting that I am gay?"

I have never seen anyone who came in with such a polished resume and surface success and happiness so quickly let someone peel away the illusion to discover that his insides didn't match his outsides. He did not anchor, lock and seal all of the wonderful attributes he uncovered about himself in two weeks. I told him it takes what it takes to come to the revelation about him and it takes what it takes to live with what he found to be true about his identity.

He went back to San Diego and over a period of several months began to unravel the lie that his marriage represented for him. He and Crystal agreed to an amicable and quiet divorce. We had a weekly phone session for several months. He stopped drinking and drugging and has been going to meetings for more than twenty years. Roger did not act out anonymously with men ever again.

After seven years of celibacy and taking care of who he was becoming, he met a man his own age, with a career that had been sober for ten years. They started dating. Slowly they got to know one another and after going out for three years, they made a life-long commitment one day at a time to live their lives together.

After being together nine years, they adopted a daughter and two years later they adopted another baby.

I spoke to Roger a few months ago and I asked him how he got from where I found him to where he was at that time.

"The most amazing part of all of this was how easy it is for me today to let people know I am gay and that I have a life partner with kids. The biggest fear I had when I started working with you was, 'What will my friends think if they know I'm gay?' When I started getting comfortable in my own skin, I began to see myself as a man who happened to love another man and have children. I learned from men and women in the same boat as me in meetings, if my friends can't accept that I'm gay then they aren't friends worth having. My ex-wife and my partner and I had dinner a couple of years ago and she said she had never seen me so happy.

She's remarried and has three kids. I cannot tell you how happy I am in my own skin. Thanks to you," Roger said.

I get a Christmas card from Roger and his partner and children every December and they seem to be as happy as any four people can be. Does he still have life challenges? What do *you* think? We still do tune-ups by phone. Do he and his male partner have disagreements? Yes. And do his daughters drive him and his partner up the wall? What else would you expect from a four-year-old and a six-year old? The difference is that after letting go of the past, an abundance of love poured out of him once he found out who he really was.

Chapter Twenty-Seven
E-Enemy.Com

———

When I first met Paula, she was working as a horse whisperer in East Texas. One of my long-time clients asked me to lunch and then to meet Paula. She and I clicked at hello. My intuition told me she could speak loud and clear to all of us animals.

She asked to book a private session with me the next day. Her burning issue was an impending divorce.

"I like Lester but I am not in love with him," she said, starting the ball rolling.

"For my years of poking and disturbing a ton of folks, most of whom were married, I always say that *being in love* was *being in sickness*. To love is a great capacity to connect. *In love* is nonsense," I said.

"I never heard that but Arta said you were not put together like the rest of us. Lester is a successful doctor and has never been unfaithful to me, as far as I know. So what grounds do I have?" she asked.

Texans, ya gotta love them. Talk about being glued together by Bubba and Wanda's silly-billy nuttiness. Paula was chewing on the succulent end of a straw sliver.

"Relationships don't work because two people never want the same thing at the same time. Dr. Lester is retooling a man's hernia and you have your mind wrapped around what makes a four-legged animal tick.

"I hereby give you permission to de-horse, excuse the expression, from your husband/doctor of twenty years and to always speak kindly of him to friends and family. Let go in love," I advised.

We hugged and she cried for a few minutes. With dry eyes she exited my hotel room office. I left the next day and she divorced her husband weeks later.

A few years went by and she called to tell me she had moved to San Diego and was deliriously happy.

"I met someone on a dating site online and he is wonderful. Sam is a lawyer who has never been married. He lives in Santa Barbara but we are thinking of relocating to Vancouver, Canada. I would like for you to meet in a session on the telephone. Are you available?" Paula asked.

Doctor, lawyer, Indian chief will be next if she stays on that dating trap. She had heard my sermon on social media and the Anti-Christ connection, but I agreed to do a session with him.

He was a Sagittarius Sun Sign with an Aries Moon. What's not to like about Sam? Everybody loves double Fire, but no one as much as he loves himself. True to nature, he bounced around like a gerbil in a big cage.

"Man, did I hit the jackpot with Paula. It was love at first sight. Her voice is so soothing that it's no wonder animals do what she tells them. I think I've found my soul mate," he blathered on and on.

Wait. Did Sam just call her his cellmate? I could have sworn he said he fell in love the minute he saw her bottom line at the bank. You think I kid. Not. He is armed and dangerous for a woman eight years older than he is. Sam is 39 and Paula is 47. Should I tell her to run from him as fast as God would have it or not? I didn't have to, Keep reading.

Sam was not a drifter. A grifter was truer to his character. Paula and Sam moved to Santa Fe, New Mexico and decided to buy an international real estate corporation much like Sotheby's. The price tag was $3 million, with a million up front and the balance over ten years. Guess who put up all the money? Si. It would take a couple of months for the transaction to be completed. She also bought them a million dollar house on five acres in the Boonies.

Paula kept her whisper business booming. As a matter of fact, she had written a successful book and was in negotiations to give Cesar Millan a run around the dog TV business with her own show.

One day Paula got a call from the consortium selling the real estate business. They asked her to come in for a private meeting without Sam.

"Paula, we did some checking and found out that Sam is not who you think he is. As a lawyer, he stole deposit receipts from clients. There were also charges of physical abuse against two former girlfriends. He is wanted by the police. There are warrants for his arrest. His credit rating is at the bottom of the barrel. We cannot allow him to be a part of this transaction. What do you want us to do?" the group leaders asked Paula.

Paula left the meeting shaking in terror spasms with the news she had just heard. She drove around all over town wondering how to approach Sam with the news. "Do I just tell him like they told me, warts and all? Could they be wrong about the information they got from the credit report agency? Jack said they talked to the Santa Barbara Police Department and got the full report on Sam's shenanigans."

When she got home, Sam greeted her with that narcissistic grin plastered on his face. When Paula walked through the door, her involuntary emotions yo-yoed between a fake smile and unbridled rage at what she'd just heard about Sam's crimes.

"I just came from a meeting with the real estate people and they told me you had warrants out for violence toward women and stealing deposit receipts from clients buying property. What do you have to say for yourself?" she asked.

Sam hung his head and shook it from side to side. When he raised it there was not a trace of make-believe signs of smarm or bravado. He walked over to Paula and with guttural rage, cold cocked her across the room.

"Listen to me, bitch. Don't go fucking around in my past. Now, get out of my house or I will throw you out. Get up and get out," Sam said.

Paula got to her feet with her face bleeding and screamed, "You get out. This is my house and we are done. It's over."

"You should have checked the documents you signed. I am listed as the sole owner of this house. You signed it over to me. Now you get out... No... I'm throwing you out," Sam said as he picked Paula up and literally threw her out of the house he stole from her.

How do I know all of these dirty details? Paula called me daily for months to report on what it took to get her property back. Sam changed the locks and when she tried to convince the court of his malfeasance, they pointed to her signature deeding it over to Sam. When the police investigated her claim of his violence, Sam said she fell. He never touched her. The police dropped her case against Sam.

What eventually happened was that because of all the things he had done, stealing money from clients and persistent follow-up by those women he had harmed, the authorities in Santa Fe and Palm Springs finally brought charges against Sam.

Forensics proved that Sam had forged Paula's name to the deed transfer. After six months she was made whole.

"Paula, let's backtrack to where all of this started. You were feeling lonely after your divorce. You did what millions of men and women do: date online.

"First of all, those dating sites all lie about their successes. Advertising in general has colluded with caching to try and make money off of a culture that is intoxicated about what this mashugana can give them," I paused for her question.

"What's mash... however you spell it?" Paula asked.

"Mashugana is Hebrew for craziness," I told her.

"So you think that all these dating dot-coms are danger-ous?" she asked.

"Absolutely," I answered. "Why would a smart, attractive, intuitive woman like you go to such silly lengths for a date? Let God take you where he leads you. If there is a man for you, you will open a door and there he will be," I said.

I told her a dozen stories about clients I had worked with who cleared away the insanity in their past. They moved forward, turning their will and their life over to the care of God. Many of them found a life partner and others determined they liked being single and free of commitment.

"Paula, our culture the last thirty or forty years has progres-sively tried to define us by doing and being what others have told us to do. Being married is the greatest hoax ever perpetrated on all of us," I said.

"If I hear you correctly, you are saying that having to marry is a concept we learn as kids. Don't people think you are gay if you don't marry and have children?" she asked.

"That's a notion spawned by fear and confusion. Why don't you stay in Sedona for a few more days and my team of practi-tioners and I will expose you to the only essence that can ever make you whole and happy. You will say hello to your Shadow, the male part of you that you have never activated," I told her.

She stayed and went through the protocol of the Sedona Intensive. Ten years later she is raising horses with a wrangler on a ranch they bought together. He and she decided they love one about but neither feels they have to marry to be happy.

Chapter Twenty-Eight
Charlotte's Web

———

I have been a big fan of Dr. Scott Peck from the time he wrote *The Road Less Traveled*, but it is *People of the Lie: the Hope for Healing Human Evil* published in 1998 that flipped my Bic. I was reaffirmed when Peck said to name the lies that people tell. He felt political regional boilerplate untruths and parochial religions take away man's capacity to know what he sees when he looks, and they take away the ability to grasp what he hears when he listens. Scott Peck is the best friend of unfettered truth in the face of the culture that excuses bad behavior because uncovering the insidious nuttiness of lying would be too disturbing to most people.

Now, let's share the backstories of three clients. The backstories are amazingly similar even though the clients have little in common other than being overlaid in narcissism.

Charlotte was one of the most beautiful women I have ever worked with. She was a former beauty queen who had been married and divorced three times by the time she was 30. Charlotte was as far away from being tapped into Mensa as she was into being accepted as a member of one of Texas' snooty country clubs. Her internal GPS was street cred and her motivation was simple: "I am the most beautiful woman in the world and my goal is to marry rich and divorce richer."

As you read this don't think Charlotte has a mother lode of self-esteem. How she talked about herself was more sociopathic than feet-on-the-ground feeling good. Her false sense of self was anchored in her back story. Her mother never married her father, who was one of the richest men in the Southwest.

Her mother had her live with her aunt who had married up, as they say in the South. Her aunt was the fulcrum to lift Charlotte from the misery and shame of her genesis.

Charlotte was a beauty queen with so-so grades. Miss then or that bolstered her image but not her sick insides.

She began to finagle and plot and tar the road to a better life in high school. She got pregnant her freshman year in college, married the rich kid and immediately put her baby up for adoption. Being saddled with raising a child was not in her game plan. She divorced the rich kid and bought a house in a different state with the settlement. Her aunt continued to manipulate her climb into a social atmosphere to which Charlotte would never belong. Charlotte was adept at hiding her marriage and baby when she won the local Miss America pageant for her city. Today she wouldn't even get to the interview with all the scrutiny and vetting these pageants do.

When I got hold of her, she was divorcing richest husband No. 3. Her self-esteem had dropped precipitously but she was wrapped in the most extreme case of narcissism that I had ever seen. She stayed three weeks, working with me and seven therapists and she did get better. Here is what her "better" looked like.

Charlotte admitted to having been sexually abused by her father. He had given her gifts and clothes and things rich girls got from their parents. She also developed a faux sense of being better than her peers in grammar school and high school.

Promiscuity started when she was 13 and she ratcheted it way up when she was a sophomore in high school. She had two abortions before she was 15. And that rich kid who got her pregnant? She was 17 then.

The most compelling breakthrough she had was to admit that she had confused her sexuality and how to get what she wanted from the sexual encounters with her father.

"When you made me take off all my make-up on day one I was pissed. When you took away my cell phone I felt as if I were lost in space. Having the hotel remove alcohol from my room and asking the hotel operator to cut the power to the telephone line in my room was the last straw. I knew I was up against someone stronger and smarter than I was," she confessed after the first week.

"Charlotte, I don't know about smarter but I do know I sense what is killing you every day of your life. You are here to get to the bottom of all the false faces you wear and the clothes and make-up you are hiding behind. All of us are living in a world that demands critical changes in the way we think and the way we act. Stay the time you booked here and when you go home, we will have a roadmap for you to get from where you've been living to the place that will free you from all the insane and destructive things you've done all your life," I said.

Her therapy included daily sessions with a licensed psychologist. Charlotte has to go to daily AA meetings. By week two she loved the meetings and the people in them. Her favorite parts of the program were the massages and reflexology.

She became as willing as a thirsty woman wanting water to do exactly what we asked her to do so she could get a different life than the one she was living. Ten years later she is sober and saner and she has not married again. She went back to college and got training to be a nurse. Charlotte proves that with the right tools applied daily, anyone can change their life.

The next case of narcissism disguising a sense of unworthiness and dependency on all kinds of drugs and booze was a wunderkund in show business. Jared was one of the brightest lights in one of the most powerful agencies in Hollywood.

Chapter Twenty-Nine
The Story of Jared

───────

One day in early spring at the turn of the century I got a phone call from a young man from Southern California who had just read my first book, *Clearing for the Millennium*. Sean was kind in his comments about the book and how it impacted him. In no time I offered to do a complimentary "Albert" session for him. He was floored at my complimentary gift as I never, ever give away my work. Once one of my sisters asked if I would give her the family discount and I told her in no uncertain terms, no! So kill me. I still feel that way, but this fellow Sean needed me and I offered.

At the end of the session he told me about his brother Jared, who was a big piece of stuff agent for actors, writers, directors and producers at one of the top agencies in Los Angeles.

"Jared has a big drug problem. His career is in high gear and his personal life is in the toilet. Will you help him?" Sean pleaded.

Newcomers who want to come to Sedona for the grueling grilling of their life first must have an evaluation, in these latter days, only on Skype. I am famous to say, "I can name that tune in one note," when I really mean to someone I am evaluating, "I had your number at hello."

Jared came into my field of vision in the days before internet overload. I have written, preached and told everyone within the sound of my voice that the world began to end with the introduction of the computer in 1953 and the overlay of credit cards in 1959. I stand by my intuitive insight, even when I am researching and reluctantly opening my emails. Can you believe a world without minute-by-minute updates on the Kardashians and their other mother, Caitlin? Spare me.

Jared called a few days later and his long and winding tale of woe and sad songs went on for more than an hour. I said little. But behind the phone receiver I was doing charade craziness like Judge Marilyn Milian from *Court TV*. Jared and I danced around his huge denial of a drug problem and he taught me everything I had never heard about how he can manage cocaine.

He was a Scorpio without the benefit of high intuition and the need to serve others. It was apparent that rocking and rolling in the fast pace of Hollywood was his pleasure, as was drugging every day. But he called me constantly with my permission.

Some former Hollywood mogul with a spread in the Caribbean allowed him to stay with him provided he give up drugs. He did, and he started to eat healthy with no Quaaludes or cocaine or marijuana. After a few months, he told his host he had to get back to work, when he really meant he was a drug addict and wanted to use.

In one of our many talks, Jared decided he wanted to come to Sedona to get well. He said he needed a couple of months. I told him the fee and he seemed to accept it. He got the Day One homework and said he had started to write. We sent a meditation tape and he said he said he was using it. He scheduled to come in August of that year.

A week before he was to arrive to begin deep tissue issue work, he called to say the fees were too high.

"Albert, will you make me a better deal than the one you quoted a few weeks ago? Don't you take insurance, dude?"

"First of all, Jared, never call me dude again. That's bullshit street cred that I never answer to," I said to him.

"Whatever," he mumbled.

"We don't take insurance because we want you, not the insurance company, to make an investment. Treatment centers depend on those companies. Sedona Intensive does not," I told him.

We hung up and continued to make arrangements to for him come in early August. He called back a few days later and cancelled.

"Your program is too expensive. Cancel my reservation," Jared said.

On his birthday, while stoned and angry, Jared hanged himself. When his will was probated, Jared had several million dollars in blue chip stocks and bonds as well as millions of dollars in paintings and other fine art.

Charming, handsome and very successful as an agent, Jared let the devils that chased him convince him to throw a rope around a high beam in his expensive house and kill himself.

One of the natural laws that we teach clients at SI is to ask the question, "Ego, are you a demon who chases me or an angel who has come to help me?" It's quite sad that we never got to give this insight to an incredible but troubled young man.

Chapter Thirty

The Lies That TJ Told

The day that I met TJ, he had bought a case of my first book, *Clearing for the Millennium*. He arranged for me to speak at his country club. A lot of people attended. At the end of the workshop, I asked him if he wanted to go through my program. He accepted immediately as did his wife. They did separate Intensives as all my work is one-on-one. Except for the 12-step meetings, the client is never in session with any other client.

From the moment he opened his mouth I knew this floor flusher from New Orleans was lying and shucking and jiving to beat the band. He was an only child. His mother was a big dick woman and his father was softer and beaten down by his own mother, and now was in the clutches of a shrew.

TJ was attractive with a smile that would make women come running into his lair. His conquests were wounded bird women who worked for him. His trick was to get one of them to work late. At the stroke of out of control sexual obsession, he would pounce and they would comply.

In time he would find couples online. They are called swingers. One of the women whose Sedona Intensive fee he paid said that they had lined up a couple of men because TJ always wanted to try the other side of obsession. She said he was ravenous.

"It knocked me over when he asked me to leave so he could have at it with the men alone," Hannah said.

The weird part of his sexual obsession was he sent a lot of these women to the Sedona Intensive. He was so split in personality that each of them from day one outed him. In the years I tried to crack the egg – help him let go of all these damaging conquests – he never confessed to one. His retort when I confronted him was, "She made that up." After a grace period, when each woman returned to work, he fired her with a pile of cash.

Not one of them ever filed sexual harassment charges against him.

His wife Elaine happened to call him when he was in Canada, supposedly on business, and a woman picked up the phone.

"Where is TJ and who are you?" Elaine asked.

"He's taking a shower. I'll bet you're just dying to know who I am," the woman said. She hung up the phone with a cackle laugh.

Elaine called me in hysterics. As she rambled and cried, she blurted out, "What am I to do? The kids and I are packing to go to the dude ranch in Wyoming."

"Call TJ back and tell him to beg me to work with him again. A week later you come and we will do couples therapy," I advised.

After a lot of "I don't have time to come to Sedona" and "If that bitch Elaine thinks she's going to get a dime from me, she's crazy," lo and behold, this narcissistic blowhard bi-sexual sociopath cleared his schedule and arrived at the appointed time.

Most of you people haven't a clue what narcissism is – especially if you are watching too many Wendy Williams or Dr. Oz television shows.

Here is the Mayo Clinic definition: A narcissistic personality disorder is a mental disorder in which people have an inflated sense of their own importance, a deep need for admiration and a lack of empathy for others. But behind this mask of ultra confidence lies a fragile self-esteem that's vulnerable to the slightest criticism.

In my world of treatment, I often see narcissism as a twin to another mental and emotional disorder, psychopathy. Psychopaths are unable to form emotional attachments or feel real empathy for others, although they often have disarming or even charming personalities.

Psychopaths are very manipulative and can easily gain people's trust. They learn to mimic emotions despite their inability to actually feel them, and they will appear normal to unsuspecting people. They are often well-educated and hold steady jobs. Some are so good at manipulation and mimicry that they have families and other long-term relationships without those around them ever suspecting their true nature.

Sexual deviancy falls into the realm of these dual addictions. My, my, my, TJ has got a trunk load of mental illness and I have the Mayo Clinic to back me up.

Since TJ was here for a week, I will capsulate what happened. TJ admitted that he had a supercalifragilisticexpialidocious sex drive that ruled his life.

"Aren't all men oversexed?" he asked.

"I will eat the competition alive before they &^%$$ with me," TJ elaborated.

Now here is the waterloo of his week with me.

My analysis:

"You are amazingly gifted, a smart aleck and as smart as a whip. But you are also irritating and a know-it-all who really has no clue how to treat a woman. Truthfully, you will screw a man or a woman or the proverbial snake. Your insecurities can never heal because when you are confronted with your foibles and peccadilloes, you have all the money in the world to run and pick up a willing slave to your addictions.

"You will never change, but when Elaine meets with us tomorrow, you will not get by with a thing. Five women who you sent to SI have 'outed' you big time — including when you were sodomized by a man and you performed fellatio on another. You know why you sent those women to me? You want them to tell me what you could not and would not," I said.

"This is not a confessional and I do not have to admit to anything," he whimpered.

"Two things, bozo, which you need to cop a plea to. One, you are a liar, a user and abuser and you have no respect for your wife or concern for your two children. Second, whether you like it or not, your children are also coming to Sedona with Elaine. I will counsel them and they will see a few other therapists.

"If Elaine decides she doesn't want to be married to you a minute longer, I have drawn up an Agreement of Separation which will spell out who has to do what and when and what is the compensation for Elaine and the children." I ended with the great stone face of someone who is in charge from this moment on.

The most tearful and stressful part of family therapy was when TJ told his children that he was in love with an executive woman who worked with him. The children screamed bloody murder because they had always looked to this woman as a surrogate — she took them shopping for clothes, managed their trust fund and both kids looked to her as someone they could always trust.

That relationship was shattered in an instant in our family pow-wow.

Elaine filed for divorce. She showed the agreement they both signed for me to her attorney. The judge read it in open court.

"I love this guy who wrote this agreement and had you sign it. The language is such accurate legalese. I am making it the basis for final adjudication of your divorce," the judge said.

Elaine got a fair settlement. TJ never changed his ways. Although the parents were awarded joint custody, the daughter asked the judge to give her permission not to see her father.

"My father will no longer hold me to a court order if it pleases the court. I do not want to be forced to see him again. He is never present for me. I do not want to see his girlfriend ever again," she wept as she spoke.

"So ordered," the judge ruled.

This saga played out several years ago. Elaine is engaged, their son is making good grades and their daughter is one of the happiest 16-year-olds in the state of Louisiana.

Where's TJ? Well some old dogs never learn to mind their manners so you can love them and let them get under the covers with you at night. But he is now close to 70 and more desperate than ever.

Chapter Thirty-One
Her Royal Highness Called Me Boss

─────────

It is amazing who seeks me out to cut the ties that bind them to a life not worth living. Shattered lives don't just happen to the rank and file among us. Even those who live in mansions and palaces with royal titles find themselves in tortured places. Trash newspapers and celebrity magazines conjure and make up so much of what they print. If millions of folks weren't so addicted to what the rich and famous were doing, these half-truths would never find their way into supermarkets and newspaper kiosks.

In a recent discussion with a couple of friends who are historian authorities, my acclaimed couple reminded me that this sort of craving and disgust with *causes célèbres* has run throughout history.

"The French monarchy was not beheaded merely because of the riotous living and vulgar extravagance of le roi et femme de roi. Oh, no, it was when Queen Marie said, `*Qu'ils mangent de la brioche,*' `Let them eat cake.' The French had their tabloids in the day that blared that line like The New York Post Page Six does daily," said m*on ami* Bill, *l'historien*.

My introduction to the Princess came from friends who were at a party with her and she began to cry over her crumbling marriage to the Prince. The small crowd of friends was stunned about her tears because the royal couple was always seen together with smiles and air kisses.

"My wife and I have a friend in Arizona who works with people in dire straits," Jonathan told the Princess. "Would you like me to call him?" he asked.

"I'd like to call him myself," the royal lady told him.

Jonathan and his wife Harriet knew I was working in New York and staying at the Hotel Carlyle. He told m'lady where I was going to be and offered to give her the number where I could be reached.

This all took place before cell phones were grafted onto everyone's ear.

"Don't bother. I am flying to New York tomorrow and I am booked into the Hotel Carlyle. I'll call him there and see if he will make time for me," the Princess said.

She did call before she arrived. Actually, the Princess woke me up. Europe is several hours ahead of New York. The chat was pleasant and I set aside a couple of days to spend with her.

I will call the Princess Madam Z from here on out. My confidentiality extends to ordinary people as well. The television show *Entertainment Tonight* used to call me frequently to ask about a certain actress with whom I have worked for more than thirty years.

"Sorry, I don't know this woman but I love her movies," was my repartee each time they tried to wedge the information out of me.

Madam Z and I met in her suite on an upper floor. When she opened the door to my knock it was love at hello. Madam Z was pretty and so bright that I had to speed my usual reaction to her questions.

"You come highly recommended by Jonathan and Harriet," were her first words to me.

"They are prejudiced. When I was in Paris, Jonathan introduced me to Harriet who he had just started dating. I did her astrological birth chart as well as compatibility with his chart. I told him this was his wife, 'if she'll have you.'"

"Well, that's so prescient of you, boss. They just celebrated their twentieth anniversary," she said.

"They also told me that you are most direct and tough as nails," she said."I could tell you a lot about the great unwashed and how nutty some of them are, but I won't. Discretion keeps you out of court." I joshed.

The first day was all about confessions and lies and betrayals. For a woman raised in an upper crust family, she amazed me. She and I were at opposite ends of the social ladder.

However, for me, all of us have lived so many lives that we innately click connect to someone with whom we apparently have nothing in common. It is what is in our memory bank that opens the door of understanding.

I did not tell her I had been a pope in a former life (and not a nice one) or a beggar who stole when his victim was not looking. If my long life has taught me anything it is that none of us is who we think we are. Many lives are opportunities to atone for past life deeds.

"Let's have lunch downstairs in the dining room. This hotel has the best cuisine in the world. When we sit down at table, look only at me. I stay here a lot and the hotel warns the guests, 'If Her Majesty is with guests never approach her table. If she nods recognition then you may speak to her,'" she advised.

We talked a lot about the Sedona Intensive. I gave her a copy of my first book, *Clearing for the Millennium*. When I said that clients are required to go to open 12-step meetings as part of the program, she balked.

"You know I am an alcoholic but the sober sort in Sedona do not have to know that," she told me.

"I have already called someone who has been a top secret security man for years. He now lives in Sedona. You will be under his care the whole time you are in Arizona.

"My staff and I decided that you will stay at a resort that, like the Hotel Carlyle, is accustomed to high-profile guests. Our security man will be outside your door at all times.

"As for 12-step meetings, I will invite a small number of people whom I will vet to make sure they will not expect to be your latest new best friend. The purpose of this arrangement is to let you hear the courage sober men and women have had to get sober and stay sober.

"Your hotel accommodations will have a kitchen and an incredible chef will cook lunch and dinner. You will be on your own for breakfast," I instructed.

We set a date two weeks hence. The financial arrangements would be made by her lady-in-waiting. She gave me her private number. I also gave her the writing assignment as well as a download of meditations. Madam Z asked about keeping a journal, so I gave her one.

"We are all set. I will call your contact for payment for the two-week Sedona Intensive."

We had a farewell dinner the second night. There was little talk but a lot of silent and invisible transference of energy between us both.

As I left her at the door to her suite, she said, "These two days have been the most freeing times I have ever spent with anyone. I will do all the writing and will see you in two weeks. Be good to you, boss, until we meet again."

She went into her room.

In a few days her lady-in-waiting said that there were some unresolved issues with her bank. Bottom line, she had to cancel because her debt to her bank was so deep and wide she could not afford to go through the program.

Through the years she has sent a letter or a card. She always writes, "I will never forget you and our time together."

Chapter Thirty-Two

The Obsessions of Laura

———

I met Laura when I was on a work trip in New York. If anyone was well turned out with beauty, style and confidence, it was she. By reputation she was called Lovable Laura. My clients are mostly referrals, as was Laura. Three of her friends who were clients of mine had been trying to get her to come see me.

When she walked through the door at the Hotel Carlyle she handed me a check for her session as well as a box of chocolates from Paris.

"I wanted to pay upfront in the event I don't like what you tell me. My friend Cassie said you love chocolate," Laura said.

"Thank you for both. I am not known to tell you what you want to hear but what I see and sense about your life. Let's get started, shall we?" I said.

Getting to know clients is easy for me. Some have said I was born to do this work. I have had sessions with empaths who have said the same thing. An empath has the ability to scan another's psyche for thoughts and feelings or for past, present and future life occurrences. Many empaths are unaware of how this actually works, and have long accepted that they were sensitive to others.

Laura's session focused on an impending marriage to a man she had dated for less than a year. We spent the whole hour on that situation. I suggested she not marry him at the end of the reading.

"Well, thanks for nothing. I will marry him whether you say so or not," Laura advised and then left my room, slamming the door.

When I counsel people, whether they act on my insights or not is none of my business. More of my work involves the healing process. The Sedona Intensive was born when so many clients asked to come here to do deeper work challenges. So many of the clients I have worked with have had addiction issues.

I didn't give Lovable Laura another thought. Her chart and my intuition told me she is very controlling and goes to any lengths to get what she wants "even if hell freezes over," as the Southern euphemism says. As a lot of girls do, two of her friends couldn't wait to tell me that when she left our session she was as mad as a wet hen.

"Why you sent me to him was stupid. He told me that I ought not to marry Jack and I did last Saturday. Keep these kinds of recommendations to yourself," Laura told both of them.

Still tending to my own business as well as not telling clients what they wanted to hear, a few years later Laura called me. By this time we had Skype, which changed the way I do business. I suggested we have another session.

"Albert, I owe you an apology. You advised me not to marry Jack and I did anyway. It lasted exactly four months. That marriage cost me more than emotional abuse but he cleaned me out financially as well," said Lovable Laura when our session started.

"I just read your new book: *You're Not Who You Think You Are*. I thought it was amazing. Your message hit me bull's eye. You have been sending me your complimentary newsletter. After I got divorced I have been reading it religiously," she reported.

"Tell me what you learned from marrying Jack?" I asked.

"I have decided I need to go through your Intensive. When can I start?" she asked.

Because names have been changed to protect the privacy of all my clients, I can let you know that she shifted from hunky athletic men to successful ones. Her latest "gotta have" man is a power broker in politics who is rich from family money. I knew who he was the minute she spoke his name. Our five days were lasered on her and him and how she could avert making another costly relationship mistake. The new man, Ted, was almost old enough to be her father.

She wrote and we processed. Laura would accuse and then excuse herself for old behavior. The writing was so detailed that I should have doubled the fee. Meditation is a part of our process. Little by little all of this work seemed to be having a positive and clean and conscious affect on her.

Part of her confession and my discovery was that she was sexually addicted to men. The current boyfriend and she have been so sexually glued together that she flies to where he is primarily to have sex. Each encounter involves more bizarre and risky interplay. Bondage and hurting in the name of love was their brand of gratification. Would they ever marry? I hoped not.

Let me be clear that hogtying and beating the meanness out of clients is not all that happens here. And to tell the truth, there is never any hogtying or beating. Someone once said I should have been a stand-up comedian.

When she was in the Sedona Intensive, she had a massage and sat for an analysis by a Human Design wizard. Laura got second opinions from a psychologist with open ears and a pure heart. She finished her day with a meditative yoga instructor who has a beautiful soul.

Laura did an incredible job unknotting and letting go of the dirty floor upon which she built her obsession about men. When

I told her about the Shadow, she was interested. We named him Larry. She understood that her Shadow was an invisible presence that was causing her difficulty.

The Shadow was on assignment to disturb any relationship that was not in her best interest. Her Shadow can act like a jealous lover. That essence will draw men to her who will not be in her best spiritual interest. That is what her Shadow was doing. Finally she seemed to unravel that mystery of "Larry."

"I am a Christian," she said. "I cannot prove that God or Jesus exist, but my faith is that I need to follow their guidelines to be happy. That's how I see the Shadow Larry. I can't prove he's in me, but if I take him on faith and let him help me, my life will be better," she added.

"Laura, in spite of what you think about me, what I know about you is that you are smarter than most people I work with. From where you came to where you are today, your life will never be the same again. Always remember that you have a tendency to glom onto a man. When you go home, you need to go to a support group, journal daily and meditate. When you write, always be honest with yourself and Larry," I advised.

She and I worked on Skype for awhile. In the second month she did not answer my Skype. That night I got an email saying that she had decided to stay with the new boyfriend.

"I appreciate all the work we have done together. You amaze me with where you took me and the admissions I made. However, Ted has promised we will be married in due time. I wish you only love and appreciation. Laura."

Those same friends that needed to tell me how much she hated our initial session reported to me that Ted had lied about other women and that Laura was on suicide watch at a hospital. The yentas kept me up-to-date by letting me know that Laura was going to a thrice-divorced psychiatrist who was the spitting image of Laura. She is still dating Ted but he will no longer be exclusive with Laura.

I tell everyone within the sound of my voice that I don't make them, God does, but I can only retool and refine them if they are ready to make the psychic changes that it requires.

As a Vedantist (look it up — it's the most amazing faith I have ever found), I put people, places and things on my prayer shrine. Laura is still there. If I know what I know, I know that prayer is as powerful as atomic bombs and/or a gaggle of tattooed trouble-makers out to do damage to your heart and soul.

Chapter Thirty-Three
The Life and Death of Anthony

—

One of the country's premier art groups in Arizona sent a lot of clients to the Intensive in the 90s. It was once a joke around the halls of that brilliant coterie of artists and agents that to work at the Phoenix Art Group you eventually have to climb the hill to Sedona and work with Albert and his posse. My bottom line about this group is that they are exceptional and were willing to experience another part of art.

One of the most loving and genius men who ever signed up for a week here was blond-haired and blue-eyed Italian Anthony, un artista di colori ad olio e acquerelli ed un pittore.

Each of us comes out the birth canal with our passage to the life ahead with a compass or a know-how manual. Tony was no different. I have said more times than reasonable that I will take an Italian over any other ethnicity, even if it's *la casa nostra*, the *Sicilian mafiosa*. A scan of my karmic ancestral tree will tell you all the times I lived and loved being Italian in Italy.

From the moment he arrived I could feel his pain. Every day he wore a smile. Anthony was grateful for everything. His great passion was painting and he had a cast of mysticism with all his oils or acrylics. Like everyone except high masters and eunuchs, Anthony oftentimes found admirers that he did not consciously draw to him collecting like fans at his doorstep.

We went through his life story – the ups and downs and all around – and nowhere did I find a magnificent obsession except when he painted.

Tony had been HIV-positive for a number of years. He experienced a lot of steady good health and then there were nosedives. Nothing erased that joy on his face and the peace he sought in painting and having people who loved his art buy it.

It was my observation that he was the darling of the Art Group. Dare I say that he was teacher's pet? No one ever said an unkind word about him but at the same time, someone in his life made him feel tortured. But living or dead, his life history will remain locked and sealed by me.

When he left the five-day program, he asked if we could work longer.

"You seem to love my paintings, so why don't I paint a large picture?" he suggested.

He did and we continued for a number of months.

"I would like to get some idea of what you would like me to paint. Let's talk and I will get some ideas," Tony said.

We sat down outside in my garden and I told him I am a dyed-in-the-wool adherent of reincarnation. At the time I had an oversized oil of Napoleon on my wall. I told Tony that I had met a Navy SEAL, vacationing with his wife, in a restaurant. On his way to being stationed in Virginia, he stopped by my house. When he saw the painting he said, "Where did you get that painting? I was Bonaparte in a former life." I joked and exclaimed, "No, I was!"

His name was Victor Meyer.

"Perhaps you both were in the French army under the command of Napoleon Bonaparte and thus thought you both were the general," Tony said.

"I love the notion that Victor and I were connected in a prior life," I told Tony.

A few months later I heard that Tony's health was failing.

"You always talked about the afterlife being better than the one in which there is so much pain and indecision," Tony said to me on the telephone one day.

Joe from the Art Group brought and hung the framed surreal picture that Tony painted. It had the most beautiful gold frame. The minute it was hung on my wall, I got word that Tony had made his transition.

The painting hangs at my desk and I look at it all day long. There are several insert cut-out photographs of both Victor and me.

Wherever you are, Tony, may God bless you, and if it be God's will, I will see you again sometime somewhere on Earth.

Chapter Thirty-Four
The Actor Caught Between Acts

This next lady, whom I will call Barbara Dupree, was referred to me by a woman I have worked with for years. A lot of people who find me are true bluebloods, or snobs with unconscionable attitudes of being better than the *hoi polloi*. They are members of clubs that are overpriced and hard to get into. Their brags are being Daughters of the American Revolution, having credit cards with unlimited open-to-buy and living on dirt in mansions that cost more than a small country's national debt.

Their children go to private schools and if they are endowed with more than money, property and prestige and have brains, they a shoo-in for Princeton, Harvard or Yale.

You are about to meet a woman whose baggage included all the above. Meet Barbara, whose name shifted for me to *bête noire* Barbara, or Bette. Unless you were raised down on the farm or holed up in an ashram, you have known someone like Bette.

Her messiest predilection was to pick up men on fancy streets, like Park Avenue or Rodeo Drive, to name a few of the cement slabs she trod. The minute her fascination was over, she gave the man of the moment a Patek Philippe or a Zenith El Primero Tour watch and sent him on his way.

"I don't like your art," Barbara said. "It is so yesterday, not centuries old like the paintings that hang in my house."

"Barbara, thank God I don't live in your house and you're only in mine an hour-and-a-half a day. When I want to see *The Coronation of Napoleon* by Jacque-Louis David or Rembrandt's *Bathsheba at Her Bath,* I will go to the Louvre. In Madrid when I have a yen to bathe in the beauty of Raphael's *The Cardinal* or Fra Angelica's *The Annunciation* and Tiepolo Gianbattista's *The Immaculate Conception,* I will stop in at the Prado," I advised.

"I knew you'd love Napoleon. I see a bit of a resemblance. I wouldn't have picked you for taking a gander at a cardinal. It must have been his red cape," she chortled.

Her friend told me I'd have my hands full with Barbara but I had no idea how deep her noire would run. In my methodology of how to crack the code to these happy wanderers who make it to my door, Bette was defended, a smart ass know-it-all, who beneath the sarcasm was a lost and wounded little girl.

In the written homework assignment, she would go from "I hate all these people, how did I ever get with them," to trying to shock me with smut and pornographic descriptions, particularly about her family. The most disturbing was the cat-and-mouse game she played with her father, which was the shoddy floor upon which she built the bad relationship she had with men.

Barbara described how she was Daddy's little girl although she had an older and younger sister. Barbara and Daddy Warbucks played a game where Barbara would sit on her father's lap and bounce until she felt his penis. During this time, the door to his study was closed. As she reached puberty, they both climaxed. This sick parlor game started when she was four or five and continued until they both knew what they were looking for when she was 15 and 16.

I gave her a copy of Dr. Kenneth M. Adams book, *Silently Seduced: When Parents Make Their Children Partners*. Adams, a leading expert on covert incest, sex addiction and childhood trauma, offers tools in his book, tools for identifying and healing from covert incestuous relationships that affect adult relationships and lives. He explains how "feeling close" with a parent is not always the source of comfort the phrase suggests, especially when that child is cheated out of a childhood by being a parent's surrogate partner.

Barbara used Adams' explanation, "The child is cheated out of a childhood by being a parent's surrogate parent," to describe what went down with her and her father. She always wanted therapists to think he molested her. Now she accepts her part in the nefarious relationship with her daddy.

"Actually, truth be told, I seduced him," she confessed.

The hardest part of the work we did in the first couple of weeks was to break her of the habit of "splitting," a term used in therapeutic circles when a patient or client denigrates one therapist to another, and vice versa.

For years we had a highly respected psychologist meet with the clients several times while they are going through the Sedona Intensive protocol. What was interesting about Barbara Dupree was she signed to come two weeks for four times in one year. She saw a lot of this noted psychologist.

"I wonder why you have Doctor IQ as support for your program. It is apparent he doesn't like women and is hiding his own stuff rather than facing what's deep within him," she said after her second session with him.

That afternoon the good doctor called me to tell me I needed to be aware of Bette's tendency to split.

"She told me that you didn't like women and that you have a lot of unresolved issues that you haven't faced," he said.

The tendency to split therapists is a device of one's Ego: Keep the therapists at each other's therapist so you can stay sick.

One of my cardinal qualities, which I embrace and nurture, is to be direct in counseling. Don't let the Ego rule and ruin the work I am trying to do.

The next day was "come to Jesus" time, as we say in the South.

"Barbara, yesterday you dissed Doctor IQ to me and when you went to him, you said the same thing about me. You are the one who paid royally for treatment, so stop sabotaging it. And if we want your opinion about either one of us, we'll ask. Tend to your own business. Continue to meditate daily, go to your daily 12-step meetings and write and most of all, listen with both ears," I chastised her.

What's that old cliché, "Rome wasn't built in a day?" Thank God pretty Barbara had preplanned to come back and forth to Sedona throughout the year because she knows that she is sicker than a lot of folks we work with. To her credit, once exposed to a fault, she makes impressive changes in that area. But her myriad of defects and Ego camouflaging low self-esteem were deep and wide.

The *bête noire* sobriquet stuck to Barbara like hot glue because of her insane outbreaks of jealousy. The most offensive stain on her *milieu* was her sharp tongue and severe criticism of other women, particularly those who were prettier, smarter, richer and happily married.

Since she was here so often that one night a few of us decided to invite Barbara to go to dinner and take in a movie. Barbara was fine at dinner because she was a newcomer and all made her the center of attention. We went to see the comedic actor Martin Lawrence in *Big Momma's House*.

The group went for coffee afterwards, most of us guffawing because the raucous humor was very hysterical.

Tim asked Barbara how she liked the movie.

"I thought it was disgusting. They would never allow that trashy movie to be shown where I live in Greenwich, Connecticut," Barbara sneered as she spit out her words.

Tim said, "Lighten up, bully Barbara. Laugh and the world laughs with you."

"Fuck you, tiny Tim. Don't tell me what kind of movies I should like just because you like low-life entertainment," Barbara chided.

"Well, Barbara, I am glad my momma wasn't here tonight or she would have washed your mouth out with soap, oh high holy one," Tim finished her off with that comment.

The next morning Barbara came into session with a couple of notes addressed to me and Tim.

"I want to make amends for my ugly Barbara behavior last night," she said. "You've got my number but I am 60 years old and I am still full of bullshit and false airs. I am so sick of me. Can you ever forgive me?" she asked.

"Barbara, life is made up of moments, some of which we regret and others we cherish. I will always keep sacred this time when you are being contrite about what happened last night. I will give Tim your letter and will read mine when I am alone with your written thoughts," I said.

We had a great session. In a few days it would be time for us to say goodbye for a while. She would come back several more times. Her load got lighter and she made tremendous changes that stayed with her through her life.

She once brought her two daughters and grandchildren to Sedona for Thanksgiving week. Of course, I had dinner with them on Turkey Day. For two days before, her daughters and one granddaughter sat with me to do their astrology charts. Each expressed how much they loved the mother/grandmother that we unearthed in the Sedona Intensive.

"I never thought she would change and that I would have to fake love for her until she died. Not anymore. Momma Barbara is exactly what we have always wanted and needed and have finally gotten," her daughter Rachel said.

Within a few months, her breast cancer began to spread like a wildfire. With great calm and readiness, Barbara recorded a message on my voice mail. They were her last words before she made her transition.

"I wanted to say goodbye to the man, with your team of therapists, who changed my life and gave me one worth living. You put up with a lot and I was extremely difficult. Promise me you will never change and will continue to challenge yourself and everyone who climbs the hill from Phoenix to uncover and discover who they were born to be. In your words, 'I will see you in my dreams.'"

God bless you, beautiful Barbara wherever you are.

Om. Tat. Sat. Om.

Chapter Thirty-Five

Medicine Woman Surrenders to Win

———

My first contact with the client who called herself Medicine Woman was in 2006. She called the office looking for a treatment center. The Sedona Intensive is more out-patient than 26 days behind locked doors. Because she lived in Phoenix, she decided to drive up I-17 to meet with me.

"You know we do not have a facility to house clients," I said to her.

She decided to have the Evaluation Session anyway.

Her addiction was drinking small bottles of vanilla extract. Vanilla is a tropical plant, mostly grown in Mexico, South America, Central America and the Caribbean. The extract from vanilla beans has various purposes. While the pods and beans are incurred without any chemical additives, the extract requires significant amount of alcohol.

In all my years of counseling I have never had a client who got their alcohol high from drinking vanilla extract.

Throughout the evaluation, Medicine Woman, which was how she wanted to be addressed, expressed deep pride in being

Navajo. Her entire birth family had died, including three brothers. Her father had been abusive to her mother and she'd had a lot of men in her life.

"For some reason I always wanted a man until he wanted me. Then I thought he was controlling and I moved on without formal good-byes," she confessed.

"Where did the idea hit you that you could alter your reality by drinking vanilla extract?" I asked.

"I love to bake cakes and cookies. One day after a painful fight with my husband – a tribal chieftain – I just started to drink the extract. After a few swigs I let go and went into that magical kingdom of fantasy," she said.

When I was growing up, I loved to hear Ethel Waters, an African-American woman from Pennsylvania, sing *His Eye is on the Sparrow*. In telling her story of emotional abuse from her tribal chieftain husband, Medicine Woman often reminded me of Waters' song because she always came back to her reliance on her faith in God and how she knew he was watching over her.

"If I am so faithful, why do I drink?" she asked.

"Why do you drink vanilla extract to get high?" I asked. "My drink of choice was J&B Scotch. Three shots of that nasty tasting stuff would send me to anywhere my Ego wanted me to go," I shared. We both had a good laugh at my silliness.

None of us drinks for the taste. We are addicted to how it makes us feel.

After the hour of evaluation, she decided to stay in Sedona for the five-day program. She and her husband had a house in Sedona.

"Give us a couple of days to get your schedule of therapists set. I can see you every day before you officially start," I advised.

She seemed relieved that she had found a program of recovery that fit her.

Medicine Woman went through the Sedona Intensive three times in ten years. She thought she was addicted to vanilla extract. My assessment was that she was a sex addict who had married a bully, an obese chieftain, who thought he could rule her like he did his tribe.

I must say that I am a bit like the smarty pants from the *Judge Judy* on television. Judge Judy will not allow hearsay about anyone or anything unless that person is in court to testify. When a client in the Sedona Intensive starts to tell me about what someone in her backstory has said, I stop them.

"Inadmissible evidence in a court of law and not allowed here. Tell your story from your point of view," I cautioned.

My philosophy does not allow drugs to treat what ails my clients. Many psychologists and psychiatrists are overmedicating their patients rather than doing the work to help their patient change without the cover-up of prescription drugs. When Medicine Woman told me about her meds, I told her to give them to me. I threw them away.

Stories have basic kinships in what I hear from my clients. Most find there was alcoholic abuse with the attendant fights and fussing that go with booze abuse in their childhood. A smaller percentage of my seekers think their childhoods were perfect. Both are skewered. 12-step sensibility has a quote that was appropriate for Medicine Woman's backstory that was overrun with weeds and bramble bushes: "There is a bit of good in the worst of us and a bit of bad in the best of us."

I have a syllabus they follow to put on the table all issues that may have played a role in whatever are their problems. Below is the format I use.

Paint me a picture of your mother and father and siblings. In describing your parents, tell me who was more dominant, loving and supportive as well as point out unattractive qualities like temper, addictions – alcoholism, drug addiction, overeating – as well as narcissistic behavior and any other qualities that were detrimental to your upbringing. In many instances a mother will have been more dominant with a take-charge personality and the father might be shy and retiring.

It was in this section of her Intensive that she laid bare the family dynamic. She tried to make the father the ogre but her mother played a big part in the emotional and oftentimes physical abuse from the father.

"I never felt my mother was at fault," Medicine Woman shared. "My father was the villain," she stressed.

"You've been watching too many soap operas. Your mother did nothing to protect her children from the monster overtaking her husband. Silence is a big crime in my book," I said.

"Albert, you do not understand the ways of tribal customs. Father is always to be honored and revered," she whimpered.

There was a pregnant pause and then I got out my whip and chair to undo tribal law.

"Oh high holy woman, I am about to amend the way of the warriors and drum thumpers. Men and woman alike need to understand that the changing line of I-ching esteems one gender equal with the other. This is the twenty-first century. Everything and everybody is out of the closet. Your father and mother were complicit in the abuse of you and your brothers," I declared.

Medicine Woman began to sob.

"Could this have been the underlining truth about why I lifted my mother up and stomped on the memory of my father?" she asked.

"Lotto, bingo, checkmate," I answered.

We worked ourselves through the table of contents for how to clean up and clear away the deep-seated misconceptions.

Was there intimacy in your family or distancing and non-communication? Were you aware of co-dependency or any enmeshment? The purpose of family dynamics is to let me know where your difficulties began and why. Everyone is sick somewhere

And all families carry secrets and shame that set up roadblocks to a happy, joyous and free life as an adult. Be rigorously honest and open about the family. None of us is a saint, not even mommy or daddy. There is a bit of bad in the best of us and some good in all of us.

Please rate your childhood on a 1-10 scale, and explain why. Were you a leader or a follower, aggressive, passive/aggressive or merely passive as a youngster? Were you competitive with siblings? Which did you like/dislike? Flesh out your childhood.

When Medicine Woman wrote and wrote and wrote all the pain and suffering of her childhood forward, a pattern emerged. She was describing how she had treated others like parents and siblings and friends and enemies in other times in other places. Her barrelful represented where she needed to accept her discomforts as karmic payback. She had diminished the self-worth of the cast of characters when she was in the role of them earlier. Medicine Woman abused others to the same degree she had been abused in this lifetime. This is Shakespeare all over again: "All the world's a stage..."

No one goes through the Sedona Intensive without realizing that they have been here many times before. They are not coerced. Rather, they are in an environment that prepares them for this concept. Those who harmed them in this lifetime are being confronted by their bad-boy and bad-girl behavior from other lives.

There are no victims. When we come back, we volunteer to confront our past sins by meeting them in those who mirror it to us by their treatment of us. The Lower World is where the deepest despair lives as well as the only place in which we can find redemption.

Her biggest secrets had to do with affairs she had had with married men. She started out at 110 pounds and by the time she married her big Indian chief, she had begun to pack on the weight.

"Medicine Woman, you were trying to defend yourself against bad-girl behavior by gaining a lot of weight. You put on the armor like a Grail knight did. Instead of looking for your soul mate you chose cell mates, men who imprisoned you," I told her.

"How do you get all of this news from what I am telling you?" she asked.

"Snake dancer from the Navajo tribe, I am smarter than you on my dumbest day," I asserted.

That's my favorite line, again from Judge Judy. There is no one in the life of jurisprudence like Judge Judy who can get a case and in make a ruling in fifteen minutes. And does she ever rule.

Medicine Woman went through the line-up of men. It was apparent she confused self-esteem with the number of men she bedded. Through this process she came into a clearing.

"Why do you think you married the tribal chief? It was because you thought your animus was so strong that soon you would be the chieftain and he would be your bitch. Little did you know his anima was so strong and unintegrated with who he is that he had made your life torturous.

"Did you read *The Invisible Partners* which I gave you?" I asked.

She hadn't. So I dismissed class for the day and she went back home and read it from cover to cover. When she came in the next day she had a halo around her head.

"I had no idea that the unintegrated Shadow starts to run our lives," she said.

"Great. You have the gist of what Jung and Sanford are trying to uncover for your freedom from relationships. You are your problem. You dragged men into your life because they had no clue that they were selling their souls for sex. It's time to either release it or get off the pot. Either take the holistic approach to marriage and heal with the chief or get a divorce and tend to your own business," I declared.

Life is a process. Each of us starts with the misinformation and control dramas of our upbringing, through religion, social ethics, politics and the ignorance of who we really are.

The endgame is to have a relationship with God and go where he leads. You must face all addictions and compulsions or you will end up in a maze without a clue where the exit is.

Chapter Thirty-Six
What Money Couldn't Buy

When the tall buffed-out 20-something gentleman walked into my room in Dallas, Texas, I did not know whether to bow or move into my attack dog mode. He had a narcissistic grin plastered on his puss that said, "I'm entitled. Kiss my coat of arms."

On the surface Lance was very pulled-together with an Ipana smile that would have won judges' hearts in the Miss America Pageant.

"Lance, switch chairs, you're sitting in my seat," I said without a hint of a smile.

I had spent a lot of preparation on this man's backstory. His astrological profile plus my highly-honed intuition is all I need to know how to help the client. He booked an hour with me at the suggestion of one of the richest doyennes plumped atop Texas society. He called her Auntie Bea. Lance probably had a lot of aunties spread around the Rio Grande.

From the moment I started with the deep dive into who and what Lance really was, the narcissistic grin never again crossed his lips. Instead he did the seat shuffle, squirming and trying to deflect with the hide-out charm he was born with. It will work with an overeducated shrink who takes years to get to first base with their patients, but I can name that tune in one note.

"Lance, when did you accept the fact that you are from a different kettle of fish than the other Vanderclimbs?" I inquired.

"What are you talking about?" Lance asked.

"You said you found the girlfriends in your IPhone at the Roadside Men's Club over on the Highway to Heaven, but in your heart you know that you will never sire a Vanderclimb IV. Dig my drift?" I asked.

And that's when truth hit a hallelujah chord. Lance would never guzzle sweet iced tea with an uplifted pinkie. Nor was he bathed in the smell of heavy Italian scent from Neiman Marcus. But he was buried under years of pretense and deflection in a wardrobe of disguises.

One of the most egregious cover-ups for men is facial hair. It is most often an indication that he is hiding something buried deeply. My intuition tells me that men have a hard time integrating their feminine nature, their Shadow. Hence, men will try to butch it up with facial hair. The villains that promote this nuttiness are in advertising and actors in films and television. Don't get me started on all the cigarettes smoked and booze gulped in these same venues.

When a client stops bullshitting and gets on the same page as who he or she really is, my tone changes into reconciliation and compassion.

Lance Vanderclimb suffered from tough women in his life and weak men who married out of necessity. His father was looking for a mother like Romulus and Remus when he married his third wife. Lance was always trying to prove himself to anybody who would look at what he was doing. He played the oil and gas game. The price of oil refers to the spot price of a barrel of benchmark crude oil. The up and downs and all around of the oil markets makes Lance loco.

He never married. Lance was too busy taking care of his sister and nieces and nephews to carve out a niche for himself. My evaluation was that Lance was girdled with the androgyny of consciousness, which is neither masculine nor feminine in nature but a balance between the two.

I have known Lance for more than thirty years. He has flourished beyond words because he supports the best for those who need him.

All rotten vines have a bumper crop of delectable fruits and vegetables. The Vanderclimbs were rooted from such a hybrid. Lance would turn out to be a bachelor at heart who had more compassion in his little finger than all the celebrated boys and girls branded by Who's Who. His grandpappy was a former governor. A brother was handsome and married with four kids and a huge success in business. By forty he was a billionaire with no silver or pewter spoons in his portfolio.

Then along came Lance's older brother, Sherman, the most unattractive and miserable human being I've ever met. At nearly 60, Sherman, unemployed for decades, was still living rent-free with his 90-year-old madre.

"Tell your mother to have Sherman call me. He will soon be paying rent or he will be living on Slipping-and-a-sliding Street," I said to Lance.

"Where's that?" Lance asked.

"It's a euphemism for Tobacco Road," I advised.

"Where's that?" Lance inquired.

This boy's been watching too much of *Keeping Up with the Kardashians.*

"It's Skid Row," I cajoled.

In a few years after meeting Lance, his 17-year old nephew Rodney went through the Sedona Intensive. At that young age he had gotten a girl pregnant but they would not abort the embryo. He stayed in the Corporate House with Scott as house manager. The two of them bonded. Rodney did much better after he left us. When he was 27 he was killed when his motorcycle hit a brick wall. The strange thing about his death was I would pick up on him mind-to-mind. He often counseled me about many of his family members.

His mother Laura went through the Sedona Intensive shortly after he did. She lived in Beverly Hills and seemed to have found firmer footing when she left our program.

Laura's daughter Ashlee booked a week here. She was adorable and very strong-willed. Ashlee had a strong bind with Rodney. She "talked" to him often. Today she is married with two children. Her life is in being a horse whisperer.

Laura's oldest son, Rawlings, had a very quirky turn of the screw. When Rawlings was 19 he apparently molested his cousin Ashton. Either fear of having the book thrown at him by the judicial system or shame for what happened, he fled to Rome where he stayed until he was 34.

Through the work we did over a number of years, including a week in Sharm el Sheikh, Egypt – mostly with the God within nudging him – he returned to Texas and was recently given probation. Today he is married to an Italian and they just had their first child. His hope is to return to Italy where he had worked as a sous chief. A *sous-chef de cuisine* (French for "under-*chef* of the kitchen") is a *chef* who is the second in command in a kitchen. The person ranking next after the head *chef.*

Last but not least is Dylan, Rodney's son that I tried to get Rodney and his girlfriend to abort. I counseled Lance that he would have to raise Dylan after Rodney's death. His nature is stubborn as well as defended. Dylan has been living with Uncle Lance since he was 10. Today he is 16 and a handful.

That makes six from the lineage of Vanderclimb. Each has been through the Sedona Intensive except Rawlings, who has been restricted by terms of his probation not to leave the state of Texas.

There are no quick fixes no matter what promises anyone makes. I saw a video of James Arthur Ray, a motivational speaker and author who was convicted of felony negligent homicide. His modus operandi is to make outlandish promises of what your tomorrow can look like if you sign up for his wealth course.

Lance and I have grown closer through the years. He is savvier than most from the world of privilege. He can spot one of the latter day pretenders from a television or a guest on a television show designed to worship at the throne of her majesty.

"What is it about this woman that I do not trust?" Lane asked.

"You have seen so many self-acclaimed self-important blowhards not to be able to see one on the street or on a show like hers," I said.

I will close with what Miss Gotrocks once said to me. "Why have I never heard of you?"

I rest my case.

Chapter Thirty-Seven
When the Roll is Called Up-Yonder

———

When I was growing up in the Bible belt, many conservative Christians waited for the Rapture like kids did Christmas. The notion that we would see granny and pappy and old friends from woebegone times was a fantasy. Even though the idea wetted our eyes and filled our hearts, the South was built on homecomings and this was to be the granddaddy of them all.

And then I woke up. Throughout my long and topsy-turvy life, I shucked many of my beliefs, knowing what is true for me. After I got sober I went all over the world. Cultures and traditions and people themselves who spoke a different language and believed in another God taught me more than the girdle of Christianity.

As time passed, darkness seemed to descend on the just and the unjust. Bigotry proliferated. The planet heated up, then below norm in winter. Violence spread exponentially. Ideologues multiplied like a virus.

There are a lot of people in this country who see a conspiracy in the movement of clouds or disagreement with not getting what their skewered mind tells them the way it should have gone.

You might think that "Who shot John Kennedy?" was the biggest cover-up in history. If that one didn't get your knickers in a wad, how about the U.S. government orchestrated the planes plowing into the World Trade center and the Pentagon?

Nothing you can dream up even comes close to the notion that there is a Heaven and you have to believe in Jesus Christ as your Lord and Savior to get in.

I have found that there are two Worlds, Upper and Lower. We descended from the Upper World when the former Archangel wanted to be God. God told him to leave Paradise and take his fallen angels with him. The riddle was the only way to return from whence we came was to turn back to God and leave Lucifer's contamination behind. God aided the return with the redemption chip embedded in each of us.

The most unsettling aspect of the mien everywhere in the twenty-first century is the nasty and mean-spiritedness of people: person to person, cause to cause, oppositional political parties to one another and also putting words in God's mouth.

When confronted with the radical and unfounded points of view of a lot of people about their religious biases, I often reply, "I spoke to Jesus last night and he said for you to stop using his name in vain." They more than not skedaddle like a dog in the wrong yard. Humor goes a long way to defuse nuttiness about any subject.

In all the years I have been in sober circles, I am reminded that our tradition, "We have no opinion on outside issues," does not keep all adherents in line with this axiom.

When I sobered up in 1980 in Long Beach, California, there was a lot of hubbub around designating some meetings as "gay." Some of us felt that sobriety was not about sexual preference but it was about practicing these principles in all our affairs. Gays screamed and complained until "gay" meetings were listed in our printed schedules of meetings, as well as on the website.

Another adage that we love is, "Live and let life," or "Tend to your own bidness (sic)," as some of us in the South like to say.

There is a fractured seam that runs through our tap roots. My worldview is that we individually and collectively created the world we now live in. Credit cards overlaid all reason and sensibility that so many of us ignored. Advertising played its part in this odium. From this book you know how I feel about social media. It has become too invasive and sired too much craziness in the name of expressing oneself.

What is the solution? When will we learn about corrections? A starting gate would be to pray to the God of your own understanding, follow that God's dictates and stop letting religious views become politics as it has through the world. Be personally responsible for how you abuse money allocations. Spend what you have to spend and don't spend what you cannot afford. Cease looking for the gurus and know-it-alls. Be your own authority.

The second paragraph of the Declaration of Independence says, "All men are created equal," which is not true in Upper World consciousness. We return to Earth to refine our souls, to do no more harm to ourselves or others, and to help when we see a need. There are those of us who believe that there were other worlds before this one we now live in.

Many see floodlights of hope in what some are calling this generation as the movement into a Golden Age – the gold being a metaphor for Alchemy of consciousness into awareness – the blue and the gold, the blueprint and the alchemy. When we see ourselves back as the Lemurians, we are seeing ourselves in higher frequency. One must not forget that time is an illusion that brings depth to physical experience.

As we say in recovery rooms, "Ya'll keep coming back, ya hear?"

There are no choices. We all keep coming back until we don't have to come back. We remain in the Perfect Place, the Upper World forever and ever and ever.

The linchpin of cleaning up the world we call home is to take personal responsibility for our own actions. The blame game has run its course. The corrections reality is in play. If it is not, we will experience the dark and dangerous life and times of past centuries of despair.

PART FIVE

Chapter Thirty-Eight

The Late and Great Mrs. Arthur Hornblow, Jr.

———

Every so often the Creator sends someone into your life who will change it more than a stable of shrinks or a room full of other recovering alcoholics. My favorite aphorism is that God is taking you where you need to go even if you won't let him.

One day I got a phone call from a woman who introduced herself as Leonora Hornblow. If she had said she was Mrs. Arthur Hornblow, Jr., I would have realized she had married well. Arthur Hornblow produced my favorite movie of all times, "Witness for the Prosecution," starring Charles Laughton, Elsa Lancaster and Marlene Dietrich and Tyrone Power. I would later find out that when she married Arthur her bridesmaids were Pamela Churchill Harriman, Claudette Colbert, Kitty Carlisle Hart and Phyllis Cerf. Don't pick them apart even if you know to whom they subsequently married.

"Darling, I found out about you from a client of yours at a dinner party last night. She was quite impressed with what you told her," Leonora explained.

"When will you be back in New York, darling?" she asked.

She's been dead for more than ten years but I can still hear her say, "Darling." I came to call her "Darling, Hornblow," although many called her "Bubbles," which she hated just as much as Elizabeth Taylor did, "Liz."

"I'll be there next week, staying at the Hotel Carlyle," I said.

"Oh, darling, my friend Kitty and I have dinner there once a week. You have good taste in hotels. I live right around the corner on Fifth Avenue. I'd like a three o'clock session with you. Could we have high tea at four?" she asked.

For years she always had a session with me at three followed by high tea in the atrium part of the dining room at four.

You should never mistake her darlingness for permissive-ness. She never suffered the most unconscious fool. Leonora could spot one across town. She tipped the doorman at her build-ing at Christmas. Darling was as generous when she ate out. If someone invited her to lunch or dinner and under tipped, she would sheepishly ask, "May I contribute a little more to the bill? He works so hard for so little." Her biggest complaint to me as she got older was ageism. "Darling, I can't find my checkbook. Can you ask your angels if they know where I put it?"

We spoke every Saturday at eleven. No matter what was going on in her life, she always asked about mine. Oftentimes I didn't want to hear what she had to say, but in hindsight I never failed to see how right she was.

Typical exchanges: "Leonora, I am so down in the dumps I can barely function," I once said to her. Pause. Pause. "Darling, are you still living in that adorable townhouse?" she asked. "Yes," I replied weakly. "Did you have three square meals this week?" she continued. "Oui," I faintly whispered. "And how is your health? Are you feeling chipper?" she asked. "I'm feeling fine," I replied. "Then shut the *&^%$* up." Pause. Pause. Pause. "Darling we'll speak same time next week. Okay?" And she hung up leaving me surprisingly feeling much better than when we were on the phone.

I had always admired Kitty Carlisle. She was an actress, singer and spokesperson for the arts. Most notably she was a panelist on *To Tell the Truth* on television from 1956 to 1978. Close friends knew she stood on her head. To say she was a fitnick would be a serious understatement. Darling Hornblow told me all about her daily exercise regime.

"How would you like to meet Kitty Carlisle Hart?" Leonora asked me over the phone.

"I'd love to, but I won't stand on my head. I can hardly stand on my tootsies," I answered.

"Bring your tuxedo and plan a work trip to New York in two weeks and I will take you to have dinner with Kitty and me."

I am not one to drool over any big piece of stuff but I had heard so much about Kitty. I did as I was told. I got to New York on a Thursday, had two days of clients and then it was to be Darling and Kitty and me at La Grenouille for dinner Saturday night.

Ring. Ring. "Hello, Albert here. May I help you?" I asked.

This was long before the name of a caller appeared on the telephone.

"Darling, it is I, Leonora, and I have made an unforgiveable mistake. Kitty's big event was last night. She had a theater renamed the Kitty Carlisle Hart Theatre and we had front row seats and then dinner afterward," she apologized. "But I got us invited to her apartment tonight," she said

Leonora and I went to Kitty's apartment where she stood on her head because I asked if it were true that she did that every day. She interrogated me as reputation had that she would. All raves and kindness from the press and gush was deserved.

But my favorite bon mot she shared that night was from her recollection of words spoken by her mother about the way time flies: "When you pass 50, every fifteen minutes it's breakfast."

In the spring of 2005 I got a telephone call from Darling Hornblow. She was moaning and said that she had fallen. After medical attention and diagnosis, the attending physician said she had a stroke. By the fall of that year, her son, Michael, whom I grew to love and adore as well as his wife, Caroline, moved her to Fearrington, North Carolina. I nudged and cajoled until Leonora said I could visit.

"Darling, I don't look like I used to. You'll know when you see me," she whispered.

On the puddle jumper out of Atlanta to Durham, North Carolina, I sat next to a man who asked what I was reading. I told him it was a manuscript I was trying to sell to my publisher at Simon & Schuster.

"'You're Not Who You Think You Are.' Now that's a fascinating title for a book," he said.

We made small talk.

"What kind of work do you do?"

"I'm an orthopedic surgeon at the Duke Hospital," he answered

"I was born with clubfeet. My granny took me to Duke when I was days old. The surgeon said he would like to do experimental correction on my gnarled feet," I explained.

"What a coincidence," he said. "Your surgeon sold me his practice a few years ago. But he still works one day a week. I know your case well. You are in the medical journals at the hospital," he told me.

No preaching here, but you will find throughout this book that I was monitored and managed from the Upper World. There are no accidents. Everything is planned in an orderly fashion, most of all learning curves like I had with drunk driving and being sentenced to those damn 12-step meetings.

When Darling Hornblow died on Nov. 5, 2005, her son asked me to speak at the memorial. Everyone who spoke was well-known except me: Christopher Cerf, son of Bennett, founding editor of Random House and a panelist on the television hit show, *What's My Line?*; producer Danny Selznick, son of David O. Selznick, Oscar winner for producing *Gone with the Wind* and *Rebecca*; Kitty Carlisle.

I was sitting next to Jeane Eddy, Leonora's dress designer, and Peter Rogers, advertising copy writer who created the popular advertising campaign, "What Becomes a Legend Most?" Jeane and I became great friends and she always took my business partner and me to lunch at the Colony Club when we were in New York.

I spoke last. It was daunting to be talking about the one person who had influenced my life more than anyone else. Remember, *I* was *her* confidante.

"I have known Leonora Hornblow more than 25 years. If you've known her long enough you may know her as Bubbles, a name she hated. I pinned the sobriquet `Darling' on her because she started most sentences with `Darling.' Throughout the years we talked every Saturday on the telephone. She sought my counsel for what was going on in her life. Today you will not find out a thing about her from me. After all, there's a sacred thing known as client confidentiality. She, simply put, was the most fascinating person I have ever met, and I have known quite a few of them, but none as prominent in my life as she was. You'll find out she was my teacher in many ways. So here are a few things I learned from her.

"While having lunch the day after 9/11 with me and my former business partner at the Hotel Carlyle, I was talking about my literary agent. 'I just love her,' I said.

"'Darling,' she said, 'You fall in love at hello.' Scott roared his approval. She was spot-on. "Soon after we met I told her that my neighbor across the street was causing trouble for me in the compound.

"'Perhaps I'll ring her doorbell and give her a piece of my mind,' I told her.

"'Stay on your side of the street,' she emphatically advised. 'Don't trouble trouble 'til trouble troubles you.'

"Leonora was not hesitant to tell me when I should dip my rotten attitude in Clorox and spray it with Aqua di Parma.

"I got to the Hotel Carlyle through the magic connections that God makes. The assistant manager of the Carlyle was a client of mine when I was staying at the Omni Berkshire Hotel on 52nd Street.

"As she left she said, 'Someone told me that you have an association with a travel agency in Birmingham, Alabama,' Carolyn said.

"'That is true,' I said, and pulled out the business card and gave it to Carolyn.

"'The next time you come to New York, stay at the Carlyle. I will honor the travel agent's discount,' she said.

"Darling's address on Fifth Avenue was 875. My lady friend in Sedona lived at 875 on a street here in Sedona.

"The impression I am leaving with you is that there are no accidents and nothing happens by chance. It is all prearranged in the Upper World to get people to others they need to meet and places they want to visit.

"When Warner Books published my first book, *Clearing for the Millennium*, Leonora had a reception for friends of mine at her apartment. Need I tell you that it was magnificently appointed? She loved Chinese red and it was beautifully evident throughout her quarters.

"She took us all to Mortimer's, where cafe society loved to see and be seen. We were seated in the window, which was the pièce de résistance. It was the favorite watering hole of Jacqueline Kennedy Onassis and other notables. I had been sober in 1997 when the book came out. In my drinking days I would have reveled in being in such a place. That night, I was grateful to Darling for planning a party for me and my friends anywhere.

"'You're sitting in Jackie O's seat,' she said.

"The owner, Glenn Bernbaum died in 1999 and the restaurant closed. A few blocks away, employees of Mortimer's opened Swifty's. Leonora was one of their investors. It catered to the highfalutin and legends in their own mind sorts. It unceremoniously closed on Jan. 13, 2016.

"I do not miss her because she has not gone anywhere. We 'speak' every day through thought impressions. God is so gracious to have let me feel an era of movie monde that I treasure the most. Through the eyes and words of Darling Leonora I was there without having to have lived in those days."

Chapter Thirty-Nine
The Comeback Kid

———

I live on a golf course in the magical kingdom of Sedona, Arizona. The colors in the rocks are red and brown and pink mixed together through eons of God's finger painting. Sedona is a soul cleanser. Many people visit Sedona for its vortexes. Page Bryant, a respected clairvoyant, coined the name "vortex" in 1980 for areas in Sedona that have highly concentrated energies conducive to prayer, meditation and healing. For hundreds of years Native Americans have performed ceremonies in Sedona.

A vortex is a colossal magnet that pulls people into its center for healing and altered consciousness. Because Sedona as a whole is known to be a spiritual hot spot, a vortex site in Sedona is a place where one can feel energies most strongly. Visitors and locals alike confess that an otherworldly transcendence overlays them and affects power thought impressions of change.

In May of 1997, I was having lunch when I noticed a waiter who was new to me. He was on the outer veranda clearing tables when I recalled the advice of Lena, the Brazilian psychic: *"When you are in your late 50s you will meet a young man who was a son of yours from a past life. You owe it to him to help him get sober and change his life path. You will remember him the minute you see him."*

In no time I knew his name was Scott and he had run away from home in Colorado with a woman friend. Thank God for cosmic energies and their determinations because he was exactly the bearded and snarly looking person I would be least likely to befriend. And to top it off, he rode a Harley motorcycle.

I sat in his station every day and gradually began to interrogate him. I told him I worked with astrological archetypes as a way to identify someone and their challenges. When I asked him his birth date, he bristled.

"I was warned about Sedona weirdoes who chanted and wore feathers in their hair – pretend Indians. I'm not interested in having you read my chart," he said, and he walked away.

The next day I sat at a table he was serving and made small talk. I ate there every day for a month, and then something unexpected happened.

"I've been thinking about having you prepare my astrology and tell me what you see. But not today... someday."

He gave me his day and time and place of birth.

"Be at my house at 4 o'clock today." I gave him my address. "Don't be late!"

At four on the dot he was in my backyard and I laid into him with no pauses or chances to build a case against the truth. Scott laughed and cried a bit but he was impressed that someone who knew nothing about him could nail him like I did.

My 12-step sponsor's wife was visiting and she and Scott and I went to a meeting that night. It was not his first 12-step meeting, but that day was the first day of more than twenty years of sobriety.

Scott wanted to work with the Sedona Intensive. I told him that when he was sober a year I would hire him.

You know what is often said about good intentions. When he was six months sober, a drug addict signed up to go through our program. The addict's parents wanted him to be closely super-vised. I decided to house him in the Corporate House with Scott as his overseer. Scott was paid very minimum wages but he never bitched about his paycheck. He upgraded his living situation by a wide margin. He was no longer waiting tables.

The month after I hired him, I took him on a five-city work trip. I had cancelled a book tour to Milan, Italy and wanted to redeem the first class fee of $6,000 to cover his tickets. After a short conversation with the Delta Air Lines big piece of stuff, the kind supervisor did it with pleasure. Today any airline supervisor would give one of those Judge Judy raucous hee-haws and dis-miss me and the idea of an airline aiding and abetting a loyal cus-tomer to use the money to buy an employee airline tickets.

Don't get me started. Social media, reality television, pol-iticians and religion and bloviator-Twitter signees are so nause-atingly disgusting I am surprised the Republic is still standing. Clearing! What bad karma gave us the Kardashians? If my mother came back from the dead she would climb back in the box. Even when I was drunk, I would have turned them off and out of my 24-inch TV.

The trip was successful and memorable. Scott shaved and loved sobriety and was so grateful to be living in a beautiful house as well as working with clients. I gave him a First Sober Birthday Party. His mother and sister and father came to the party. When he spoke, Scott shed tears of joy.

Scott had always had a problematic relationship with his father. I got the bright idea to fly his dad to a hotel in Boca Raton, Florida do they could spend several days talking and hopefully coming to terms with one another. The agreement was that Scott would not let his dad pay for anything. Apparently it worked because to this day they are closer than most sons with their fathers.

Scott's core issue was a lack of self-esteem. Several times in our working relationship, he wanted to quit. We would talk and oftentimes he was reduced to tears. His strength of self-esteem came over a long period of time. We are wont to say in 12-step recovery that we are unlearning a lot of the reasons we drank alcoholically. Time and a lot of inventories as well as 12-step meetings did the trick.

Twenty years later I can say with no equivocation that he is the nicest person I have ever met. He's savvy and his instincts are much sharper than mine. In the second year he worked at the company, he came to me and laid down the law.

"This company has too much debt. Stop spending and get out of debt," he said.

Within 18 months the company was solvent. Time to time we would borrow money to stay afloat, but he would pay back all of the debt in record time. Can you imagine in these days of rolling in debt, over-consuming, perusing Paul Stuart to see what you couldn't live without? Scott couldn't, wouldn't and didn't. All those years ago I could never have imagined living debt-free. But I am.

Monsieur also taught me to belly-laugh. He has such an infectious laugh — but he also could turn his lip up like a child about to see dark clouds in a sunny sky.

But what knowing Scott has really done for me is to see a man who got sober with my help, to see him stand on his own two feet with the help of a God of his own understanding.

When Scott was 30 he met a girl named Alison in his Tuesday morning yoga class. She asked him out but he said she was too young. She got a Bachelor of Arts and a Master's Degree in English. She went her way and he stayed put in Sedona.

A few years later, Scott's brother Chip got married in Las Vegas. The day after the wedding Scott had an epiphany. He wanted to get married and have children.

He came back to Sedona and went to his Tuesday morning yoga class. Alison was on the floor waiting, for the class to start. He joined her. They started dating. On Oct. 3, 2009, they got married and I officiated. Livia and Augusta were born the next October. Today Scott lives in Colorado and sells real estate and works as a firefighter in Denver.

No matter what he does or where my life takes me, there will never be anyone to take his place. He and I refer to our meeting as a God shot and where God has taken him and his family is because they were willing to go where the Higher Power took them.

Chapter Forty

Rex Reed and the Welles at the Dakota

———

"On an arctic iceberg or in the middle of Macy's, the voice on the phone could have belonged to only one person. Part Fanny Skeffington and part Margo Channing but all Bette Davis."

— Rex Reed, *Conversations in the Raw.*

Travel back to 1969. I am in my garden on a Sunday morning in Peachtree Battle in Atlanta, sober as a judge — ha-ha — reading *Conversations in the Raw* by newcomer Rex Reed.

In a nutshell with *Conversations in the Raw*, the second of his four best-selling celebrity profile collections, he turns his focus on cult legends such as Bette Davis and Jean Seberg, international superstars like Simone Signoret, screen idols, Ingrid Bergman and Paul Newman.

That afternoon I dropped into at a local "see and be seen" bar on Peachtree Avenue sitting by a fascinating woman of about 40. I introduce myself.

The minute she said, "My name is Sally Sue and I am an editor at *Atlanta Magazine*," the light bulb burned bright.

"I have a good friend who is dying to have me do a profile for your magazine. He's just written a fabulous book that they're all talking about in Palm Beach and Malibu and Southampton – everywhere that everybody who's anybody hangs out," I titillated her.

"Who is he and what's the book?" Sally Sue asked.

"Let me get us another drink," I murmured. "Give me a double Scotch on the rocks and Sally Sue, for you?" I asked.

"I'll have a Crown Royal with a splash," she said.

"He's Rex Reed and his new book is *Conversations in the Raw*," I said.

"You won't believe it but my assistant put that book on my desk today," Sally Sue exclaimed.

"It's a small world. I believe it is called synchronicity. You and I have just met. I mention doing a profile on Rex Reed. His new book is on your desk," I gloated.

"Come to my office tomorrow and let's talk about you doing that profile," said Sally Sue.

We had a meeting of the minds.

"Albert, we will only pay you $500 if the profile is published. We will reimburse you for roundtrip air, meals and lodging in New York. Give me a hug. I love this project already," Sally Sue said.

Rex Reed lived in one of the most prestigious buildings on the Upper West Side, the Dakota. It is a bastion of gothic meets classical overwhelming grandeur. There is a guardian at the gate and a sentry to announce you. I was pre-screened and approved for entry by Rex.

It was obvious from hello that Reed loved jumping into the lives of movie stars and their backstories. There was no secret to his success. It's all chutzpah and great writing. To his credit, he was somewhat self-effacing. To tell the truth I liked him from the moment we met. I still like to read what he writes.

It ain't what it used to be. He started when people bought a magazine or newspaper just because they wanted to read what he wrote about anybody.

There was very little "getting to know you" chitchat. Rex Reed knows how to enliven one of his profiles.

"Why in the world would *Atlanta Magazine* want to do a profile on me?" he asked.

"Did you read *Conversations in the Raw* after you wrote it?" I asked.

After a few hours of digging and saving as well as throwing out stuff we talked about, we went to lunch at a diner. There was a long counter and a few tables and chairs. There was a sign that warned you, "Tables bear a minimum coverage." A cover charge was customary in New York when I lived there in the mid-60s.

"Let's get a table. We can eat up the minimum," Rex said.

I know he was born in Fort Worth but what he said about eating up the minimum was so Southern Baptist.

"Rex, I love your apartment and am knocked out by the Dakota itself. If I ever moved back to New York I'd love to live here," I said.

"You couldn't afford it," he said matter-of-factly.

What was amusing about Rex Reed is that he writes like he talks. Time does strange things to the glitterati, a word he often uses to describe famous people, especially movie stars. I have friends in his building and they report that he has assumed mannerisms that show he has had a radical makeover without the plastic surgeon. They see Rex on the subway. He wears a stone-cold demeanor when he is on the elevator with others.

Going on fifty years later, his apartment should bring a pretty penny. But housing in Gotham City is like an elevator. It goes up and drops down – oftentimes way down.

His writing has become crueler and more staccato like the rat-a-tat-tat of a machine gun. In his early profiles, Rex Reed let his subjects indict themselves by how they acted and what they said. If you lived in New York for more than fifty years and had to deal with celebrities that newspapers and magazines would pay you to write about like they do Rex, you might mosey into jade-like copy like he has.

Ageism is rampant everywhere. His publishing sources realize that the hungry yenta-like readers are always looking for a fresh bitch and a savage bite in the prose they buy for their public. I remember when Liz Smith wrote for top publications and now she shares a column with a parvenu co-writer.

The nice thing about Rex Reed is that today he could make a killing on what his apartment at the Dakota would sell for. Rex could get enough to buy his own Ponderosa in Fort Worth.

And then I met the Welles in 2000. Dennis is tall, distinguished, a big piece of stuff in international advertising. He was twice president of the Ad Club as well as chairman of a large advertising conglomerate. The day he first sat with me, he had a breakfast meeting where his current ad agency was merging with another ad group.

I look at the world through a different lens. For all his accomplishments, what he's done to help others who need it anonymously is what I most admire about Dennis.

Yolanda Welles is a showstopper. She and Dennis met while working together in advertising. She is an actor, a M.E.L.T. accredited instructor and made an award-winning commercial in the Czech Republic a number of years ago. Today she sits on the board of a national theatre company. Yolanda does amazing work with breath, especially with actors and those who need to improve their effectiveness with public speaking.

Daughter Alana Welles was 16 when we met. Dennis had won the bid for a catered dinner in a townhouse on the Upper East Side. There were several people there hobnobbing and schmoozing.

"Did you ever think about going to Yale?" I asked

Alana was sitting directly across from me.

She was not thrilled with me or the astrology which I use in my work. But that's often how it is when we bring personal biases into a social gathering. Later we became inseparable.

"Maybe, but why do you ask?" she replied.

"My intuition told me," I said.

A couple of years later she applied to Yale. By that time she and I were a bit closer. That Christmas I sent her charms for a necklace that could have spelled YALE, but I did not send "A" or "E" in case she did not get into this Ivy League School. Included in the package was a book, *Great Women of Yale*.

My gifts for the Welles arrived on December 15. On December 19, she learned she had been accepted into Yale.

"How did you know?" Alana asked me on the phone.

I said, "I'd tell you but then I'd have to kill you." No, that's what a Navy Seal says if you ask where he's been or where he was going. Rather, I told her that I never really know how and why I pick up things I should not know about people I have just met in a session.

When she was graduating from Yale, I called to tell her that I had an intuitive notion that she would make Phi Beta Kappa.

"Principe (my nickname in Italian), don't say that. My grades are not good enough."

Alana called a few days later and said sheepishly and softly, "I got into Phi Beta Kappa."

Alana is an opera singer who has sung all over the world. She speaks five languages and does translations. She is so amazingly humble and thrifty. For one of my birthdays in New York, her parents told her to take me to dinner wherever I wanted to dine. Together we chose an Italian restaurant. When the bill came she nearly fainted. For years later she trembled whenever that dinner date is referenced.

And then there is Braden Alec Welles, who my former business partner dubbed "The Kid." The Kid was 11 when we met. I used to refer to him as "knee-high to a grasshopper" because he was small in stature. Today he is skyscraper height and he played championship basketball at Poly Prep Country Day School in Brooklyn. And don't get coaxed into a tennis match with him. At his tennis club in Southampton, he was reigning champion for years.

When Braden had his first session with me, he was wide-eyed and somewhat entranced, his rapt attention hung on my every word.

"Are there any questions?" I asked.

"I want to quit the school I am at right around the corner from where I live and go to Poly Prep Country Day School in Brooklyn. What do you see about that?" he asked.

The Kid was savvier than most kids his age. But I knew that his current high school was where bright lights reached for the stars for their future careers. I also figured his parents might want him to stay put. But the God of Braden's understanding might be putting the thought in his head to transfer.

"Braden, get on the bus and time how long it takes you to get to Poly Prep and back again. Then ask yourself whether or not you want to devote that much time to get to school where now it is just around the corner," I advised.

He did exactly that the next day and called to say he still wanted to transfer.

"Okay, Kid, don't let the door hit you in the ass on the way out of your fancy pants school," I did not say, but instead, "You did the right thing. Now tell your parents your decision."

Ring. Ring. Ring.

"Albert, it's Dennis Welles. I hope you didn't tell Braden he could transfer to Poly Prep."

"Dennis, I did not discuss your session with me with Braden. I won't discuss my time with him with you. Thanks for calling," I said, and slammed the phone down.

Years ago Braden stayed with me and my Wire Haired Fox Terrier, Mr. Darby, in Sedona. Braden slept on the pull-out sofa bed in the living room. Mr. Darby slept with Braden both nights he was with us. I was furious with Mr. Darby and told the dog so loudly in front of Braden.

When Braden got home he emailed me a very brilliant note about how much Mr. Darby loved me and that I ought to ask myself where the jealousy came from since the dog stayed with him two nights. I was thankful and never again felt jealous of Mr. Darby and anyone he was close to or seemed to like a lot.

When Dennis went through the Sedona Intensive, he bought a house on his lunch break. Yolanda came out a week or so later to approve the purchase before it went to escrow. She asked me to look at the house and tell her what I thought.

"Yolanda, I love the house. It is one of the most attractive I have ever seen in town. When I sold John Travolta a house a few years ago I got the seller to give him all the furniture. Ask for the furniture," I advised.

She did and they said yes and they bought the house. We had a lot of good times here. Dennis is a chef extraordinaire so he cooked for Christmas, New Year's Eve and other special occasions. We swam together at the Hilton Spa and laughed and cried a little as well.

Oct. 5, 2016 they sold the house. The Welles were here only a few weeks a year. Mr. Darby and I love them but we will go to New York and Southampton and they will come back to Sedona time to time.

Chapter Forty-One

Her Name is Bishop Reverend Doctor Barbara King

———

It comes as no surprise to those who sit on the front row of my life that I prefer blacks to whites. I had always been a Republican until I heard Barack Hussein Obama speak at the Democratic Convention a few years before he was nominated and elected the 44th President of the United States.

From that moment in time I drifted back to Blanche, who ironed for my family in the 50s. I wrote about Blanche in my book, *Signs and Wonders,* in 2003. Like President Obama, Blanche inspired me and lifted my soul to the highest octave I resonate with.

Publishers expect an author to do all he can to promote his book. Get on television or be interviewed by the *The New York Times* or try to book the Halle Casser-Jane syndicated radio show. It also helps to get speaking engagements, which is how I met Barbara King. I wrote her a letter and told her I would like to speak at her church, Hillside Chapel & Truth Center in Atlanta, Georgia.

"Hello, this is Albert Gaulden," I answered the ring.

"This is Barbara King, pastor of the Hillside Chapel & Truth Center in Atlanta. You wrote me asking to speak at my church," she said.

"Wow. I am flattered you called me from my letter. Thank you, Dr. King," I groveled.

This happened to me with Dr. Gina Cerminara, with Elizabeth Kubler-Ross and now with Dr. King. Someone touched from above said that when this happens, you have been together before in a previous life. It is also how you click-connect with someone on an airplane, someone sitting across from you in a restaurant or when you bump into someone on the street in a foreign country.

"You wrote asking me if you could speak at Hillside," she said.

"Yes, but let me tell you that in two weeks I am speaking at the Unity Church in Birmingham. Atlanta's pretty close. I am sure you would want to check anyone out before you agree to them being invited to speak at your church," I offered.

"You are reading my mind, Dr. Gaulden," she said.

I am not a doctor but that is how someone like Dr. King refers to someone who seems to be in the business of helping people find their way. It is a term of respect.

I spoke at Unity Church of Birmingham where Jerry Bartholow was pastor. Through James Redfield, author of *The Celestine Prophecy* and a client and close friend, I was asked to speak in April 2009 on my new book *You're Not Who You Think You Are*. Barbara King decided to come hear what I had to say before offering me an opportunity to speak at Hillside Chapel & Truth Center.

Dr. King sat in the front row after being palavered over by Bartholow and anybody who knew that King was a big piece of stuff. When I got up to speak, I said how happy I was that Dr. King had come all the way from Atlanta so we could meet.

Within minutes of my probing and irritating and cajoling the congregation about trying to find out who they really were, Barbara King fell fast asleep.

We had a late supper at Bottega Cafe on Highland Avenue. We sat outside and rehashed how we had met.

"Albert, I am so sorry I fell asleep while you were speaking. You must think I am disrespectful," she confessed.

Without missing a beat I said, "Barbara, you got it on the inner planes."

She told me for years afterward that my response endeared me to her for life.

I spoke at Hillside Chapel & Truth Center a few months later. That Sunday afternoon I conducted a workshop on the book. Many clients booked appointments with me. That gesture drew me closer to the church and its congregation.

A year later, Dr. King called and asked to go through the Sedona Intensive.

"Just look at me as a client who has come to you for help. No special privileges please," she pleaded.

Barbara had an amazing experience in her week in Sedona. No inside information will be shared. Barbara often speaks to her congregation about her Intensive in very plain language about what happened to her.

The Light Foundation is a not-for-profit organization started by graduates of the Sedona Intensive. In the spirit of giving back and sharing, each member of the founding board of directors wanted to help those who could not afford the Intensive program to get assistance to do so. In 2005, the board decided to under-write a dinner to celebrate my sobriety birthday every five years.

In 2010, Dr. King was the keynote speaker at the gala. King is an honorary chieftain of a tribe in Ghana, West Africa. Well over six feet tall, King took the podium in full tribal dress from the top of her head to her ankles.

For half an hour she mesmerized the room of more than eighty people with her talk, "The Power of a Great Idea," touching upon Nelson Mandela and how courage stirred her to act on ideas that came from God. I am reminded of something that Ray Stannard, one of the founders of *American Magazine* and a major writer about race relations in the South in the 1920s, said about power and ideas. "It is not short of amazing, the power of a great idea to weld men together."

In my life I would rate her speech with the charisma and delivery of President John F. Kennedy, President Barack Obama and Madame Johan Sadat.

What endears Barbara to me is her steadfastness in being who she is, authentic and determined to touch the lives of those who are in her presence. What she has to say is spellbinding.

The timbre and resonance of her voice reminds me of another Barbara, Barbara Jordan. Barbara Jordan was a lawyer, civil rights activist and congresswoman from Texas. She's best-known for her eloquent opening statement at the House Judiciary Committee hearings on the impeachment of President Nixon. Jordan was the first African-American woman to deliver a keynote address at a Democratic National Convention.

Few people have that ability. There are those who have platforms on television who have a great need to make people laugh. Tiring and boring, but they motor on. Dr. King can stand silent and speechless at a lectern and mesmerize her audiences with her radiant presence. But when she speaks, all ears are attuned to what they have come to hear.

I will always love and adore her. If you ever hear she will be speaking at a church or venue near you, run as fast as God will have it to listen to her. She will change your life in the first sentence.

Chapter Forty-Two
The Strange Gift of Mr. Darby

Marilyn and her friend Lorraine from Canada had just arrived to start my personal growth program. Marilyn sat on the sofa and Lorraine in an overstuffed chair facing me. My Wire Fox Terrier, Mr. Darby, was sitting near me.

I used to put him in a separate room until he mind-to-mind telepathically said, "Daddy, I am a healer just like you. Let me work with the client under the table."

So I always let him be in the room where I work with those who seek me out.

Suddenly Mr. Darby jumped onto Marilyn's lap and lay down. Marilyn said nothing but I could tell from her body language that she was uncomfortable about something.

The client sees me five days as well as work with other practitioners. When Marilyn started her program, Mr. Darby did what he always does. He went under the table and I assumed he did what he told me was healing.

Marilyn was married with a couple of children. Clients write a life history guided by a structured outline I give them. Initially I felt she was in a distressful marriage. He husband seemed to be a bully. Time to time she resisted his anger and raised voice. Marilyn never seemed to have serious doubts about her marriage.

On the third day as we started she began to weep. Her outburst astonished me because she had seemed like a cool collected customer.

"What's troubling you?" I asked. "Is it Mr. Darby?" I inquired.

"No. That's the point I wanted to bring up. He has been healing me even when I was terrified of him," she answered.

At the mention of his name, the dog came out from under the table and was wagging his tail.

"When he jumped into my lap on Sunday afternoon I was mortified. At seven years old, I was bitten by a big dog and he mangled my arm and leg. A surgeon was able to work with manipulation and casts. In four months I was good as new," she explained.

"Marilyn, had I known this I would have kept him out of the room," I said.

"No, no, no," she exclaimed. "Mr. Darby has been sitting on my feet every day I have been in this room with both of you. This dog is a healer," she said, and began to sob again.

When she started to cry, Mr. Darby went back under the table and sat down on her feet again.

"My children have always wanted a dog. I refused. I did a poor job of letting them know what happened when I was a child. This morning when I was waiting for the valet to bring my car, a dog walked over to me and I instinctively petted him and he licked my hand.

"You need to understand I know that Mr. Darby was a huge piece in the puzzle of why I came to see you and your therapists. When he sat on my feet he was helping release the toxic layers of my emotional body. This dog is a wizard.

"Between appointments, I called my daughter and told her that she and her brother could each pick a dog. I told her that they would be responsible to feed and walk the dogs. I felt they needed to exercise their pets if they chose to get them," Marilyn finished. She was now smiling and then laughing.

In the last two months I had a man and a woman who were having difficulty with their legs. They had a lot of massages as requested while in the Sedona Intensive and were lathered with lotion.

Mr. Darby licked their legs every day they were here. When I told the vet he said that dogs are liable to lick lotions and other oily substances. When I told both Michal and Martha the news from the animal doctor they said Mr. Darby was a four-legged magician.

"I could barely walk when I came here and after four days of his sitting on my feet and licking my legs I am tons better," Martha said.

Michael had confirmed the same thing – weeks apart.

My history with Mr. Darby started with the Welles, who I call First Family. Yolanda Welles grew up with Wire Fox Terriers. When I met them they had a rescue Cocker Spaniel named Belle. Within months of my knowing the Welles, she died.

Yolanda was determined to get a Wire Fox Terrier and she did. They named the puppy Curtsey. When I met Curtsey I adored her and said if I ever get a dog, it will be a Wire Fox Terrier.

For two years I searched breeders in the United States. Some were so strange, asking me for my financial statement and other invasive questions.

"I'm trying to buy a Wire Fox Terrier, not join a country club or buy a house," I told one nosy breeder before we got around to pictures over the internet.

I gave up and got my dog fix from animals in the neighbor-hood. In January 2009, I got on the internet and typed in Wire Fox Terrier. When the pages came up I saw a tiny picture of a dog and clicked on that site. I called the woman and over two hours agreed to buy the puppy whose picture was on the site.

"That is a picture of Darby who was born on October 5 last year. He has the best temperament of any Wire Fox Terrier we have ever bred. Had you not called, we were going to take his picture off the site because we decided to keep him," the woman named Millie said.

I was going to Egypt in February and turning another year older on March 6.

"Millie, can you fly him to me on March 6? I will call him my birthday present to myself," I told her.

That is the story of Mr. Darby and me. I named him Mister because he has great bloodlines. He was going to be the second therapist in the room with me and my clients. Each and every one of them is convinced that he and I are a team.

He had been included in this anthology of people who have had a major impact on my life because I know I knew him before. I am convinced that mind-to-mind, he drew me to the computer.

"Time is of the essence," he "told" me and I obeyed.

Mr. Darby is one of the most important "people" I have ever known.

Denouement

The Doomsday Clock – Two Minutes to Midnight

The following information was published by Reuters News Agency in an article from *Science News* dated Jan. 22, 2017.

"Rising threats from climate change and nuclear arsenals prompted the scientists who maintain the Doomsday Clock, a symbolic countdown to global catastrophe, to move it two minutes closer to midnight on Thursday, its first shift in three years.

"The Doomsday Clock, devised by the Chicago-based Bulletin of the Atomic Scientists, now stands at three minutes to midnight, or doomsday.

"It has been adjusted 18 times since its creation in 1947. It has been set as close as two minutes to midnight, in 1953 when the United States tested a hydrogen bomb, and as far as 17 minutes from midnight, in 1991 as the Cold War expired.

"It was last adjusted in January 2012, when it was moved one minute closer to midnight."

I wanted to talk a bit about the Doomsday Clock because all my efforts have always been about the individual not the collective. Inspirationalists like Churchill and Lincoln served to lift millions of people from despair, but it has always been my message for the one as he or she affects the many.

And dare I say that I am not at all concerned about either the clock of doom or the tick-tocks of boon.

We have all been here before. The Creator decided to have teachers and writers establish means for man to make corrections in his fallen angel choice and puppet to his egocentric self. What happened was those who were entrusted with the message of redemption and change became afflicted by the devil it was supposed to conquer and lead others back to their birthright, precious child of God.

Addictions became the avenue God used to allow man to stay attached to his lower self until a flicker of remembrance of his true identity enlivened itself enough to allow him to return to true self. Addiction was the pathway to bottoming out. The High Self within each of us abetted the journey back to who we were born to be.

What I came to understand is that my Ego was a friend and not an enemy. As a butterfly starts out in the cocoon and emerges with wings to soar and pollinate and bring beauty to nature, I had to understand the mystery of rebirth through making an ally of my dark side. The Ego morphed into my friend when my Shadow made itself known to me.

There are so many distractions that the Lower World has to shield us from our birth right. As God rules the Upper World, through a separation from him, the Supra Ego has dominion over the Lower World.

When you hit a low point of despair, Natural Law makes it possible for each of us to remember the Creator and ignites a desire to come back to Divine Light.

By Natural Law, it is paramount that you repeat aloud, "Ego, are you a devil that chases me or an angel who has come to help me?"

With that intonation you have now shape-shifted from ego-centric self to the precious child of God you were always meant to be.

Politics and religion are broken. All political parties say anything to win. They make promises they cannot keep. They are pretenders, the Hatfields and McCoys, opposing sides in latter day America. No wonder children are so misguided when they hear and see the vile and half-truths candidates use against one another. Some analysts believe that the current president of the United States used fake stories to topple his opponent.

The religions in this country are no better than the Muslims they vilify. Does anyone not see the hatred and murderous deeds done in the name of the Republic by so-called Christians? The notion that we have separation of Church and State in America is ludicrous. No Constitution will ever be able to right the wrongs that these religious zealots have done to contaminate the moral fiber of our nation.

As someone who knows that we recycle life after life, I don't allow that to misguide me. No matter what mean-spirited politicos and religious meanness does to our nation, or what others do to theirs, we will return from whence we came. There will be a price to pay for how we preached and played the game of bully pulpit. It is called deep freeze until we decontaminate.

God is watching. He is called a lot of different names but each represents the same Divine Creator.

Acknowledgements

My deepest thanks and appreciation will always be to Mrs. Arthur Hornblow, Jr., better known as Darling Leonora, whom I consider a soulmate. Your portrait hangs above my desk to remind me that you are always as close as a thought impression.

I say *Grazie mille* to Michael and Caroline Hornblow for being true friends. Michael read unfinished manuscripts and offered brilliant insights.

To James and Salle-Merrill Redfield I want to thank you for being side by side by side on this journey called life. And especially to Salle I am forever grateful for all the delicious Southern dinners in Birmingham.

For Joanne Davis I will always be grateful for buying my first book and all the times we have spent together. I may not see you but I will always find you inside me where it counts.

I want to thank my Wire Fox Terrier Mr. Darby for urging me to go online and see his picture when he was a few months old. I called and bought him but not before other breeders made me loopy about their requirements for selling me a dog.

To Andrew Bell, I am extremely grateful to you for just being in my life, but especially because you read chapters of this book long before they had gelled and became what it is today.

To David Bell, you are one of the stalwarts in my life. To Gail Galvani Bell, you and I are soul mates in so many ways. To Ashley Tripp Bell, "Diva," I am forever grateful to know you and to acknowledge your voice as one of the greatest ever heard on the planet to lift the human spirit. When I hear "Un bel Di Vedremo" I will always think of you.

To Livia and Augusta Carney whom I call the Gorgeous Geniuses, my thanks for all the joy you bring to me.

To Scott Carney who worked with me for years and added so much to the book and to my life, I will be eternally grateful. And to Alison, his size zero wife, what a quartet are the Carneys in my life.

To my Saturday Morning 12-step meeting my deep-felt thanks for all you mean to me every week.

To Cathy and Paul Friedman for the true friendship they have extended to me. I fell for Cathy at hello.

To Carole Marcus Pizitz for your capacity to always be true to yourself; to tell the truth even if many of us can't hear it. You are a treasure to the world.

To June Iseman for the talks and comfort I have felt throughout our long and precious relationships.

To Sue and Don Mozzone, your love and support made me a better person.

To my mother Maggie and to my dad, "Ty," you were my best teachers when I was finally able to recognize it. You are both gone but will never be forgotten by me.

To Amber and Dr. Jay Kaplan for all the love and support and medical reports Mr. Darby and I got from you. And I'll add a shout out to Mia, Chelsea and Julia, the beautiful Kaplan daughters.

I want to thank Larry Kirshbaum, who was CEO of Warner Books when my first book, *Clearing for the Millennium,* was published in 1997 and who is now an agent with Waxman Leavell Literary Agency, for his never-ending support of me and my work. You will always be my Angel.

Kudos and eternal thanksgiving to Karin Price Mueller who made this book a lot better because she did a brilliant edit as she did with *You're Not Who You Think You Are* and several other projects. We writers are only as good as a brilliant editor like Karin makes us in the final draft.

To my adorable and loving sisters, Jeannie Gaulden Barron and Margie Gaulden Gilbert for their loving support and capacity to move beyond differences.

Bibliography

Achebe, Chinua.*When Things Fall Apart: Heart Advice for Difficult Times*. London: Heinemann, 1958; New York: Astor Honor, 1959.

Baigent, Michael, Richard Leigh and Henry Lincoln. *Holy Blood, Holy Grail*. New York: Delta Trade Paperbacks, 1982.

Berg, Yehuda. *The Power of Kabbalah: Thirteen Principles to Overcome Challenges and Achieve Fulfillment*. Los Angeles: Kabbalah Publishing, January 1, 2011.

Butterworth, Eric. *Discover the Power Within You: A Guide to the Unexplored Depths Within*. New York: HarperOne 2008.

Carson, Rachel. *Silent Spring*. New York: Houghton Mifflin, 1961.

Cerminara, Dr. Gina. *Many Mansions*. New York, New American Library,1967.Coelho, Paolo. *The Alchemist*. San Francisco: HarperSanFrancisco, 1998.

Dossey, Dr. Larry. *Recovering the Soul: A Scientific and SpiritualSearch*. New York: Bantam Books, 1989.

Fiore, Edith. *Encounters: A Psychologist Reveals Case Studies ofAbductions by Extraterrestrials*. New York: Ballantine Books, 1989.

Fiore, Dr. Edith. *The Unquiet Dead: A Psychologist Treats Spirit Possession*. New York: Ballantine Books, 1986.

Fiore, Dr. Edith. *You Have Been Here Before*. New York: Ballantine Books, 1986.

Fox, Emmet. *The Sermon on the Mount: The Key to Success in Life*. New York: HarperOne, 2009.

Friedman, Thomas L. *Thank You For Being Late*. New York: Farrar, Straus and Giroux, 2016.

Gibbon, Edward. *The Christians and the Fall of Rome*. New York: Penguin Books, 1994.

Gladwell, Malcolm. *Tipping Point: How Little Things Can Make a Big Difference*. Boston: Little, Brown, 2000.

Hirschfield, Jerry. *My Ego, My Higher Power and I*. Farmingdale, NY: Coleman Publishing Inc, 1990.

Hopcke, Robert H. *There Are No Accidents Synchronicity and the Stories of Our Lives*. New York: Riverhead Books, 1997.

Isherwood, Christopher, translator. *How to Know God, the Yoga Aphorisms of Pantajali*. Hollywood: Vedanta Press, 1953;

Jung, Carl. *The Portable Jung*. Edited by Joseph Campbell. New York: Penguin Books, 1971.

Jung, Carl. *The Essential Jung, Selected Writings*. Edited by Anthony Storr. Princeton, NJ: Princeton University Press, 1961.

The Kabbalistic Bible Technology for the Soul edited by Yehuda Berg. Los Angeles: The Kabbalah Centre International Inc., 2004

Kaplan, Richard. *Awakening to Zen*. New York: Scribner, 1997;

Osho. *The Secret of Secrets: Talks on the Secret of the Golden Flower*. Hong Kong: Tao Publishing Pvt., Ltd., 1982.

Peck, Dr. Scott. *People of the Lie: The Hope for Healing Human Evil*. New York: Touchstone, 1983.

Redfield, James. *The Celestine Prophecy*. New York: Grand Central Publishing, 1993.

Sanford, John B. Invisible *Partners: The Invisible Partners: How theMale and Female in Each of Us Affects Our Relationships*. New York: Paulist Press, 1979.

Sri Ramakrishna Math. *The Gospel According to Sri Ramakrishna*, Madras, 1930.

Swami Prabhavananda. *Realizing God: Lectures on Vedanta by SwamiPrabhavananda*. Edited by Edith Dickinson. Tipple Advaita Ashrama, 2010.

Rabbi Joseph Telushkin, William Morrow et al. *Jewish Literacy The Most Important Things to Know About the Jewish Religion, Its People and Its History*. William Morrow, 1991

Wilson, Colin. *Rudolph Steiner The Man and His Vision*. London: Aeon Books, 1985.

Wolinsky, Stephen. *Trances People Live Healing Approaches in Quantum Psychology*. Bramble Books, 1992.